The Mystic Christ

The light of non-duality and the path of love as
revealed in the life and teachings of Jesus.

Ethan Walker III

Devi Press
PO Box 5081, Norman, OK 73070
www.devipress.com

Published by:

Devi Press
PO Box 5081
Norman, OK 73070
405-447-0364
www.devipress.com
Contact the author at: ethan@devipress.com

Library of Congress Control Number, 2003103581

Printed in the United States of America
Oklahoma City, Oklahoma
ISBN # 0-9729317-0-8

Mystic

One who professes a knowledge of spiritual truth
or a feeling of union with the divine,
reached through direct experience.

Christ

The anointed one;
the divine manifestation of God incarnating in the flesh
for the purpose of destroying ignorance.
The word "Christ" is also used to denote the
all-pervading eternally personified presence of God
as opposed to the formless impersonal aspect.
Christ is the universal undivided soul.

Other books by the author include:

Soft Moon Shining:
Poems for the Mother of the universe

Finding God's Love:
The theory and practice of love and devotion as a spiritual path

A brief description of these books can be found in the back of this book.
They may be thoroughly explored and purchased on-line at
www.devipress.com or call 405-447-0364 for a free brochure.

Acknowledgments

I wish to offer my sincere and heartfelt gratitude to the many who helped in the reading and refining of this work. First is the Divine Mother of the Universe and Her incarnation as Ammachi by whose grace alone this work was conceived and came to fruition. Next is my wife and best friend Marsha whose brilliant sunshine editing scattered the clouds of murky sentences and obscure phrases. I would like to thank everyone who bothered to read it. Thank you to spiritual brothers Rev. Ray Eppler, Tupper Lienke, Scott Burr, Michael Wilson, Dr. Tom Boyd, Rev. Terry Dearmore and spiritual sister Abhaya and brother John for their thorough reading, commentary and input.

This book is dedicated to

All seekers of truth everywhere,
my grandsons, Ethan V and Andy,
and all of my grandchildren who are yet unborn.

Wisdom

And what is Wisdom?

Wisdom is knowing we are all one.
Love is what it feels like,
and Compassion is what it acts like.

Love

Compassion

Contents

Synopsis

I. Happiness, as the kingdom of heaven, is an attainable goal not only in the "hereafter" but right now, not only on a personal level but worldwide.

    A. To reveal this path is the purpose of the life and teachings of the world's great masters such as Jesus, Buddha, Mohammed and Krishna.

    B. This goal requires focused effort on our parts.

II. The ego, or sense of separation as "I" and "mine," is the obstacle to the kingdom of heaven and the source of our unhappiness.

III. The practice of love and compassion is the path taught by Jesus and others for the removal of the obstacle.

    A. Love is the antithesis of the ego. Love is "I'm in it for you," and ego is "What's in it for me?"

    B. Love is the primal cosmological phenomenon.

IV. There is an underlying living intelligent Supreme Being whose very nature is love and who supports and animates the universe and all of the beings in it.

    A. Direct experience of this Supreme Being is the goal of human existence.

        i. Love is the surest path to this direct experience.

    B. All of us are continuously united in this unfathomable Being, the I AM, even though this truth may be obscured by the darkness of the ego.

Preface

This book is a discussion of various scriptures in the Old and New Testaments with the majority of these being quotes from Jesus. Also included are numerous parallel and appropriate commentaries by Ammachi (Holy Mother) whom the author regards as his teacher and mentor. Therefore, some introduction to Ammachi is necessary for those who have not acquainted themselves with the Holy Mother. In October of 2002, Ammachi was awarded the prestigious international Ghandi-King award. This award is named after Mahatma Ghandi and Martin Luther King, Jr. and is given each year to the person who has contributed the most to non-violence in this world. Prior to that she was one of a few delegates chosen to represent India at the Parliament of Religions also held at the United Nations building. Ammachi believes that all of the world's major religions are paths to God.

Ammachi was born in 1953 to a poor family of fisher folk in southern India. From a very young age she was absorbed in God, which culminated in her merging completely with God while she was still a teenager. This is a fascinating story best left to her biography (see Bibliography). Her path is love, and her life is one of unending and unparalleled compassion. Jesus willingly died on the cross for our benefit. Ammachi spends ten or twelve hours of most days of the week hugging all comers, consoling them and blessing them with her divine love. To date it is calculated that she has hugged over twenty million people. In India it is not uncommon for her to hug ten to twenty thousand in a single sitting. Can we imagine ourselves even lifting our arm to make the embrace ten or twenty thousand times in a single day? Ten to twelve or more hours she will sit hugging without ever getting up to attend to bodily needs. At the end of each hugging session, at four, five, or six o'clock in the morning, she will still be smiling, fresh, and taking just as much time with each person as she did when the first pilgrim arrived in her lap. Many people have reported miraculous healings and spiritual awakenings, but most importantly, we feel the unimaginably powerful love that pours out of her like a great untamed river. Like Jesus, she sacrifices the whole of her being every day for our welfare. To find a person with this much love is extremely rare and fortuitous.

She asks nothing but gives everything. No collection plate is passed. There is nothing to join. She does not ask that we reconstruct our beliefs or pledge allegiance to her or her organization. Members of any faith are welcome and encouraged to excel in their own chosen paths. The Holy Mother will help them. This is truly an event in human history that is without precedent. Ammachi is pure unconditional love incarnate. And what is love? God is love.

Introduction

At the end of our days on this earth, after all our successes and failures, the measure of worth for our life will be how much we have loved. AMMACHI

It is the nature of man to seek happiness. *The Mystic Christ* is an exploration of this instinctive pursuit. This inquiry naturally leads directly to love because love and love alone makes life beautiful. Love is the wine of divine intoxication that fills the cup of our mortal lives with the happiness that we seek. It is the love we give to God and others that makes our lives full of meaning and pregnant with joy as each moment so lived gives birth to the splendor of the Infinite Reality.

Within the all-encompassing embrace of this Eternal Presence are other things we must consider in order for love to be fulfilled. These are the attitude of the mind toward God, man and our own selves. So it must be said that *The Mystic Christ* is also an exploration of the mind. We will undertake an introspective examination to discover why love (and therefore happiness) has been lost and how it may be rediscovered. Our measuring stick will be the life and teachings of Jesus.

We will also embark on a quest for innocence because innocence is the fertile soil in which love sprouts, flourishes, blooms and yields the sweet fruit of immortal bliss. Without innocence, we are left with the hard barren rock of pompous arrogance and its twin—guilt and shame; the fruit of this is suffering.

To find love, it will be necessary to cut away the knotted jungle of our own self-centered existences. This task is not for the faint of heart. However, it is the only way for us to truly love God and to love one another. There is no other path to salvation. Cutting away this jungle of deluded narcissistic self-absorption is what Jesus had in mind when he said:

> *"Do not suppose that I have come to bring peace to the earth.*
> *I did not come to bring peace, but a sword."*
>
> Matthew 10:34 , NIV

The sword, in this case, exists solely for the liberation of the soul that it may soar into the boundless sky of love. It is a sword of uncompromising compassion.

We will examine this essential question of faith: Are we all separate from each other and God, or are we connected? If we are separate, then it is every man for himself; get yours first before someone else gets it. If we are connected, then our attitudes and treatment of others will be kind and compassionate. Regardless of our decisions, it is absolutely certain we will reap what we sow.

If we are truly connected, then we must experience this truth inwardly as personal revelation in order for it to affect our lives in any lasting and meaningful way. Furthermore, if this deep personal change is not forthcoming for the practitioners of any faith, then the laws, dogma and doctrine of that faith often become the unwitting apocalypse of suffering and despair which history reveals as religious bigotry, persecution and intolerance. During the period of the Inquisition tens of thousands were deprived of their property, banished or executed by burning at the stake because of their beliefs. This attitude still exists today, smoldering in the dark depths of our collective unconscious, constantly calling for its consort, ignorance, to unlock the gates of hell and unleash its fury. Bigotry, prejudice, intolerance and ethnic cleansing are but a few of its names. It was this attitude that Jesus challenged at the cost of his own life.

We are trapped in mortal prison cells of flesh and blood cohabiting in the larger prison compound of the world. As a vehicle for liberation, religion reveals a very narrow and arduous path of rebirth and resurrection that ultimately frees the soul from the confines of the prison forever.

Throughout history and in all religions, very few of us have become aware of our own self-perpetuating bondage, and still fewer have perceived the need to change as the result of having gripped and shaken the iron bars of our own self-centered prison. Most of us are content to remain as we are, not realizing that the awful price is separation from God.

Personal spiritual change is painfully difficult. Spiritual change leaves us naked and empty. The thundering waves of radical non-duality revealed by the life and teachings of Jesus Christ will come crashing down on our illusory sand castle of "I" and "mine" which, up to the point of transformation, will have stood basking in the artificial light of endless unfulfilled desires. If this change, this rebirth, this resurrection, this enlightenment, this transformation has not utterly shattered our world and our conception of ourselves, then we are not ripe for the kingdom.

Unless we have realized the temporary nature of the alluring pleasures of the world, and unless we have begun to understand that it is the illusory ego, the "I" and the "mine" and its desires, which are the source of our suffering and our separation from God, we will not be able to commit to the painful process of gripping the arrow of ignorance, thus pulling it from the flesh of the mind.

Because of this, the profound and transforming teaching which Jesus brought to the world is rejected or ignored by most of us today, just as it was by his contemporaries 2000 years ago. The hard sayings of the Master have been diluted by our egocentric self-view, or they have simply been ignored.

This book is written for Christians who harbor a feeling of concern, sensing that there is more to salvation than simply mouthing the words, "I believe in Jesus." This book is written for anyone who is willing to embrace the possibility that salvation is a deep and fundamental change that must take place at the very root of the human psyche. This book is written for all seekers who see that Christ was a revolutionary and that a great civil war must be fought on the battlefield of our own minds. This book is written for anyone who has begun to understand that salvation must happen here and now as we labor to bring each moment into the fullness of God's infinite love.

1

We are All Brothers & Sisters

Both read the Bible day and night.
But thou read'st black where I read white.

WILLIAM BLAKE

We are all brothers and sisters bound like pearls on the same string or light bulbs connected by one wire and illumined by the same electricity – the same "one living" Supreme Being. There is absolutely no one who is excluded. Love is another name for this unity. This is the true core and the central issue of the life and teachings of Jesus. The goal of our human existence is to experience this directly in the depths of our own beings.

Discovering, experiencing and then practicing this unity is the beginning of the end of human mental and emotional suffering. From the point of view of one who is merged in the reality of this unity, it would make no sense whatsoever to steal, lie, murder or covet another man's wife or property. It would be the same as committing these acts against one's own self. Who would find it reasonable to steal one's own car from one's own garage? To a person who is merged in the awareness of our divine unity, the ideas and emotions of greed, jealousy and hatred are laughable and invoke a sense of compassion and sadness toward those who are prisoners of these afflictions. Like prodigal sons and daughters, most of us have somehow wandered away from the awareness of our connectedness. Our own consciences and our sense of compassion toward others are echoes of this long forgotten unity.

The truth of our connectedness is no longer available as a topic of speculation. Our unity has been clearly revealed in quantum physics. Bell's Theorem, which has been scientifically demonstrated, states that objects (and that includes us) have no local existence of their own (*Quantum Reality* by Nick Herbert). Rather, everything is connected, and everything simultaneously affects everything else. A butterfly flapping its wings on Jupiter will affect us even though the effect will be minute. In other words, the universe is not a lot of separate objects. The universe is a bowl of gelatin, and if we poke it on one side it will wiggle on the other. If this is true, then our notion of being separate individuals is an illusion.

It is this seeing of "nothing separate" that Jesus refers to as single-eyed seeing.

> *The light of the body is the eye: if therefore thine eye be single, thy whole body shall be full of light. But if thine eye be evil, thy whole body shall be full of darkness. If therefore the light that is in thee be darkness, how great is that darkness!*
>
> MATTHEW 6:22-23, KJV

Here Jesus is not talking about the two eyes in our heads. In this scripture he only uses "eye" in the singular form. By this he means our understanding, our vision, our mind's eye if you will. If our "eye be single" then we have the vision of the unity of life. We see the unity of all that exists which is seeing with a "single eye." When we have the "single eye" of non-duality, then we see as Jesus sees. In the *Gospel of Thomas*, Jesus again expresses the concept of non-duality:

> Jesus said, "When you make the two one, you will become the sons of man, and when you say, 'Mountain, move away,' it will move away."
>
> GOSPEL OF THOMAS, NAG HAMMADI LIBRARY, VERSE 106

The root of all sin is simply ignorance of our true nature – our oneness in the omnipresent Divine. Sin sees separation while Truth sees unity. Sin accuses and judges others to be good or bad, worthy of our love or worthy of our scorn. Truth sees others as our brothers and sisters regardless of their wrong actions. Truth is a like mother who will never stop loving her children and regards their wrong doings as simply mischief that has to be corrected. This mother also sees the innocent children even when they have become grown men and women, and she will continue to love them all even if they make mistakes. This is how Jesus wants us to see.

In order for us to arrive at this all-encompassing love, we must have a direct experience of our oneness in Christ. That experience comes as a flash of lightning from out of the east and illuminates far into the west (Matthew 24:27), and for a brief moment the landscape of our own being is revealed, and our lives are forever changed. In that flash of insight we are born again, escaping the prison of our separateness, and the path to God is opened.

> *On that day you will realize that I am in my Father, and you are in me, and I am in you.* JOHN 14:20, NIV

In the preceding scripture, Jesus doesn't say that on that day we will *become* one with him and the Father. This is very important. He says that on that day we will emerge from our ignorance and *realize* the condition of our oneness that has always existed. We will see that we are in God and God is in us. We will see clearly that it has always been this way, but we had forgotten it. As the prodigal sons and daughters, we will have returned home to the origin of our being by vanquishing the illusion that we are separate.

> *For them I sanctify myself, that they too may be truly sanctified. My prayer is not for them alone. I pray also for those who will believe in me through their message, that all of them may be one, Father, just as you are in me and I am in you. May they also be in us so that the world may believe that you have sent me. I have given them the glory that you gave me, that they may be one as we are one: in them and you in me. May they be brought to complete unity to let the world know that you sent me and have loved them even as you have loved me.*
> JOHN 17:19-23, NIV [emphsis added]

In this scripture Jesus makes direct reference to oneness and the potential for realizing oneness.

The Pharisees thought that Jesus' claim to be one with God was blasphemous, and they were preparing to stone him to death for saying it. Jesus points out that others have also been referred to as "Gods," and it was written in their scriptures:

> "We are not stoning you for any of these," replied the Jews, "but for blasphemy, because you, a mere man, claim to be God." Jesus answered them, "Is it not written in your Law, 'I have said you are gods'? If he called them 'gods,' to whom the word of God came—and the Scripture cannot be broken—what about the one whom the Father set apart as his very own and sent into the world? Why then do you accuse me of blasphemy because I said, 'I am God's Son'?   JOHN 10:33-36, NIV

In Psalms we read:

> I said, "You are 'gods;' you are all sons of the Most High."
> PSALM 82:6, NIV

Paul tells us that God is not only over all but also that God is simultaneously existing through everyone and everything and is within everyone and everything.

> There is one body and one Spirit—just as you were called to one hope when you were called—one Lord, one faith, one baptism; one God and Father of all, who is over all and through all and in all.   EPHESIANS 4:4-6, NIV

And again in John's First Epistle, John tells us that we are of God and that God is in us.

> You, dear children, are from God and have overcome them, because the one who is in you is greater than the one who is in the world.   1 JOHN 4:4, NIV

To see God everywhere and in everyone is the goal of our human existence. Everyone, without exception, is our brother and sister. This divine kinship also extends to mountains, rivers, plants, planets, suns and universes. Everything is alive with God's infinite consciousness.

2

The Nature of Man

We are trying to learn how to see God, or the Pure Essence, in everything and everybody and not the demon in them, even in the wicked. If you see the demon in others, the very same negative forces will swallow you up and you yourself will become a demon in the end.

AMMACHI, AWAKEN CHILDREN, VOL. 3

In this chapter we will begin by examining man's exit from the Garden of Eden in order to demonstrate that the "fall of man" did not corrupt the essential nature of humankind. Then we will take up the primal question: If we are not evil, then just who or what are we?

IS MAN GOOD OR BAD?

There is a common belief among many Christians that the core nature of every person is evil and that we are all miserable, wretched sinners. This belief takes root because we have not probed any deeper than the mind with regard to the nature of our own being. It is the mind that harbors evil. If we believe that we are the mind, then one can more easily come to the conclusion that the real nature of man is evil. We see humans acting selfishly and assume this is the bottom of the human well.

Deeper than the mind is the core of our existence, which is pure awareness: the very presence of God. Observation and introspection can prove that we are not the mind. Consider our own minds which are nothing more than the sum of our thoughts and emotions. We ourselves, as awareness, observe the mind. This means that we are *not* the mind. If we are the observers of the mind then we cannot be the mind. In conversation we say, "I have a mind," and not "I am the mind." To illustrate, if we are reading a newspaper it is proof that we are something other than the newspaper. This brings us to our point. We are not the mind or the body, and any corruption in these does not affect the quality of our true Self. The core of every person is eternally pure. There is no original sin but only original innocence.

These opposing points of view, man is good or man is evil, have a profound affect on our culture, politics and approach to life. A democracy depends on the attitude that man is basically good. The people of a democratic nation will collectively make constructive decisions. Thus, the best depository of power is with the people. A free society in which anyone can criticize political leaders also depends on the attitude that an informed and freethinking populace will make the best decisions. Open debate is encouraged because the good in man will ultimately prevail. In the United States the constitution guarantees free speech. We tolerate publications that display a broad spectrum of views because the overall benefit of a free exchange of ideas will outweigh the negative impact of publications that promote man's lower aspects such as hatred or licentiousness. Most will rise above these base attributes because the nature of man is inherently good. We can be trusted.

The belief that man is basically evil cultivates an atmosphere of distrust and suspicion. This will always encourage various elitist groups to see themselves as the bearers of the true interpretation of reality. It then becomes their duty to subdue the unenlightened masses and impose the will of the few on the many. Once empowered they will eliminate political dissent under penalty of harassment, imprisonment or death. Intellectuals, professors and practitioners of the various arts are suppressed. Individual liberties must be curtailed to save the ignorant masses from themselves. The few can never trust the many because the many are perceived as being morally, intellectually and spiritually inferior. The many are not capable of making good decisions.

ADAM AND EVE

The orthodox idea that all humans are inherently evil comes primarily from the Old Testament account of Adam and Eve. In this story the first couple broke God's commandment prohibiting eating the fruit of the tree of the knowledge of good and evil, and so they and all future generations were cursed. It is assumed that this disobedience and the curse that followed destroyed and replaced the good that had resulted from being created in the image of God (Genesis 1:27). From this assumption arises the doctrine that the core of man's being is wicked. Even if God did curse Adam and Eve, that does not mean the original nature of Adam and Eve was changed. We should note that Jesus never mentioned the idea of original sin or that the core of human beings is evil.

The belief in an original sin, resulting from the disobedience of Adam and Eve, was eventually extended to include all of nature. Nature became something worthy of suspicion – she was not to be trusted. The doctrine of original sin held death and sex to be *???* the unnatural consequence of the fall of Adam and Eve. This point of view gained its first significant toe-hold in 399 when it was promoted by Augustine (354-430 C.E.) in his *Confessions*. The widely held view prior to Augustine proposed that nature, having been created by God in the first place, was inherently good, and that man is morally free because he was created in the image of God. Death and procreation were seen as natural processes created by God and thus divinely sanctioned. At the time of Augustine, this naturalist point of view was championed by Pelagius, a British monk and theologian, and the two waged a verbal war which resulted in actual rioting in the streets of Rome in 417 between the supporters and detractors of each. When Pelagius arrived in Rome at the beginning of the 5th century, he was immediately struck by the moral laxity created by Augustine's doctrine of <u>total depravity</u> which had arisen out of the concept of *??/* original sin. Total depravity meant that all humans after the fall

*marked by a strong emphasis on the sovereignty of God, the depravity of mankind, and the doctrine of predestination.

John Calving The theological system of Calvin and his followers *

A state of corruption due to original sin held calvinism to infect every part of man's nature and to make the natural man obey God.

The Nature of Man 11 to know or

were incapable of overcoming their sinful nature. Pelagius felt this encouraged laziness by abandoning the importance of human effort. He reasoned that total depravity irrevocably binds us to the conditions of the fall of Adam and Eve, thus allowing the human psyche to avoid all blame. In other words, we all sin because of Adam and Eve, and there is nothing we can do about it. Augustine and his followers eventually succeeded in persuading Pope Zosimus to excommunicate Pelagius even though the Pope had previously declared him to be orthodox. Pelagius died shortly thereafter, but his followers refused to give up. Julian of Eclanum, an Italian bishop, engaged Augustine in a battle that consumed the last twelve years of Augustine's life. Julian believed that Augustine's primal error was to assume that nature, in its present state, was a punishment. Julian also pointed out that it was ludicrous to imagine that Adam and Eve had the power to alter the fundamental structure of God's universe. Unfortunately, present day Christians have assumed the idea of original sin to be chiseled in stone by some divine mandate and therefore beyond examination.*

As Metaphor

First of all, let us explore the idea that the story of Adam and Eve is a metaphor and should not be taken literally. If it is a metaphor then "God's curse" is a metaphor. The very "forbidden tree" is obviously metaphorical because it is a tree of "good and evil," as opposed to a fig tree or an apple tree. The tree represents something that happened to the condition of the human mind. As further proof, God tells Adam that if he eats of the fruit of the tree of the knowledge of good and evil he shall surely die (Genesis 2:17). As the story goes, Adam and Eve ate the fruit, and they did not die. Rather, Adam lived another 900 years. This story represents a spiritual death, and eating the fruit represents the birth of the ego or sense of being separate from God and each other. In spite of these calamities, our basic original nature has remained unchanged and essentially divine.

---

* A more detailed account of this intriguing bit of history can be found in chapter 6 of the book *Adam, Eve and the Serpent* by Elaine Pagels.

Cain's Wife

If we are still not willing to accept part or all of the Garden of Eden story as a metaphor for the birth of the ego, then we must at least consider that Adam and Eve were not the first persons. If they were not the first persons then those descended from the "other parents" will not be required to be branded as "inherently evil" because their parents did not disobey God.

Adam and Eve were not the first persons because Cain, after slaying Abel, went to the land of Nod and lay with his wife (Genesis 4:17). They had a son, Enoch, and Cain began building a city. For whom is he building a city? In fact, there is much marrying and begetting with Cain being Adam and Eve's only living child.

> *Cain lay with his wife, and she became pregnant and gave birth to Enoch. Cain was then building a city, and he named it after his son Enoch. To Enoch was born Irad, and Irad was the father of Mehujael, and Mehujael was the father of Methushael, and Methushael was the father of Lamech. Lamech married two women, one named Adah and the other Zillah. Adah gave birth to Jabal; he was the father of those who live in tents and raise livestock. His brother's name was Jubal; he was the father of all who play the harp and flute. Zillah also had a son, Tubal-Cain, who forged all kinds of tools out of bronze and iron. Tubal-Cain's sister was Naamah. Lamech said to his wives, "Adah and Zillah, listen to me; wives of Lamech, hear my words. I have killed a man for wounding me, a young man for injuring me. If Cain is avenged seven times, then Lamech seventy-seven times."* GENESIS 4:17-24, NIV

Only after all of this happened did Adam and Eve conceive their third child Seth. Some have attempted to explain the presence of these many "other wives" by saying Adam and Eve had the girl children who became the wives listed above. In the following verse it is clear that there were no other "daughters" or any children at all in between Cain, Abel and Seth.

> *Adam lay with his wife again, and she gave birth to a son and named him Seth, saying, "God has granted me another child in place of Abel, since Cain killed him."* GENESIS 4:25, NIV

Further indicating that Cain's wife was not the child of Adam and
Eve, we read in Genesis 1:28 that after God created <u>man</u> he told
them to go and "replenish" the earth. To replenish means to re-
stock, add to or build up what is already there.

Genesis does not mention any other children that were born to
Adam and Eve in the interim separating Cain, Abel and Seth, but
it does say that later, Adam and Eve had other male and female
children (Genesis 5:4). Genesis reveals that *only* after Seth was
born did Adam and Eve beget other children.

> *After Seth was born, Adam lived 800 years and had other*
> *sons and daughters.*   GENESIS 5:4, NIV

GOD PLANNED IT THAT WAY

At this point we will take yet another avenue and examine God's
intentions with regard to the Garden of Eden story. It is entirely
likely that God intended for all of these events to take place; that
God himself put the original seed of the ego in man. This would
put man in the position of being inherently innocent by nature.

Adam and Eve were brand new. They had no experience with actions and consequences. Putting two innocent and naïve "children" named Adam and Eve in the Garden of Eden and then
pointing out the "tree" is like leaving your own three- and five-
year-old children at home alone and asking them not to eat the
cookies in the cookie jar. Or maybe it was more like leaving a
loaded 45 on the dresser table and telling your 12-year-old not to
play with it while you are gone to the store. If we take the position
that God did not intend for Adam and Eve to eat the fruit, then
we are faced with the uncomfortable view that God had an enormous lapse of judgement. What was God thinking? Did he fail to
consult his own omniscience? Surely God was aware that the serpent was craftier and subtler than all the other creatures. Yet God
allowed this foreboding mix of characters and circumstances to
intermingle. The serpent's punishment was simply to crawl on
his belly the rest of his days and eat dust. And if God had not previously warned the serpent about tempting Eve, then why is the
serpent to blame for his naivete? Why should he be punished? If

God did warn the serpent then God must have seen this train wreck coming.

If we are to accept the banishment of Adam and Eve as punishment, then where is God's mercy? Because of them the very ground was cursed. They and everyone after them would have to sweat and toil for their food and reap thistles and thorns. Worst of all, Adam, Eve and the serpent were not the only ones to be banished from the Garden. All of the other animals were put out as well. We know they were also in the Garden because Genesis refers to the serpent as being craftier than all the other wild animals (Genesis 3:1). What did the other animals do wrong? There should only be humans and snakes in this world. If we accept the punishment view of the Garden of Eden story in which God is most certainly a negligent parent, then we are brought to the unsettling position that God is the guilty one, and humans are innocent.

Those who favor "inherent evil" and a literal interpretation of the fall of man will argue that God gave us free will. This is supposed to explain God's lack of judgement and mercy. Adam and Eve were like children. Does God not shepherd his flock? Could God not give them a second chance? Also, the serpent did not have free will. God could have prevented the serpent from interacting with Adam and Eve.

A more reasonable and loving view would be to say that God planned it just the way it happened. The serpent is a symbol for our sense of separateness, or "I" and "mine," which we will refer to as the ego. The reason that God allowed this is the same reason that God permits Satan to continue to tempt us. The reason for the fall and for Satan is to give humankind the opportunity to grow. One cannot grow strong in spirit if one does not have resistance that must be overcome. God can at any time choose *not* to allow Satan to roam the streets of our world. After all, God can do as he likes with Satan.

Without Satan to challenge us, we would not grow. We would not continue to evolve. We would spend eternity lazing on the bank of some idyllic river in the Garden of Eden as spiritually inept, thumb-sucking souls. Perhaps God wanted some adult company, and that required that we be tempted and tested in order to become spiritually mature. We are evolving to the point of knowing God directly and intimately, to the point of becoming as God is.

SEPARATED FROM GOD

We must understand that the curse, which is to live an ego-centered existence apart from God, is something that is not part of our true original nature. Man was created in God's image, which means that the essential nature of man is good (Genesis 1:27). Also, the breath of life that God breathed into the clay body of man is God's nature. Jesus tells us that the kingdom of God is within us (Luke 17:21). If that is true, then our essential nature is God's kingdom. Because we embraced the ego, we were cast out of the Garden of Eden which symbolically represents losing touch with our inner kingdom. The ego is something separate, like a parasite that sucks the life out of its host. Forgetfulness of our true nature does not change our true nature. We are simply ignorant of it. Yet, it is still there; we could not exist without it.

Holding the position that man's original nature is evil or sinful is not supported by anything Jesus said or did. In fact, the contrary is true. Jesus said we should love one another even as our own selves. This would not make sense if we were all evil to the core. He would be asking us to love evil. If we understand that our true nature is God or Christ then unconditional love for everyone makes sense. Jesus said that what we do to the least of human beings, we also do to him (Matthew 25:45). This also supports the idea that we are all Christ in our deepest heart even though we have lost touch with that through the delusion of the ego.

The truth is that humankind is created in the image of God. Therefore, taking the position of "inherent evil" is simply ignorance. By doing so we are saying that God is evil. If humankind was created in God's image, and if humankind is inherently evil, then God is inherently evil.

So Who Are We?

You are the "I" which is in me and I am the "you" which is in you. The feeling of difference is due to the blindness of igno-rance. In truth, nothing is separate.
AMMACHI - OMKARA DIVYA PORULE, PART 1

In the beginning God created all that exists (Genesis 1:1). Cre-ation was formed out of God because prior to creation, there was only God. There was no other God; there was nothing but the one living God. Therefore, there is nothing that can now exist apart from God. We are part of him. We are all God stuff. John ex-presses this idea:

> *Through him all things were made; without him nothing was made that has been made. In him was life, and that life was the light of men.* JOHN 1:3-4, NIV

Genesis underscores this truth by stating that we are all made in God's image:

> *So God created man in his own image, in the image of God created he him; male and female created he them.*
> GENESIS 1:27, KJV

And Mohammed said:

> *Every child is born of the nature of purity and submission to God.* MOHAMMED, HADITH OF BUKHARI 23:112

Because we are made from God and in God's image, it is possible for us to know God directly. It is God's life that dwells in us as our own being:

> *And the Lord God formed man of the dust of the ground, and breathed into his nostrils the breath of life; and man became a living soul.* GENESIS 2:7, KJV

God's breath is the "being" in us. God's breath is the "is" in us. God's breath is the I AM in us. There is still a faint awareness of this which arises as our sense of conscience and our feelings of compassion. It is our God-given destiny to make the awareness of this full and complete.

A human being whose mind is permanently and irrevocably absorbed in the truth of our oneness is a Christ. The difference between Jesus the Christ and a mortal person is that Jesus abides absolutely in the truth of our oneness in God and a mortal person is ignorant of this. The mind conditions our reality.

Jesus lived his life for the purpose of bringing us into the truth that we are not a limited ego or a mortal body but a ray of the Divine. We will become like Jesus. This is evidenced by the following scripture:

> *Verily, verily, I say unto you, He that believeth on me, the works that I do shall he do also; and greater works than these shall he do; because I go unto my Father.*   JOHN 14:12, KJV

We begin to see that most everything about our worldly existence, including radio, TV, culture, history, schooling and religion, is rooted in the untruth that we are separate. The world is perpetually chanting its mantra, "We are all separate." We are deluded as though dreaming, and we reinforce the illusion to each other. From the time we are born, our parents and mentors, deluded by the I-am-the-body idea, instill the separatist pseudo-reality in us just as their parents and mentors presented it to them. And so the baton has been passed for eons.

Occasionally God incarnates as a human being to give us the opportunity to escape from our prison, to awaken from our dream and arise from the dead. Because we are entranced in the stupor of our separateness, we are dead even though we appear to walk, talk and live our lives. Jesus expresses his view of the "walking dead" in the following scripture:

> *But Jesus said unto him, Follow me; and let the dead bury their dead.*   MATTHEW 8:22, KJV

I Am That I Am

The very center of everything that we are, the foundation of our very existence, the ground of our being can be most accurately expressed with the words "I AM." There is only one living I AM from which every being in the universe continuously derives its existence. This concept is well established in other religious philosophies. The Hindu Vedas (scriptures) call this Brahman; Buddhists call it Buddha Nature; Jewish Kabbalists call it Einsoph, while Moses revealed God's self-imposed name as I AM. In other disciplines, the all-inhabiting I AM is referred to as "Self," as opposed to "self" which describes the separate individual.

> *"I tell you the truth," Jesus answered, "before Abraham was born, I am!"*
> JOHN 8:58, NIV

The eternal Christ, speaking through the body we call Jesus, declared his existence as having predated Abraham. This is why we see the curious use of the present tense I AM instead of the past tense "I was" or "I existed." In the state of being which is Christ's consciousness there is no past or future but only the eternally present shining singularity of existence. Now let's look at a very enigmatic and penetrating scripture.

> *And Moses said unto God, "Behold, when I come unto the children of Israel, and shall say unto them, 'The God of your fathers hath sent me unto you;' and they shall say to me, 'What is his name?' What shall I say unto them?" And God said unto Moses, "I AM THAT I AM:" and he said, "Thus shalt thou say unto the children of Israel, I AM hath sent me unto you."*
> EXODUS 3:13-14, KJV

The name of God was a household word for all Jews up until this event. Everyone knew it was "Yahweh" or "Elohim" (in the Old Testament there are various Hebrew words for God). Leading up to this event the Bible says Yahweh or Elohim many times. For at least 1,800 years since Abraham, every Jew knew God's name. In light of this, we should ask why Moses found himself in a quandary. Why was he puzzled as to what to say to the children of Israel concerning whom he had been talking to? Why didn't Moses think he could simply come down from the mountain and say, "I have been talking to Yahweh?"

Moses knew that what he was experiencing was *not* what the children of Israel conceived God to be. Moses did not want to say Yahweh (Jehovah) because he knew the Israelites would have the wrong idea. He knew that his experience was beyond description, and therefore, he was perplexed as to how to portray it. How was he to describe the core of existence which is pure awareness–consciousness–bliss? How could he describe God as being the center of every being–the Is-ness that hears all sounds and sees all sights and tastes all tastes? Moses gave God the opportunity to say his name, and God did not reply with Yahweh. God said very plainly that his name is I AM. Not only that, God said He *is* that I AM. I AM is pure existence.

The same I AM that is God is also the very core of our own existence. With some introspection we can see or feel that we are always I AM. When we are awake we are I AM, and when we are asleep we are I AM, and when we are in deep sleep we are still I AM. Through all of the changing states of our mind, I AM remains the changeless observer or witness of all activity and inactivity.

Whether we see an object with our eyes or hear a sound with our ears, it is I AM that is common to the two different experiences. The I AM, our underlying awareness, realizes the events. I AM is formless, unchanging, immutable, without beginning or end, without birth or death and IS regardless of the condition of or the presence of an ego and a body. The I AM is not a thing or an object, but rather it is experience itself or spirit. Jesus says:

> God is a Spirit: and they that worship him must worship him in spirit and in truth.   JOHN 4:24, KJV

I AM is pure awareness and is utterly unaffected by any activity of body, mind and senses in the same way that a movie screen displays burning buildings or raging floods without itself being burned or soaked.

Krishna says:

> *Weapons cannot hurt the Spirit and fire can never burn Him.*
> *Untouched is He by drenching waters, untouched is He by*
> *parching winds. Beyond the power of sword and fire, beyond*
> *the power of waters and winds, the Spirit is everlasting, omni-*
> *present, never-changing, never-moving, ever One. Invisible is*
> *He to mortal eyes, beyond thought and beyond change. Know*
> *that He is, and cease from sorrow.*
>
> KRISHNA, BHAGAVAD GITA, 2:23-25

How can it be that there are seemingly so many individual beings, yet all of them have their existence in the same I AM? This
is God's slight-of-hand. The universe and all of us in it are holographic. In other words, each part contains the sum of the whole.
The following prayer from the Hindu Vedas reveals this mystery.

> *That is the Whole, this is the Whole;*
> *From the Whole, the Whole arises;*
> *Taking away the Whole from the Whole,*
> *The Whole remains.*
>
> YAJUR VEDA, BRHADARANYAKA UPANISHAD, 5.1

A holographic picture has a unique property. If we take a pair of
scissors and cut the picture into ten pieces, we will have ten
whole and complete reproductions of the one original. As another
analogy, we can say that each person and each creature is like a
spoke on a wheel with God as the hub. At every moment God is
the very life which supports us and *is* us. Take away the hub, and
there is no wheel, and there are no spokes. In yet another analogy
we can liken each individual to a lens on the eye of a fly which
has hundreds of individual pictures but only one observer behind
it. God is the observer and each individual being is a lens on the
eye. Or we can say that each individual mind is a mirror, and one
mind looking at another is like two mirrors opposing each other,
which creates the appearance of limitless images trailing off into
infinity. In reality there is only one being and one God appearing
as "the many." God is like an endless fountain that bubbles up
from the center of our being as light, life and love. For most of us

ᴛne awareness of this is very dim and obscure. What Jesus taught was rediscovering this wellspring of eternal life.

> Jesus answered, "Everyone who drinks this water [ordinary well water] will be thirsty again, but whoever drinks the water I give him will never thirst. Indeed, the water I give him will become in him a spring of water welling up to eternal life."
> JOHN 4:13-14, NIV [brackets by author]

ARE WE GOD?

In our search for a complete revelation regarding our true nature, we are compelled to approach our abiding unity in God's being from the practical point of view. It is not correct to say, "I am God" if our minds do not also experience everything else as God. When those of us who are still groping in the darkness of separateness say, "I am God," we are stating it is our ego that is God. We are living in the delusion of "I AM a separate ego" and "I AM a separate body." Our minds are currently not capable of being I AM without adding individualistic notions to it. This is the error that is to be corrected through spiritual practice. As discussed previously, the question of whether we are a Christ or a mortal human being has only to do with the condition of the mind. Jesus says that by simply believing with only the faith of a mustard seed we will be able to command a mountain to move (Matthew 7:20). This supports the idea that both the problem and the solution have to do with the condition of the mind.

A question appeared in the October 21, 1999 edition of *The Daily Oklahoman* newspaper posed to Dr. Billy Graham in his daily column. The reader asks, "In my view, we are all 'little gods' and part of the Divine Force that fills the universe. We need to realize that we are each divine as well as human. Isn't this what the Bible really teaches?" In Dr. Graham's reply, he states that the Bible does not teach this but instead teaches that God is separate from us and that He is far greater than we are. He uses the analogy that even though we may have inherited certain physical characteristics from our father and mother, we are nonetheless quite separate from our father and mother. The points of view of both the reader and Dr. Graham have substance. While it is true that God is in everyone, everyone's mind is not in God, and in this way Dr. Graham is correct. At the same time, our true Self is not the mind but the I AM, and so the reader is also correct. We might consider amending Dr. Graham's statement that God is separate from us to read, "we are separate from God." It is the illusion of the ego in our minds that has imposed the illusion of separation on God. In truth, God has never been separated from us. In the Koran, the holy book of Islam, we read:

> We created man; and We know what his soul whispers within him, and We are nearer to him than his jugular vein.
>
> KORAN 50:16

THE KINGDOM OF GOD IS WITHIN US

> If the attitude of duality increases, the mind will fall deep into the darkness of illusion. Therefore, let us seek the Self and know who we are before the mind loses its luster.
>
> AMMACHI, OMKARA DIVYA PORULE, PART 1

Can it be true that God is within us?

> And when he was demanded of the Pharisees, when the kingdom of God should come, he answered them and said, The kingdom of God cometh not with observation: Neither shall they say, Lo here! or, lo there! for, behold, the kingdom of God is within you.
>
> LUKE 17:20-21, KJV

The word "within" as it appears in the King James Bible has been translated in some modern bibles as "among." The King James Version and the New International Version both say "within." The Greek word "*entos*" is ambiguous and can be translated as either "within" or "among." The tendency of modern translators to use "among" indicates their inability to accept the idea that God could be within us. These interpreters believe Jesus intended to say he himself was among them. However, this does not tally with preceding statements in the passage. There are two things that point away from interpreting this scripture to mean "among." Item number one: Jesus says the kingdom of God cannot be observed. Therefore, Jesus could not have been talking about himself. He was observable. Item number two: Jesus says the kingdom of God is not a place. It is neither "here" nor "there." Thus, Jesus could not have been referring to himself. Occupying a position in time and space, his audience could describe him as being "here" or "there." By saying that the kingdom of God cannot be observed, Jesus is telling us that it cannot be seen with the eyes because the I AM is pure awareness. It has no form. It is not a thing. We must take all physical descriptions of the kingdom, such as streets paved with gold and pearly gates, as metaphors because these things can be "observed."

God is love, and love comes from our own hearts further under-scoring the truth that we must look within ourselves to find God. Love is another word for God in the same way that heat and light are both qualities of fire. Love is heat and I AM is light. If the kingdom of God is to be found within our own being then who or what is God according to the New Testament? God is *love* (1 John 4:8 and 4:16). Like the I AM, love is not observable, and so love complies with the Master's advice that the kingdom of God does not come by observation. Love comes from the great sun of infinite life and bubbles up through the wellspring of our own inner hearts. We will never directly experience love anywhere but in our own hearts.

In the following scripture we read Jesus speaking of the Spirit of truth as being within us.

> *Even the Spirit of truth; whom the world cannot receive, be-cause it seeth him not, neither knoweth him: but ye know him; for he dwelleth with you, and shall be in you.*
> JOHN 14:17, KJV

It is understandable that we would not be able to easily accept the idea that God is within us if we have no awareness that we are all connected. However, Bell's Theorem in quantum physics clearly demonstrates that we *are* all connected, thus debunking once and for all the illusion that we are a lot of separate individuals like so many marbles in a coffee can. This connection is at the very core of each of us. It is within us.

ONE WITH GOD

The call to Unity is the message of all scriptures which declare that everyone is the One Self. Understand that everyone is the Self only, which is the Essence of the Vedic teaching. Even the grains of sand are ever declaring this Truth. The quiescent mind can hear that Voice, the Voice of the Unmoving Self.
AMMACHI, OMKARA DIVYA PORULE, PART 2

We can begin to see that the testimony of our five senses is an oppressive tyrant that perpetually seeks to crush the idea that we are all, at the core, absolutely one and inseparable. The feeling of oneness fully contradicts what we have learned from the time we were children about who we are and what the world is. For this reason, oneness or non-duality (non-duality means that there is not the duality of a separate "me" and a separate "God" and a separate "world") is very difficult for most of us to accept, and Jesus knew this. Few will even agree to consider such a possibility because it means surrendering what we now hold to be precious. Non-duality is to the ego as salt is to a slug. To a worldly person, the proposition of non-duality is laughable. A worldly person sees only through the five senses and, therefore, sees only diversity. Think of the spectrum of vibrations beginning with physical objects and ending with cosmic rays. This spectrum is really a seamless progression of vibrations from slow to fast, big to small. There are no hard lines that can be drawn to segment this seamless whole. Like the colors in a rainbow, there are no hard edges where one color stops and another begins. The five senses perceive only fragments or sections of this seamless whole of vibrations. Thus, the illusion of separateness or fragmentation appears in the mind.

And the light shineth in the darkness; and the darkness apprehended it not.
JOHN 1:5, KJV

Because knowledge of the truth is not readily grasped, it is called the "secret" teaching or is referred to as the "mystery." The mind that is wholly absorbed in the ego and the outer world does not have the necessary spiritual equipment to see it. Such a mind lacks subtlety. These persons are described in the parable of the ten virgins. Five failed to keep their lamps maintained and thus missed their opportunity to marry Christ spiritually. Jesus said:

> At that time the kingdom of heaven will be like ten virgins who took their lamps and went out to meet the bridegroom. Five of them were foolish and five were wise. The foolish ones took their lamps but did not take any oil with them. The wise, however, took oil in jars along with their lamps. The bridegroom was a long time in coming, and they all became drowsy and fell asleep.
>
> At midnight the cry rang out: "Here's the bridegroom! Come out to meet him!"
>
> Then all the virgins woke up and trimmed their lamps. The foolish ones said to the wise, "Give us some of your oil; our lamps are going out."
>
> "No," they replied, "there may not be enough for both us and you. Instead, go to those who sell oil and buy some for yourselves."
>
> But while they were on their way to buy the oil, the bridegroom arrived. The virgins who were ready went in with him to the wedding banquet. And the door was shut.
>
> Later the others also came. "Sir! Sir!" they said. "Open the door for us!"
>
> But he replied, "I tell you the truth, I don't know you."
>
> Therefore keep watch, because you do not know the day or the hour.   MATTHEW 25:1-13, NIV

One must do spiritual practices to cleanse the mind of its obsession with the objects of the world. Without spiritual practice, the mind will remain blind and deaf. Six times in the four gospels Jesus used the following phrase:

He that hath ears to hear, let him hear. MATTHEW 11:15, KJV

In the Koran we read:

> *They have hearts with which they do not understand, and
> they have eyes with which they do not see, and they have ears
> with which they do not hear.* KORAN, 7:179

Jesus and the Koran are saying those who have developed a subtle
mind will have the ears of spiritual understanding. For those who
were capable, he gladly revealed the truth. In Matthew the Lord
elaborates on this idea.

> *The disciples came to him and asked, "Why do you speak to the
> people in parables?"*
>
> *He replied, "The knowledge of the secrets of the kingdom of
> heaven has been given to you, but not to them. Whoever has
> will be given more, and he will have an abundance. Whoever
> does not have, even what he has will be taken from him. This is
> why I speak to them in parables:*
>
> *"Though seeing, they do not see; though hearing, they do not
> hear or understand. In them is fulfilled the prophecy of Isaiah:
> 'You will be ever hearing but never understanding; you will be
> ever seeing but never perceiving. For this people's heart has be-
> come calloused; they hardly hear with their ears, and they have
> closed their eyes. Otherwise they might see with their eyes, hear
> with their ears, understand with their hearts and turn, and I
> would heal them.'"* MATTHEW 13:10-15, NIV

Jesus understood that the truth of our oneness and the implica-
tions of death for the ego would be resisted by all who still cher-
ished their desires, attachments and bodily existence. The
Pharisees resisted it. In the above scripture, the "haves," those
who had developed deeper vision, would be "added to" because
they would be fertile soil for the wisdom and love of the Christ.
The "have nots," those who had no understanding but lived only
for the ego and the body, would lose whatever they had by denying the Christ when they had come face to face with him. They

would have to reap the seeds of their denial and be plunged into an even greater ignorance.

In Mark, Jesus refers to four types of persons who hear the truth (the "word").

> *The farmer sows the word. Some people are like seed along the path, where the word is sown. As soon as they hear it, Satan comes and takes away the word that was sown in them. Others, like seed sown on rocky places, hear the word and at once receive it with joy. But since they have no root, they last only a short time. When trouble or persecution comes because of the word, they quickly fall away. Still others, like seed sown among thorns, hear the word; but the worries of this life, the deceitfulness of wealth and the desires for other things come in and choke the word, making it unfruitful. Others, like seed sown on good soil, hear the word, accept it, and produce a crop—thirty, sixty or even a hundred times what was sown."*
> MARK 4:14-20, NIV

The first type of person hears the truth of our oneness in God but the darkness of the ego rejects it immediately. Such a person laughs at the truth and has contempt for it. The second type of person hears the truth and finds joy in it but has no sufficient depth of understanding to make a commitment to it. As soon as a choice has to be made between the inevitable conflicts such as being abandoned by worldly seeking friends, this person gives up. The third person encounters conflicts with desires and attachments to the objects of the world and has not sufficient spiritual strength to abandon them, and so he chooses the world and drops the truth. The last type of person hears the truth and accepts it, enduring the inevitable conflicts with the opinions of others and the habitual sense-bound pleasure seeking of the mind. Only in the latter person does the truth bear fruit.

Five hundred years before Jesus, Lao Tzu, a Chinese philosopher and "knower" of the Christ wrote the spiritual classic the *Tao Te Ching* or *Book of the Way*. In this text Lao Tzu makes the same observation as Jesus as to different levels of comprehension regarding the mystery of our being (here referred to as the Tao or "way").

When the best student hears about the Way
He practices it assiduously;
When the average student hears about the Way
It seems to him one moment there and gone the next;
When the worst student hears about the Way
He laughs out loud.
If he did not laugh
It would be unworthy of being the Way.

TAO TE CHING, TRANSLATED BY D.C. LAU,
PUBLISHED BY PENQUIN CLASSICS

When we use phrases like, "become as Jesus," or "merge in God," what we mean is that the ego dies, and God remains as the un-covered truth. God is always there in us, but we are blinded by the ego. To say there was a time God was not with us or in us is to say that God is not omnipresent. Before creation there was only God, and so there can only be God now. It is important to remem-ber that the ego which we currently regard to be our individual self is not God. The ego is not "something," but rather it is a delu-sion in the mind.

Be ye therefore perfect, even as your Father which is in heaven
is perfect.   MATTHEW 5:48, KJV

Here Jesus tells us to be that perfection even as God is perfect. He tells us to be as God is. In the following passage Ammachi says the same:

Having attained human form, we should elevate ourselves to
the Divine. We should surrender our individual selves totally
to God and thus become perfect.

AMMACHI, OMKARA DIVYA PORULE, PART 6

And who is God? God is the I AM. We must be the I AM which is real and not an ego which is make-believe.

The disciple is not above his master: but every one that is per-
fect shall be as his master.   LUKE 6:40, KJV

In the preceding scripture, Jesus tells us that as long as the ego remains, we are students, disciples. Therefore, we take a subservient position to Jesus and regard him as our master. He goes on to say that we can become perfect, and then we shall be *as* the master. We shall be as Christ is. Jesus continues to reveal the mystery of our oneness in Christ in the following scripture.

> *For I was hungry and you gave me something to eat, I was thirsty and you gave me something to drink, I was a stranger and you invited me in, I needed clothes and you clothed me, I was sick and you looked after me, I was in prison and you came to visit me.*
>
> *Then the righteous will answer him, "Lord, when did we see you hungry and feed you, or thirsty and give you something to drink? When did we see you a stranger and invite you in, or needing clothes and clothe you? When did we see you sick or in prison and go to visit you?"*
>
> *The King will reply, "I tell you the truth, whatever you did for one of the least of these brothers of mine, you did for me."*
>
> *Then he will say to those on his left, "Depart from me, you who are cursed, into the eternal fire prepared for the devil and his angels. For I was hungry and you gave me nothing to eat, I was thirsty and you gave me nothing to drink, I was a stranger and you did not invite me in, I needed clothes and you did not clothe me, I was sick and in prison and you did not look after me."*
>
> *They also will answer, "Lord, when did we see you hungry or thirsty or a stranger or needing clothes or sick or in prison, and did not help you?"*
>
> *He will reply, "I tell you the truth, whatever you did not do for one of the least of these, you did not do for me."*
>
> MATTHEW 25:35-45, NIV

Jesus is affirming that Christ (who is one with the father – the I AM) is absolutely and positively the true being of every person –

even those who are guilty of every crime! Christ is one with every murderer, rapist, pedophile and thief, and whatever we do to the least of these, we do to Christ. Jesus does not mean that they should not be in prison. We can be harmless as doves but wise as serpents (Matthew 10:16). Rather he is making a point about what our attitudes should be. This truth is so difficult to see from our present egocentric view of reality that even the "righteous" will be confused by this. Even the righteous will ask when they had ever seen Jesus hungry or when he was a stranger or was sick or in prison. Most will be baffled. Then Jesus explains that every human being is the same as him. By this he affirms that we are all one in Christ, we have always been one in Christ, and we will always be one in Christ. Whatever kindness we extend to the least among all human beings, we extend to Christ. And if we fail to provide this kindness to even the least among human beings, we have failed to provide the same to Christ. Jesus is telling us that we should regard every person as the same as himself. In the light of understanding revealed in our essential and original oneness in Christ, this makes perfect sense.

> Ye have heard that it hath been said, "An eye for an eye, and a tooth for a tooth:" But I say unto you, That ye resist not evil: but whosoever shall smite thee on thy right cheek, turn to him the other also. And if any man will sue thee at the law, and take away thy coat, let him have thy cloak also. And whosoever shall compel thee to go a mile, go with him twain. Give to him that asketh thee, and from him that would borrow of thee turn not thou away.

> Ye have heard that it hath been said, "Thou shalt love thy neighbour, and hate thine enemy." But I say unto you, Love your enemies, bless them that curse you, do good to them that hate you, and pray for them which despitefully use you, and persecute you; That ye may be the children of your Father which is in heaven: for he maketh his sun to rise on the evil and on the good, and sendeth rain on the just and on the unjust. For if ye love them which love you, what reward have ye? do not even the publicans the same? And if ye salute your brethren only, what do ye more than others? do not even the

publicans so? Be ye therefore perfect, even as your Father
which is in heaven is perfect.   MATTHEW 5:38-48, KJV

Again, if we understand that we are all connected in Christ then
the above scripture is clearly revealed. If our own flesh and blood
brother hit us we would turn the other cheek to him. If he asked
for our coat we would give him our cloak as well, and if he asked
us to walk a mile with him we would go two miles. If our brother
stole a car and went to prison for six months we would not abandon him. We would visit him often with no sense of condemnation. We would feel compassion for him, thinking he had simply
made a mistake. We should see every person as we would this
flesh and blood brother. This is because we actually are all brothers and sisters born of and having our being in the same father—
the I AM. With this view our love for others should be like the
sun which rises on the evil and the good and the rain which falls
on the just and the unjust. Jesus is saying our love should be unconditionally and universally given to anyone and everyone. In
this way we merge in God.

BE AS A LITTLE CHILD

The childlike innocence deep within you is God.
                    AMMACHI, AWAKEN CHILDREN, VOL. 6

Innocence does not mean naivete. For us, innocence means being childlike as opposed to childish. Innocence, along with love,
is the hallmark of the true or original nature of mankind. The
quality of innocence is a recurring theme in all major religions.
Seeing others with an attitude of acceptance and love, no matter
who they are or what they have done, is innocence. This is the reflection of our underlying unity that does not judge others to be
good or bad. This is how a child sees others. A child makes no
judgements as to religion, race, social status, wealth or education.
A five-year-old will play with anyone equally. "Equally" is the operative word. This is the innocence that was overthrown by the
ego in a pre-pubescent coup d'etat, thus causing us to accept or
reject others based on a set of conditions that we have con-

structed in our minds. This process of acceptance and rejection denies the truth that we are all one in Christ. It is a denial of God. Unless we regain this innocence, Jesus tells us that we are absolutely not getting into heaven. To pass judgement is to drive a wedge between ourselves and other persons, which destroys the feeling of unity and the presence of love.

> And he said: "I tell you the truth, unless you change and become like little children, you will <u>never</u> enter the kingdom of heaven."　　　　　　　　　MATTHEW 18:3, NIV [emphsis added]

We would profit to ponder this deeply. The Lord is flatly stating that unless we have reclaimed our innocence, we will not get into heaven. There are those who believe this passage has only to do with having faith in Jesus such as the faith of an innocent child. This is wishful thinking as most of us know we do not possess the innocence of our five-year-old daughter or nephew. If Jesus had meant innocent faith in himself instead of a broad based innocence, then the Lord would have said, "Unless you change and have faith in me as a little child would..." Certainly innocent faith in Jesus would be included in the innocence of a small child. However, the innocence that Jesus is talking about is much more than that. Let's look at the passage in context:

> At that time the disciples came to Jesus and asked, "Who is the greatest in the kingdom of heaven?"
>
> He called a little child and had him stand among them. And he said: "I tell you the truth, unless you change and become like little children, you will never enter the kingdom of heaven. Therefore, whoever humbles himself like this child is the greatest in the kingdom of heaven.　　　MATTHEW 18:1-4, NIV

As we can see, the topic of conversation is far from any idea of confessing one's belief in Jesus. Also, the idea that this scripture simply means innocent faith in Jesus makes no sense because Jesus was already talking to his most faithful, namely the disciples. He is telling the disciples that they must change and become as little children even though they were already faithful. Jesus is talking about humility. Jesus is telling them they must be humble like a little child. It is no wonder that many attempts are made to soften this scripture. With an understanding of the ego and its obscuring power, we can begin to glimpse the full impact and meaning of this scripture. As long as our ego prevails, there will be no innocence, and there will be no heaven.

To return to the Garden of Innocence, we must have a fundamental change in our mind and heart. Are we able to love everyone equally as the Master instructs in Matthew 5:44-45? Are we capable of *sincerely* praying for our enemies? If not, then we have fallen short.

Because it is so important to understand what it is to be innocent like a child, we will explore the Holy Mother Ammachi's discourse on innocence.

> *Ammachi: Look at a child. The child is not at all concerned about the past or the future. Whatever the child does, is done with total participation. The child is fully present in whatever he does, he cannot do anything partially. Children live in the present; this is why people feel so drawn to them. You cannot really dislike a child, because the ugliness of the ego is not present in the child.*
>
> *A child can attract anyone's attention; even the most cold-hearted person will have some feelings toward a child, unless the person is a demonic monster. This attraction is due to the innocence of the child. When you are free from the grip of the ego, you, yourself, will become as innocent and playful as a child.*
>
> *Most human beings live with one foot planted in the dead past, and the other in the future, which is not real. The future is an unreal dream which has yet to happen. You cannot be sure that it will actually happen in your case. The future is uncertain; it may or may not occur, and yet, the most intelligent human beings constantly worry and dream about the future, or they brood and cry recollecting the dead fossils of the past. Both the past and the future should disappear. Only then will you be able to live in this moment; for, it is in this mo-*

ment that you experience reality. This moment alone is real. The past and the future are unreal.

Jesus makes the same point as Ammachi regarding living in the present moment:

Consider the ravens: They do not sow or reap, they have no storeroom or barn; yet God feeds them. And how much more valuable you are than birds! Who of you by worrying can add a single hour to his life? Since you cannot do this very little thing, why do you worry about the rest? LUKE 12:24-26, NIV

The Holy Mother, Ammachi continues her talk on innocence:

Just as a child lives fully in the present, when you love, let your whole being be present in that love, without any divisions or reservations. Don't do anything partially, do it fully by being in the present moment. Don't brood on the past, and don't cling to it. Forget the past and stop dreaming about the future. Express yourself by being fully present, right now. Nothing, neither the regrets of the past nor the anxieties about the future, should interfere with the flow as you express your inner feelings. Let go of everything, and let your whole being flow through your mood. This is exactly what a child does.

A child doesn't have any attachments to the past nor does he worry about the future. When a child says, 'Mummy, I like you so much!' he really means it. Through his kisses, looks, and loving ways he expresses himself with his whole being. The child doesn't recall the scolding or thrashing he was given yesterday, nor is he upset because the toy he so badly wanted wasn't bought for him; and he has no worries about tomorrow. He doesn't hold onto anything. The child simply loves and forgets. A child can never do anything partially. Whenever he does anything, he is fully present. Doing something partially is possible only when there is an ego.

Whatever a child does is not related to any memories. The child is in the present moment, and whether he is feeling love or anger, it is being fully expressed. But he will soon forget it

and pass on to the next moment. A child's expression, whether it be anger or love, are never caused by attachment. That is why even the anger of a child has a certain beauty. It is purely natural and spontaneous, and whatever is expressed sponta-neously, without any interference of the ego, has a beauty and charm of its own. But you have to be innocent to be that spon-taneous. This is why even the anger of a Mahatma (great soul) is beautiful, because the Mahatma is absolutely pure and innocent. His expressions are spontaneous, direct, and utterly natural. He is not reacting out of the past. He just is, right here, in this moment.

A grownup's anger is ugly. Nobody likes a person when he is angry. But the anger of a child is different. When a child is angry, the father, mother or someone else will lift the child into their arms and embrace him. They will kiss the child and do all they can to calm him down. Whereas the anger of a grownup is repulsive and will arouse the anger in others, a child's anger invokes our love and sympathy. It is the presence of the ego in the grownup, and its absence in the child, that makes the difference.

You can only be attached if you have an ego. The "ego makes you attached to the past, and as long as the ego's attachment to the past exists, you cannot express anything fully. Your ev-ery word and action will be tainted by the ego. The past creeps up before you and creates a fence between yourself and what-ever you do or say. Whatever you wish to express is first filtered through the fence of the past; thus the child or the innocence within, is completely blocked.

A child has no ego, no past or future. The child has no attach-ments, and because of this, he is able to express himself fully, without any prejudices or preconceived ideas.

Grownups believe they have grownup, that they should no longer be like children, and that childlike qualities are some-thing to be ashamed of. But what really has grown up in the grownup is the ego. The body, intellect, and ego may have grown, but the heart, i.e., such essential qualities as love and *compassion, is on its death-bed. People think they have become mature adults. But are they really grown up and mature?*

The body has changed from a child's body into a grownup body, but the inner personality is still undeveloped.

If you continue to cling to the past, you cannot call it maturity. Of course, you can find people with a so-called mature ego, but among them you will not find a truly mature human being. A person with a mature ego may behave in a decent and refined way, but he still acts and speaks in the light of his past. His words and actions in the present are rooted in his past experiences. He has made many mistakes in the past. He has learned a lot from all those experiences; and now, whenever he says or does anything, he is careful not to repeat the same mistakes and not to say something foolish, because he knows from experience that this could create problems. So he chooses his words carefully and acts with deliberation. This shows that the past is still working within him, in a subtle, refined, and powerful way. We may call this maturity, intellectual maturity or maturity of the ego—but it is not real maturity.

Real, genuine maturity develops when you drop the ego and you stop dwelling in the past. When the inner Self is allowed to express itself, without being tainted or interrupted by the ego, a spontaneous and genuine maturity unfolds.

Grow without allowing your innocence to be destroyed; and as you grow, remain humble in all circumstances. Your physical growth should not affect the child within. Let your intellect become sharper, let your mind gain more clarity and vigor, but along with the development of your faculties, the feelings of the heart should also be allowed to grow. Such growth is perfect growth in perfect proportion. It will help you maintain a healthy and intelligent attitude towards life, in every possible situation. This verily is the fundamental foundation of life, which allows you to experience a loving and intelligent relationship with everyone and everything.

AMMACHI, AWAKEN CHILDREN, VOL. 8

Jesus comments again in Luke on the importance of being as a little child. He tells us that the secrets of the kingdom are not revealed by knowledge of scripture or philosophy. The mysteries can only be glimpsed from the high mountaintop of innocence. True knowledge has to do with the heart and not the intellect. Children are still in touch with their hearts, whereas in most adults the heart has been reduced to a dim spark or obscured completely by the darkness of the ego.

> *At that time Jesus, full of joy through the Holy Spirit, said, "I praise you, Father, Lord of heaven and earth, because you have hidden these things from the wise and learned, and revealed them to little children. Yes, Father, for this was your good pleasure."*   LUKE 10:21, NIV

Again mirroring Jesus' comment on childlike innocence and humility Ammachi says:

> *To be truly humble is to bow down, not just with your body but with your entire being. You should feel with your whole being that you are nothing, not just before the Master or a few selected souls, but before all of creation.*
>   AMMACHI, AWAKEN CHILDREN, VOL. 8

To be nothing is salvation, and yet "nothing" does not mean that existence stops. It means that our individual self no longer claims to own any part of life including our own. In that way of experiencing, how can we continue to regard ourselves as an individual? And yet, everything remains as it is. Our individuality is defined by what we possess. To not possess anything including (and especially) our own selves is to be truly liberated.

In summary, the essential core nature of man is God and is good. However, we have lost touch with God within us like the prodigal son. This "losing touch" is represented by the story of the fall of Adam and Eve and also by Satan being cast out of heaven and separated from God. The sense of separation is the ego, and it is the ego, like mud on a looking glass, that prevents us from seeing our true nature.

3

The Nature of Evil

The battlefield of Kurukshetra* is there both outside and inside. Symbolically, it is the constant war which is fought within each one of us between righteousness and unrighteousness, vice and virtue, untruth and truth, evil and good, the demons and God.   AMMACHI, AWAKEN CHILDREN, VOL. 1

In this chapter we will explore the question of unhappiness and its causes. Why do we experience pain, suffering and calamity, and what should we do about it? Where does fear and anxiety come from, and how do we get rid of it? We will dive to the very source of our deepest infirmities in order to assess the damage. Armed with this knowledge, we will be inspired to find a course of action to rectify it.

DOES EVIL EXIST?

To say that we are all God flies in the face of our everyday experience. We are reluctant to believe that Adolph Hitler or Jack the Ripper is God. Even if we admit that they might be God in the depths of their souls, we are still pained to reconcile their actions with a reality in which only God exists. If only God exists, why is there evil? Why does God allow people like Hitler and the Ripper to inflict so much suffering on others? This philosophical question has been in circulation for ages.

---

* From the religious epic The Mahabharata which also gives us the *Bhagavad Gita* wherein Lord Krishna reveals the Way to his friend Arjuna.

The minds of our two examples were inclined to perform evil actions because they did not have the wisdom of unity. The absence of wisdom and love meant that their minds were ignorant of God and their own true nature. Without this "knowing" they became self-serving. They lost touch with the universal harmony of the cosmos. Their view of life became small, narrow and dark. Lacking the discrimination to set a course that conformed to the universal order, they were ships without rudders. Chaos was the result.

There are evil acts in the world because people have created them in their minds. With regard to human beings, evil is any act or thought that harms nature or others for the sole purpose of fulfilling a selfish end. Evil is the ego in action in the same way that compassion is love in action. Suffering, on the other hand, is not necessarily evil. Suffering is necessary for this world of duality to exist. One cannot have pleasure without pain, good without bad or hot without cold. The river of God's awareness flows between the banks of pleasure and pain. Suffering is also our greatest teacher. From it we eventually learn to abandon the pleasure fields of the senses and turn towards God, who is the only lasting source of happiness.

All deeper spiritual questions such as the existence of evil can be addressed from two points of view with both being paradoxically true at the same time. There is the absolute point of view and the relative point of view.

From the absolute point of view, there is only God. There is nothing that exists outside of God. From this absolute way of seeing, evil is an illusion and not real. In our conversations we speak of evil as though it were a real substantial entity, but in fact, it is an imagined reality having its existence only in our mind. Sufferers of schizophrenia hear voices and hallucinate, so it is difficult to convince these persons that the apparitions are in their own mind. In the same way evil is the hallucination of separateness. Can we say that the lake we see in the desert as a mirage is part of the desert? In the same way, we cannot say that evil is part of God. It is only an appearance.

On the other hand, from the relative point of view, it will not help those of us caught in the quicksand of suffering to simply say evil is not real. That would be like telling a starving man that he is not the body in order to appease his hunger. Evil may ultimately be an illusion, but the problem is that we believe that the darkness and the untruth of our ego is real. Evil is the result. We see real evil actions in the world. In this way of seeing, evil is real and the ignorance that causes it should be resisted with all the vigor we can muster.

THE PERSONIFICATION OF EVIL

Satan is a Hebrew word pronounced Suh-tawn'. The name Satan is derived from a root word meaning "to oppose" or "to be or to act as an adversary." In some Old Testament scriptures, he is not malevolent and was sent by the Lord as a protector. Examples of passages using this interpretation include:

> But God was incensed at his going; so an angel of the LORD placed himself in his way as an adversary [Hebrew: satan].
> NUMBERS 22:22

> He shall not march down with us to the battle, or else he may become an adversary [Heb: satan] in battle. 1 SAMUEL 29:4

> Appoint a wicked man over him; may an accuser [Heb: satan] stand at his right side. PSALM 109:6

In Job 1:6-8, Satan is the servant of God and does nothing without the permission of God. He appears along with the other "ben Elohim" (sons of God) implying that he is one of the angel-ministers of Yahweh. The Jewish tradition has a very different view of Satan than does orthodox Christianity. Judaism believes Satan works for God and has a job to do, which is to test, prod and thereby bring humans into spiritual maturity.

With regard to the human mind, Satan is our evil inclination or the ego. The ego is that which hides the knowledge of our true nature with the illusion of separateness. This illusion comes from our mistaken identifications with the body and its senses in the same way that the hot midday sun causes the mirage of a lake to appear on the desert floor. This illusion, in turn, gives rise to the sense of "I" and "mine" like yeast that is mixed into flour and water. Ignorance of our true nature is the root sin that manifests in various forms such as greed, selfishness, hatred, covetousness, envy and vanity. From these arise a plethora of emotional sufferings such as strife, grief, anxiety and fear.

The personification of all egos (the collective ego) is called Satan in the biblical scriptures. This collective ego has a unified intelligence of its own which works purposefully to maintain the illusion of separateness. So there are forces of ignorance that seek to perpetuate ignorance both within and without. Using the paradigm of Carl Jung's *collective unconscious*, we see there is a pooling of the egoistic inclinations of all people. These negative, self-centered tendencies exert themselves as though functioning as a single intelligent being. It is the direction of these forces to encourage egoistic tendencies in the thoughts and feelings of us all. In so doing it perpetuates itself.

Hindu and Buddhist traditions also have their "Satan" and a hierarchy of demons (known as "asuras" in Sanskrit). Buddha was sorely tested by Mara the tempter just prior to his enlightenment as he sat under the Bodhi tree. Among other things, the Buddha was offered the kingship of all lands, and beautiful nymphs tried to seduce him. The central difference between these traditions and the Christian concept is that Hinduism, Buddhism and Judaism accept the occurrence of these negative forces as part of the whole of existence. There is a sense of integration whereby absolutely nothing is excluded. Good and bad are seen as interdependent whereby it is not possible for one to exist without the other. Even so, these paths are clearly focused on transcending or purifying the demonic and egoistic qualities that have taken up residence in our minds.

In the orthodox Christian view, Satan unilaterally rebelled against God and was cast out of heaven by Archangel Michael after a great war (Revelation 12:7). Satan then inherited an earth that is also separate from God, which Satan then set about to further corrupt and destroy. This reveals our underlying collective schizophrenia – the footprint of the ego. Such a unilateral rebellion in heaven without God willing it is not possible. Once the universe is divided into "us" and "them," or the children of God and the children of Satan, the next step is the demonization of our enemies or anyone that opposes us for any reason whatsoever. This plays into the ego's self-centered pursuit of its selfish ends, and we are now able to rationalize and justify killing others, ethnic cleansing and theft of land and possessions. For the ego, such a schism is perfect. It is also easy to understand how the demonization of tormentors could arise from 300 years of the Roman martyr factory whereby thousands of Christians were tormented or killed. In stark contrast to the demonization of our foes is Jesus' recommendation that we love our enemies and pray for those who persecute us (Matthew 5:44), that our love should be for everyone in the same way that the rain falls on the just and the unjust (Matthew 5:45). This is also the spirit of Mahatma Ghandi, Martin Luther King, Jr. and the Dalai Lama. From this schism of God and Satan also arises the idea that nature is inherently corrupt and evil. This brings us to an adversarial relationship with nature. She becomes something we must conquer and subdue rather than a partner warranting our love and cooperation.

How the Ego Works

With the relinquishing of all thought and egotism, the enlightened one is liberated through not clinging.
BUDDHA, MAJJHIMA NIKAYA 72:15

It is important that we try to understand the mechanism of the ego. By doing this, we can begin to discriminate between the real and the unreal, the permanent and the impermanent, the delusional and the sane. Once we understand what it is about us that is unreal, we can begin to glimpse our true nature. We will see that the ego is a liar and a thief and that it is the source of all the fear, tension, misery and war that has possessed humankind through the centuries. Hell is the shadow of the ego. Wherever there is ego, hell is sure to follow. The ego is like something that is borrowed. It doesn't really belong to us. Hell is what comes to collect the debt.

The ego is our sense of separateness as "I" and "mine" and arises from identification with the body. We have become blinded by the ego, thinking that we are the ego, and the more we think we are the ego, the more deeply we sink into spiritual darkness. In truth, we are spiritual beings who have been imprisoned in bodies by the belief that we *are* these bodies. Ego (Satan) does everything possible to continue to persuade us that we are mere mortal fleshly beings. Satan is our jailer and holds the door to our cell closed by means of our own desires and attachments. We could walk out right now–today–but we are unable to do so because we are spiritually blind like a horse with blinders and see only materially through the five senses. Our desires are the whip that drives us into this morbid existence.

Sri Krishna says:

> It is greedy desire and wrath, born of passion, the great evil, the sum of destruction: this is the enemy of the soul. All is clouded by desire: as fire by smoke, as a mirror by dust, as an unborn babe by its covering. Wisdom is clouded by desire, the ever-present enemy of the wise, desire in its innumerable forms, which like a fire cannot find satisfaction. Desire has found a place in man's senses and mind and reason. Through these it blinds the soul, after having overclouded wisdom.
> KRISHNA, BHAGAVAD GITA 3:37-40

The ego is composed of attachments which are things we like and things we don't like. From these attachments arise various desires which are the engine of rebirth in this earthly plane. We desire to possess that which is pleasurable, and we desire to avoid that which is unpleasant.

Our mistaken identification with the body gives rise to the illusory "I thought," which is further defined and developed by our association with various likes and dislikes. This development of the ego is to be expected. How could it be otherwise? Our own body appears to be separate from all others, thus the "I thought," or thought of being a separate individual, arises.

We know from our previous discussion of Bell's Theorem that we are not separate. If we are not separate then the ego is an illusion. If we look at a map of the United States we can trace our fingers around the border of our own state. However, if we were to go to the actual border location, we would see no such line. The ego is like this. It is an imaginary line drawn in the sand of our minds. This "I" that we imagine to be our own self, separate from others and from God, is only a concept in our mind. We go through life unaware that this ego we assume to be so real is actually no more than a bundle of thoughts. We continue this assumption because we have never stopped to investigate our egos, our own minds nor the source of our awareness. We have simply never stopped to ponder the question, "Who am I?"

We continue to enhance the illusion of being separate by clothing this "I thought" in colorful robes of identity such as name, age, nationality, food preferences, race, social status, religious beliefs and political persuasions. These trappings of identity are impermanent and are not our real selves. Furthermore, our identification with them leads us to reject others because they don't look or act like us or believe as we do. Their differences threaten our own self-ordained identities, creating a reaction of fear. About this Paul says:

> There is neither Jew nor Greek, slave nor free, male nor female, for you are all one in Christ Jesus.
> GALATIANS 3:28, NIV

For those of us who are absorbed in the ego, it is difficult to comprehend how we might exist without an ego in the same way, a city dweller cannot imagine living as a farmer, and a farmer cannot imagine living in the city. We have no experience with any other mode of existence. We have long forgotten any other point of reference, and our ego-centered view is all we know. The mind recoils in horror at the idea of abandoning the ego questioning how we could do business or even brush our teeth.

For one who has merged in God, the ego is dead. We may observe that person still making conversation and taking care of business. We may assume s/he has an ego, but s/he does not. The body and mind are still functioning, but such a person does not feel that s/he *is* the body and mind. Rather s/he feels that s/he is simply the observer of these comings and goings like one sitting on the beach watching one wave after another roll into the sand, break and slide back into the infinite ocean of being. Many of Jesus' most profound sayings can only be understood as a description of the absence of ego.

> *If someone strikes you on one cheek, turn to him the other*
> *also. If someone takes your cloak, do not stop him from taking*
> *your tunic.*   LUKE 6:29, NIV

Buddha said:

> *Overcome anger by love, overcome evil by good.*
>   DHAMMAPADA, 17:3

It is the ego that is offended and strikes back, and it is the ego that ignores the opportunity to help another. One who is without an ego will not have an "I" to be offended. There will not be a "me" who experiences loss.

> *Bless those who curse you, pray for those who mistreat you.*
>   LUKE 6:28, NIV

Only the ego feels mistreated. One can mistreat a dog, but it will quickly repay us with love because it does not have an ego. To one in whom the ego has been vanquished there is never a feeling of being mistreated or slighted. Such a one is the embodiment of humility.

> *Consider the ravens: They do not sow or reap, they have no*
> *storeroom or barn; yet God feeds them. And how much more*
> *valuable you are than birds!*   LUKE 12:24, NIV

As the ego is diminished, the sense of separation from life is also diminished. This person moves beyond faith and merges in actual "knowing." There is a sense of unbroken communion with all life and a sense of utter trust. There is no thought for the outcome of one's own physical circumstances because there is no one to be concerned about it. The egoistic anxiety is replaced with the knowledge of an all-pervading intelligence and love. In fact one becomes this "knowledge." This "knowing" produces a total and irrevocable trust in God like a small child trusts its mommy and daddy. Everything that comes, good and bad, is seen as God's will.

> *Blessed are the poor in spirit: for theirs is the kingdom of heaven.* MATTHEW 5:3, KJV

In the above scripture, the Greek word from which "poor" is translated is "ptochos," which means to be as a beggar or pauper living off alms that are begged for. By poor in spirit, Jesus does not mean to be unenlightened or ignorant but rather the opposite. Jesus means one who *is* enlightened. Such a one relies utterly on God for everything like a beggar with his cup held out. A person who lives life with this attitude will attain the kingdom of heaven. Such a person is totally bankrupt and has no ego left. There is no "I" or "me" that imagines itself to be in control of anything. For one who has made the ultimate sacrifice of his own ego, only God is in control. This idea is again expressed by Jesus:

> *Jesus saw infants being suckled. He said to his disciples, "These infants being suckled are like those who enter the kingdom."*
> GOSPEL OF THOMAS, NAG HAMMADI LIBRARY, VERSE 22

For Jesus, the body, mind and personality are a mask that can be put on or taken off at any time. For the purpose of restoring righteousness, God puts on a mask called Jesus and appears as one of us talking on our level. Even so, Jesus never for an instant succumbs to confusion about his identity with the eternal. He never mistakes the limited mask for his real Self. There is never any sense of attachment to the mask. The rest of us see ourselves as the mask and have no awareness of who is behind the mask.

If we continue to embrace our own egos then we will lose everything and gain nothing. This is because God is everything and the ego is nothing. As long as we cling to the egoistic delusion, we will be subject to suffering and death. We will be shipwrecked on an island of bad dreams divorced from divine truth. We will not know God. We must abandon the illusory ego in order to be with God. One cannot serve both God and mammon (Matthew 6:24), and oil and water will not mix.

Krishna comments to his friend Arjuna:

> From the world of the senses, Arjuna, comes heat and comes cold, and pleasure and pain. They come and they go: they are transient. Arise above them strong soul. The man whom these cannot move, whose soul is one, beyond pleasure and pain, is worthy of life in Eternity. The unreal never is: the Real never is not. This truth indeed has been seen by those who can see the true. Interwoven in his creation, the Spirit is beyond destruction. No one can bring to an end the Spirit which is everlasting. For beyond time He dwells in these bodies, though these bodies have an end in their time; but He remains immeasurable, immortal. KRISHNA, BHAGAVAD GITA 2:14-18

Jesus says:

> Then he said to them all: "If anyone would come after me, he must deny himself and take up his cross daily and follow me. For whoever wants to save his life will lose it, but whoever loses his life for me will save it." LUKE 9:23-24, NIV

Jesus is saying that if we try to save the ego we will lose life eternal. In India, monkeys are captured by putting a few nuts in the bottom of a jar with a narrow opening. The opening is large enough for the monkey's hand to go into the jar but narrow enough to prevent pulling the hand out if it is laden with nuts. The monkey reaches in, grabs the nuts and then refuses to let go and escape even as he screams and cries piteously at the approach of his captors. So too, we refuse to let go of the ego and escape into the boundless bliss of the Divine. Jesus is telling us again and again to abandon the self-centered ego and the illusion of separateness, and in so doing we will gain immortality.

And the Lord God commanded the man, saying, "Of every tree of the garden thou mayest freely eat: But of the tree of the knowledge of good and evil, thou shalt not eat of it: for in the day that thou eatest thereof thou shalt surely die."

GENESIS 2:16-17, KJV

The ego, or sense of being separate, is "the knowledge of good and evil." In order for something to be good or evil there must be an individual "I" to reference as the subject of good and evil. In other words good and evil are relative only to the individual ego. Therefore, eating the fruit of the knowledge of good and evil is the birth of the ego or the "I thought." Prior to that we existed in innocence. The dying that surely comes in the last three words of this scripture is not the death of the physical body. If that was the case, Adam and Eve would have died the same day they ate the fruit, but they did not. This kind of dying is the death of innocence caused by the coming of the ego. Since the ego and the attachments that clothe it are impermanent, we experience death again and again as we struggle vainly to cling to the perishable, the impermanent. The ego and the objects of the senses come as a wolf in sheep's clothing promising happiness. The fruit of this egocentricity and misplaced attention is bitterness, sorrow and suffering. As these impermanent things fade away, we suffer loss and death again and again and again.

The ego doesn't want us looking for God because when we find God, the illusion of being an ego will be destroyed. It will mean the end of our self-centered existence and all of its negative emotions and the reclaiming of the Garden of Eden. One cannot see God and continue to live as a separate person. Each and every day we will watch the mind carefully and destroy our divisiveness. We will stop separating and start uniting. We will stop hating and start loving. We will stop judging and start accepting. We will stop gossiping and start understanding. We will battle constantly against those habitual points of view that deny the oneness that Christ professes. This is what Paul meant by saying that he dies daily (Corinthians 15:31). Every day the stake of truth must be driven deeper into the heart of the ego. We will stop living to gratify the body and the senses which only inflames the "I am the body" illusion. This in turn pushes us deeper and deeper into the

darkness of a self-absorbed, self-centered, ego-intoxicated existence. By constant introspection and self-examination, we can put
an end to the ego's tireless efforts to validate its own illusory existence. It is our good fortune to be able to dig deeply into our
own library of desires and attachments and review them carefully.
Why do we think intellectuals are snobs? Why do we dislike for-
eigners? Why do we criticize those who do not dress as we do?
Why do we think that only those who believe as we do are going
to heaven? Why are we annoyed by a braggart? Why are we not
able to love everyone – what is it about us that prevents us from
doing so? A child can do these things, but we have forgotten how.

The ego wants us to believe that we are somehow basically corrupt in nature and that there is nothing about us that can be
trusted. And who does the ego think we should trust? The ego!
The ego may say we should trust God, but what the ego really
means is that we should trust our ego-centered beliefs and prejudices. Unless we understand the nature of the ego, it is difficult to
see this distinction. The ego is positively petrified to ponder "going within." The ego wants us to believe that going within will
deliver us to the same sea monsters that awaited thirteenth century sailors who considered sailing to the "edge of the world." The
ego doesn't want us to surrender to life or to love because the ego
must always be in control. It is afraid that it will die otherwise.
And it will.

BLINDED BY IGNORANCE

> The mind is the ego which makes you very self-centered. But
> instead of being self-centered you should be centered in the
> Self, the real center of your existence. For this to happen, the
> Mind should be extinguished. The ego should die. Only then
> can you be established in the state of sakshi bhava (witness
> consciousness).   AMMACHI, AWAKEN CHILDREN, VOL. 7

The ego's apparent existence is only borrowed from the I AM,
much like a shadow that appears to move about and seems to
have its own existence. Because we do not know God, we are un-

aware of how our existence can be managed without the ego. We would joyously give up our attachment to the ego if we could glimpse the true reality of our own beings. Jesus explains this in the following parables.

> The kingdom of heaven is like treasure hidden in a field. When a man found it, he hid it again, and then in his joy went and sold all he had and bought that field.
>
> Again, the kingdom of heaven is like a merchant looking for fine pearls. When he found one of great value, he went away and sold everything he had and bought it. MATTHEW 13:44-46

In both parables, a man discovers God (the treasure and the pearl) and gladly sells the ego and his worldly attachments to get back to God permanently.

Buddha says:

> If by giving up limited pleasures one sees far-reaching happiness, the wise one leaves aside limited pleasures, looking to far-reaching happiness. DHAMMAPADA 21:1

Once God has been discovered and we have tasted the sweetness of the Divine, we will give up everything for that. All excess baggage must be thrown overboard if our balloon is to rise into the stratosphere of God consciousness. There is no compromise here. There is only one way. Jesus was very clear about abandoning the separatist ego and its identification with the body.

> And he said unto his disciples, "Therefore I say unto you, take no thought for your life, what ye shall eat; neither for the body, what ye shall put on. The life is more than meat, and the body is more than raiment. Consider the ravens: for they neither sow nor reap; which neither have storehouse nor barn; and God feedeth them: how much more are ye better than the fowls? And which of you with taking thought can add to his stature one cubit? If ye then be not able to do that thing which is least, why take ye thought for the rest? Consider the lilies how they grow: they toil not, they spin not; and yet I say unto you, that

Solomon in all his glory was not arrayed like one of these. If then God so clothe the grass, which is to day in the field, and to morrow is cast into the oven; how much more will he clothe you, O ye of little faith? And seek not ye what ye shall eat, or what ye shall drink, neither be ye of doubtful mind. For all these things do the nations of the world seek after: and your Father knoweth that ye have need of these things. But rather seek ye the kingdom of God; and all these things shall be added unto you.

LUKE 12:22-31, KJV

If our lives come from God and are connected to God as the innermost aspect of our being, then we can never be away from God. We will see that God is in us and also everywhere at once. One who sees this way has no anxiety about having food to eat or clothes to wear. Such a person accepts what God brings and is secure in this direct communion with God. We can contemplate the Lord and let the Lord take care of the rest. Even the joys of family life are for sale when it comes to raising the funds to purchase the pearl of great price.

"I tell you the truth," Jesus said to them, "no one who has left home or wife or brothers or parents or children for the sake of the kingdom of God will fail to receive many times as much in this age and, in the age to come, eternal life."

LUKE 18:29-30, NIV

If anyone comes to me and does not hate his father and mother, his wife and children, his brothers and sisters—yes, even his own life—he cannot be my disciple. LUKE 14:26, NIV

"Yes, even his own life" means the ego, our individual existence – the "I" and the "mine."

Why does Jesus encourage us to abandon our relationships with significant others or at least abandon them in our minds if not physically? Jesus does not imply that we should stop loving these people. What he means is that we should stop expecting other people to be a source for our own happiness. We should turn to God alone for happiness. Deep and lasting happiness cannot come from any external source, be it person, place or thing. If we abide in the fullness of Christ, we will love these people and all people without expecting anything in return. Our love will be without conditions.

Avoiding Harmful Actions

> *Maya, the Great Power of Illusion, is pushing us back from progressing (spiritually). We are spending our days in body-consciousness with a heart full of sorrow. What a pity that the devil of desire, which affects us through illusory temptations, kicks us into the dark abyss of Maya (illusion), making us food for the god of Death. If you get caught in the grip of the devil of desire, woe to you for you will lose your soul. All worries will come to an end if only you give up your desires and keep your hopes in God alone.*
> AMMACHI, OMKARA DIVYA PORULE, PART 4

Various "evil" acts illustrate the point of view of the ego. Sinful actions, driven by our desires, are symptoms of the ego. Conversely, living a moral life is a symptom of becoming egoless. However, it is not enough to take an aspirin for a broken leg. The leg itself must be repaired. In like manner it is not enough to blindly follow moral laws. One must root out the cause of immoral actions, the ego. We may cut a weed off at the ground, but it will surely grow back. To eliminate the weed, the root must be taken out. The ego is the root.

To remain in the ego is to remain in hell. To go more deeply into the ego is to go more deeply into hell. Excessive fascination with bodily pleasures increases the I-am-the-body delusion in the mind, which in turn gives rise to increased self-centeredness and selfishness. Let's try to illustrate this mechanism. Imagine sitting down to a delicious meal at our favorite restaurant. As we take each bite, we chew it, and the body experiences pleasure. This programs the habitual mind to identify eating, chewing and bodily pleasure with happiness. Happiness then is experienced as being dependent on the body because a body is necessary for chewing and eating. Thus, the pleasure reinforces the I-am-the-body illusion, and we become more deeply identified with the body. This is why Ammachi says that in order to get the "taste of the heart" one must abandon the "taste of the tongue."

With the mind focused more on the body, our world shrinks until the ego is all that remains in the mind's field of view. Serving the whims of the body and the ego becomes one's sole occupation. Concern for others becomes a failing light that shrivels to a dim spark far away on the distant horizon of our awareness. Then it disappears altogether. When that happens we are utterly lost, and only God's direct intervention can find us. With this understanding, sex, food and other physical pleasures are not seen as being evil in themselves. Let's repeat this for emphasis: sex, food and other physical pleasures are not evil. Rather, evil is the ego which is fed by identifying with the body. Most of us can avoid neither food nor sex, but we can consider diminishing their importance.

We avoid negative habits like greed, jealousy and envy because they increase the feeling of being separate from others, and this hides the truth of our connectedness. We avoid pride because it increases the sense of separation. The ego will exclude others (they are poor; they are dirty; they are sinful; they are pagans; they are are somehow less than me, me, me) in order to make itself appear to be real. It is the presence of Satan (the ego) and his lieutenants (anger, vanity, arrogance, greed, etc.) in the mind that must be overcome. Jesus makes it clear in the following scripture that the mind must be controlled.

> But I say unto you, That whosoever looketh on a woman to lust
> after her hath committed adultery with her already in his heart.
> MATTHEW 5:28, KJV

And again the Lord tells us that it is the condition of the mind that is of paramount importance by equating anger with murder.

> You have heard that it was said to the people long ago, "Do
> not murder, and anyone who murders will be subject to judg-
> ment." But I tell you that anyone who is angry with his
> brother will be subject to judgment.   MATTHEW 5:21-22, NIV

What we think and feel can defile us as certainly as the physical act. If the mind becomes obsessed with personal pleasures, then the ego will be inflated by the dark obscuring power of selfishness, and separation from God will be the bitter fruit. It is the mind conditioned by desires that separates us from God.

Lord Krishna comments on this:

> When a man surrenders all desires that come to the heart and by the grace of God finds the joy of God, then his soul has indeed found peace. He whose mind is untroubled by sorrows, and for pleasures he has no longings, beyond passion, and fear and anger, he is the sage of unwavering mind. Who everywhere is free from all ties, who neither rejoices nor sorrows if fortune is good or ill, his is a serene wisdom. When in recollection he withdraws all his senses from the attractions of the pleasures of sense, even as a tortoise withdraws all its limbs, then his is a serene wisdom. Pleasures of sense, but not desires, disappear from the austere soul. Even desires disappear when the soul has seen the Supreme. The restless violence of the senses impetuously carries away the mind of even a wise man striving towards perfection. KRISHNA, BHAGAVAD GITA, 2:55-60

One who does not examine, come to understand, and finally control his or her own mind is lost. From the first day of our birth the world puts a self-centered view of reality into our mind, which is in error by one hundred eighty degrees. Therefore, these blind errant notions and habitual ways of thinking will have to be removed stone by stone.

THE PHARISEES

> Whatever is not understood, whatever is beyond the ordinary intellect, people want to destroy. They consider it as strange, unreasonable and illogical. Their egos cannot bear it. Not having an ego is unknown to them; therefore, they want to get rid of such egoless phenomena. They are afraid. They fear that such people will destroy their ego and make others egoless as well. If

the whole world becomes egoless, then the big, inflated egos will have no existence. They want the ego and the world to exist forever, for without the ego and the world, they cannot possess, acquire, enjoy and indulge. For them life is for that, not for becoming egoless. AMMACHI, AWAKEN CHILDREN, VOL.4

There is a humorous story. A man was expelled from his church, and he complained to God, "They won't let me in. I'm such a sinner." God replied, "They won't let me in either!" This story illustrates the narrow exclusionary attitude of the Pharisees in Jesus' time. The Pharisees were the dominant Jewish religious sect, and they sought to expel Jesus from their midst because he did not conform to their own view of religious interpretation. They decided to kill him because his teachings and his expanding popularity threatened them.

Studying the Pharisees is of great value in understanding the meaning of Jesus' life and teachings. In the drama of the four gospels, the Pharisees played the part of the anti-Christ, and Jesus frequently used them as an example of what not to do or what not to be like. Understanding who opposed Jesus and why will give us a more focused picture of the Master's teachings.

We will always have the Pharisees with us as they represent the narrow, dogmatic, legalistic, fundamentalist mindset that appears as vigorously in our present day as it did then. It was this same mindset that claimed to be the exclusive and singular chosen people of God in Deuteronomy 7:6 and, with that egoistic delusion of moral invincibility in hand, justified the wholesale slaughter of every man, woman and child in 1 Samuel 15:3. It was this mindset that burned thousands of Europeans at the stake in the Inquisition. The Pharisaic mindset appears in all religions as that which opposes truth by embracing the ego in the guise of religion. This mindset has several characteristics:

1. There is very little or no awareness of love. It is never discussed, much less practiced.
2. They alone are in possession of the true interpretation of reality.

3. No one can leave with blessings. Those who do leave are considered to have failed, having fallen into the influence of evil forces.
4. There are strict prohibitions against visiting any other paths or teachers.

To be fair, we must mention that there were many good Pharisees with deep spiritual understanding. Hillel was the leading Pharisee in the late 1st century B.C.E. and became the foremost authority on the oral tradition of Judaism that complimented the written law of the Torah. The central issue of his teaching was that mercy, kindness and compassion were at the core of all scripture and law. Paul was born a Jew and trained to be a Pharisee. In the following scripture Jesus encounters a wise Pharisee.

> *One of the teachers of the law came and heard them debating. Noticing that Jesus had given them a good answer, he asked him, "Of all the commandments, which is the most important?"*
>
> *"The most important one," answered Jesus, "is this: Hear, O Israel, the Lord our God, the Lord is one. Love the Lord your God with all your heart and with all your soul and with all your mind and with all your strength. The second is this: Love your neighbor as yourself. There is no commandment greater than these."*
>
> *"Well said, teacher," the man replied. "You are right in saying that God is one and there is no other but him. To love him with all your heart, with all your understanding and with all your strength, and to love your neighbor as yourself is more important than all burnt offerings and sacrifices."*
>
> *When Jesus saw that he had answered wisely, he said to him, "You are not far from the kingdom of God." And from then on no one dared ask him any more questions.*
>
> MARK 12:28-34, NIV

The Pharisees were learned and strict observers of religious law. According to the Rabbinic tradition, they were part of a direct line of preservers of the oral law from Ezra and the Men of the Great

Synagogue. The Pharisees believed in personal resurrection, retribution after death and a blending of predestination and free will. Most importantly was their insistence on the authority of oral law which, according to them, had been revealed to Moses along with the Torah (written law) and had equal authority with it.

The Pharisees were, for the most part, non-political with their religious values placed so far beyond other considerations that they were willing to embrace foreign rule rather than submit to any impious rulers in their own government. On one occasion, three different Pharisaic delegations appeared before Mark Antony pleading for the removal of Herod. This was done at great personal danger to the delegates.

The Pharisaic leaders often looked upon the religious laxity of the masses with disdain, and in an attempt to encourage greater ritualistic strictness, organized themselves into special fraternities (*haburot*; thus, the members were known as *haberim*). In spite of their strictness, the Pharisees enjoyed a wide popular following and were considered the spiritual spokesmen of the masses at the time of Jesus' ministry.

It is important to have a picture of the Pharisees as individuals. They were zealous religious practitioners. They followed the law with great sincerity and determination. This law not only included the Ten Commandments but a multitude of rules dealing with everyday affairs such as how to prepare food. Also, the Pharisees practiced many religious rituals on a daily basis with exact prescribed formulae. The typical Pharisee prayed to God before every meal and attended the temple regularly. The typical Pharisee was in an upper economic class, probably educated, and was considered to be an ideal citizen—a pillar of the community. No one would ever question their devotion to God. They would refer to God and praise God frequently in their common conversation with others. They could often be seen walking through town with their prayer beads on display. They would never do any work on the Sabbath in order to keep it holy.

Seeing through their displays of piety, Jesus refers to the Pharisees as hypocrites. In the original Greek text, the word for hypocrite is *hupokrites* which means literally an actor under an assumed character. At the time of Jesus, actors wore masks. The Pharisees were actors, and their righteousness was their mask. Beneath their righteous appearance is not love of God but the ego. Their religiosity was nothing more than a means to purchase the intoxicating drug of self-importance.

> *So when you give to the needy, do not announce it with trumpets, as the hypocrites do in the synagogues and on the streets, to be honored by men. I tell you the truth, they have received their reward in full.*   MATTHEW 6:2, NIV

> *And when you pray, do not be like the hypocrites, for they love to pray standing in the synagogues and on the street corners to be seen by men. I tell you the truth, they have received their reward in full.*   MATTHEW 6:5, NIV

> *When you fast, do not look somber as the hypocrites do, for they disfigure their faces to show men they are fasting. I tell you the truth, they have received their reward in full.*
>   MATTHEW 6:16, NIV

> *Woe to you, teachers of the law and Pharisees, you hypocrites! You give a tenth of your spices—mint, dill and cummin. But you have neglected the more important matters of the law—justice, mercy and faithfulness. You should have practiced the latter, without neglecting the former.*   MATTHEW 23:23, NIV

> *As he taught, Jesus said, "Watch out for the teachers of the law. They like to walk around in flowing robes and be greeted in the marketplaces, and have the most important seats in the synagogues and the places of honor at banquets. They devour widows' houses and for a show make lengthy prayers. Such men will be punished most severely."*   MARK 12:38-40, NIV

The ego of the Pharisees had adopted religion with its intricate tapestry of laws, doctrines and dogmas as an identity—as clothing. These distinctions granted the ego its charter to an imaginary existence. The maintenance of that identity was expensive. First their egos needed the approval of others because the ego is by nature insecure. Secondly their egos needed sinners as a backdrop against which to define their sense of righteousness. The result of this is more sinister. Without sinners there could be no contrast, and their own egos would lack clear definition. In order for the ego to be clearly defined, the position of righteousness must be practiced to the satisfaction of others, and the sinners must be reviled, spat upon and condemned. Jesus gave the following parable to those who were feeling righteous:

> *Two men went up to the temple to pray, one a Pharisee and the other a tax collector. The Pharisee stood up and prayed about himself: "God, I thank you that I am not like other men—robbers, evildoers, adulterers—or even like this tax collector. I fast twice a week and give a tenth of all I get."*

> *But the tax collector stood at a distance. He would not even look up to heaven, but beat his breast and said, "God, have mercy on me, a sinner." I tell you that this man, rather than the other, went home justified before God. For everyone who exalts himself will be humbled, and he who humbles himself will be exalted.*
> LUKE 18:10-14, NIV

The very foundation of these "men of God" is not love of God but ego—Satan. The more intense is the ego and sense of "I" and "mine," the more zealous one must be in religious practice, appearance and persecution of the unrighteous.

> *He said to them, "You are the ones who justify yourselves in the eyes of men, but God knows your hearts. What is highly valued among men is detestable in God's sight."* LUKE 16:15, NIV

Lord Krishna chastens this Pharisaic mindset thousands of years before Jesus:

> *There are men who have no vision, and yet they speak many words. They follow the letter of the Vedas (scriptures), and they say: "there is nothing but this." Their soul is warped with selfish desires, and their heaven is a selfish desire. They have prayers for pleasures and power, the reward of which is earthly rebirth. Those who love pleasure and power hear and follow*

their words; they have not the determination ever to be one
with the One.   KRISHNA, BHAGAVAD GITA 2:42-44

The greater the ego, the further one is from God and His kingdom. On the outside, the Pharisees appeared to be pure and obsessively religious, but on the inside there were only worms and scorpions. Two thousand years later, we still see the same mentality in great abundance worldwide. It appears in every religion.

> *Woe to you, teachers of the law and Pharisees, you hypocrites!*
> *You clean the outside of the cup and dish, but inside they are*
> *full of greed and self-indulgence.* MATTHEW 23:25, NIV

> *Woe to you, teachers of the law and Pharisees, you hypocrites!*
> *You are like whitewashed tombs, which look beautiful on the*
> *outside but on the inside are full of dead men's bones and ev-*
> *erything unclean.*   MATTHEW 23:27, NIV

On another occasion while teaching in the temple, the chief priests and temple elders confront Jesus. After some discussion Jesus pulls their masks off again.

> *Jesus said to them, "I tell you the truth, the tax collectors and*
> *the prostitutes are entering the kingdom of God ahead of you."*
>   MATTHEW 21:31, NIV

Jesus uses tax collectors as a reference because in his time the Romans would appoint tax collectors and allow them to collect more than the tax as a wage for their work. As a result there was much graft, corruption and extortion causing the populace to despise them. And again Jesus was fearless in exposing the egoistic narcissism of self-importance.

> *For I tell you that unless your righteousness surpasses that of*
> *the Pharisees and the teachers of the law, you will certainly*
> *not enter the kingdom of heaven.*   MATTHEW 5:20, NIV

The multitudes were astounded and shocked at these sayings because the people to whom he was speaking were the upright pillars of the religious community. They appeared to do everything as perfectly as it could be done according to everyone's understanding. Everyone thought the Pharisees would be the *first* into heaven, yet Jesus was telling the Pharisees that they would be the last into heaven. The Pharisees were more astounded than the multitudes. It's no wonder they executed him. Hell hath no fury like an ego scorned.

For all of his rebuking, Jesus loved even the Pharisees because he saw their true nature. Jesus knew that God was hidden inside of them waiting to be realized. His words were pointed and forceful because he knew it was his only chance to break through the hardened shell of their ego. He scolded them out of love. He put his own life in peril to save them. In the end he forgave the very ones who had him put to death. He knew they had acted out of ignorance and blindness.

> Then said Jesus, "Father, forgive them; for they know not what they do."
> LUKE 23:34 KJV

The Pharisaic mindset reappeared in the Christian bishops and deacons in the second century C.E. who claimed sole right to interpret and dispense the Christ by way of apostolic succession. The Pharisaic mindset also appeared in the inquisitors who put tens of thousands to death in Europe for disagreeing with the church's interpretations of the life of Christ. As before, these neo-Pharisees were convinced that they were doing God's work.

> They will put you out of the synagogue; in fact, a time is coming when anyone who kills you will think he is offering a service to God.
> JOHN 16:2, NIV

In the following scripture a futuristic eerieness seeps through the Lord's words. If Christ were to come today, no doubt many who profess to be Christians would not recognize him (or her). They would try to destroy the Christ again, all the while proclaiming that if they had lived at the time of Christ, they would definitely not have been among his tormentors.

> Woe to you, teachers of the law and Pharisees, you hypocrites! You build tombs for the prophets and decorate the graves of

the righteous. And you say, "If we had lived in the days of our forefathers, we would not have taken part with them in shedding the blood of the prophets." So you testify against yourselves that you are the descendants of those who murdered the prophets. Fill up, then, the measure of the sin of your forefathers! You snakes! You brood of vipers! How will you escape being condemned to hell? MATTHEW 23:29-33 NIV

By understanding the Pharisees of Jesus' time, we are able to recognize them in our own time. Just like those who are truly devoted and humble, our Neo-Pharisee attends church, Sunday school and Wednesday night prayer meetings without fail. He reads the Bible regularly and can quote scripture chapter and verse. He makes a show of praying before meals, especially in restaurants so others can witness his piety. He thinks wealth is God's gift to the righteous, and he wants his. He will aspire to a position of prominence within the church so that he may be esteemed by others, all the while publicly proclaiming that God himself had called him to serve. If he is not the minister, he will want to be a deacon or a lay minister. When confronted with the prospect of giving to the poor he will justify the unworthiness of the poor by saying they could get jobs if they wanted to. However, he will give money to Christian Ministry projects to save others from a non-Christian fate. He likes to drop comments about God into everyday conversation so that others may also admire his beautiful garments of religiosity. He does not feel compassion. He professes love only for his own "brethren," and the concept of universal and equal love for everyone is utterly incomprehensible to him. He claims not to judge because the scripture says not to, but his mind is filled with disgust and is revolted when in the presence of sinners and those of other faiths. His focus for relieving the problems of the world is more scripture, more discipline and more law—never more love, more compassion or more forgiveness. Our Neo-Pharisee laughs at the idea of merging in Christ or that God is in all of us because the very concept would tear down the castle walls of his self-created identity. God cannot be the center of his existence because that is the throne on which his own ego sits. God must be imprisoned in a heaven far away or the ego's dreamlike enchantment will be threatened. Our Neo-Pharisee is inflexible, intolerant and rigid in all things because his ego is so great. Day and night, his thoughts revolve around himself. Because his ego is so large, he must work very hard at its maintenance. Because of this, he evangelizes and proselytizes with an obsessive zeal to convert others to his narrow view. There's safety in numbers.

> *Woe to you, teachers of the law and Pharisees, you hypocrites! You travel over land and sea to win a single convert, and when he becomes one, you make him twice as much a son of hell as you are.*   MATTHEW 23:15, NIV

In the *Gospel of Thomas* we read:

> *Jesus said, "The Pharisees and the scribes have taken the keys of knowledge (gnosis) and hidden them. They themselves have not entered, nor have they allowed to enter those who wish to."*
> GOSPEL OF THOMAS, NAG HAMMADI LIBRARY, VERSE 39

2,000 years later nothing has changed. The study of the Pharisees brings us to the question as to who will recognize Christ when he returns. His return will not be grandiose as some think with the sky parting and trumpets blazing. Rather, it will be subtle, and most will not recognize him, and this will especially be true for the entrenched orthodoxy just as it was 2,000 years ago. As revealed in the parable of the 10 virgins, only those who have trimmed their wicks with childlike innocence and filled their lamps with the oil of love will recognize his return. As it was for the Pharisees, the mode of Jesus' return will be very unexpected.

WEALTH

> *To have God in us is a struggle in the beginning, but if we persist, it will lead us to everlasting bliss and happiness. All struggles will end. To embrace the world is easy and things go smoothly in the beginning, but this will culminate in never-ending sorrow and suffering. We are free to choose one or the other.*
> AMMACHI, AWAKEN CHILDREN, VOL. 4

It is worthwhile to examine the issue of wealth as an example of our expectation and dependence on external sources of happiness. This is not an attempt to roast wealthy people in particular. Because everyone commonly understands wealth and the desire for it, it is useful as a tool to explain the underpinnings of the ego. This discussion will apply to all desires that make happiness dependent on persons, places and things outside of ourselves.

At the writing of this book, it is somewhat common for orthodox ministers to preach the coming of wealth as a spiritual dowry bestowed on us by God as a reward for our faith. This was also the view of the Pharisees at the time of Jesus' appearance, and wealth was looked upon as a sign that the wealthy person had found favor with God. That is why Jesus' position on wealth was just as shocking to those who heard it then as for those of us who read it now. Jesus tells us that getting and possessing wealth is to be avoided. In the Lord's opinion, wealth should be regarded as a curse or at best a millstone around one's spiritual neck. The best that can be done with wealth is to give it to the poor. Many people then and now do not want to hear this. Preachers wishing to lure wealthy patrons to the donation basket will be tempted to distort the Lord's position on wealth. It is quite common in these days, and especially with smaller churches, to pay the minister with a percentage of the weekly donations.

As Jesus started on his way, a man ran up to him and fell on his knees before him. "Good teacher," he asked, "what must I do to inherit eternal life?"

"Why do you call me good?" Jesus answered. "No one is good—except God alone. You know the commandments: Do not murder, do not commit adultery, do not steal, do not give false testimony, do not defraud, honor your father and mother."

"Teacher," he declared, "all these I have kept since I was a boy." Jesus looked at him and loved him. "One thing you lack," he said. "Go, sell everything you have and give to the poor, and you will have treasure in heaven. Then come, follow me." At this the man's face fell. He went away sad, because he had great wealth.

Jesus looked around and said to his disciples, "How hard it is for the rich to enter the kingdom of God!" The disciples were amazed at his words. But Jesus said again, "Children, how hard it is to enter the kingdom of God! It is easier for a camel to go through the eye of a needle than for a rich man to enter the kingdom of God."

The disciples were even more amazed and said to each other, "Who then can be saved?"

Jesus looked at them and said, "With man this is impossible, but not with God; all things are possible with God."

MARK 10:17-27, NIV

For centuries, this saying has been a major stumbling block for Christians who still have an appetite for the pleasure, security, and comforts that money can provide. All cultures in all nations glorify and, in a secular way, worship wealth. This scripture disputes a fundamental aspect of our cultural psyche. From the day we are born until the day we die we hear the world's mantra, "Make money and buy things to be happy."

Buddha says:

Riches make most people greedy, and so are like caravans lurching down the road to perdition. Any possession that increases the sin of selfishness or does nothing to confirm one's wish to renounce what one has is nothing but a drawback in disguise.

JATAKAMALA 5:5 & 15

There have been numerous attempts to soften Mark 10:17 by implying that the "eye of the needle" was a physical place, albeit very narrow, that a camel might possibly get through. Another twist proposes that the Greek word *kamilos* meaning "cable" or "rope" is similar to the word *kamelos* meaning "camel" and that a mistake was made somewhere along the way in the translation. It is easier to imagine getting a rope instead of a camel through the eye of a needle but this explanation is still not too comforting. These salves are an attempt to soften the words "eye of the needle," but such palliatives do not tally with the rest of the scripture. Prior to the camel metaphor, Jesus says very plainly, "How hard it is for the rich to enter the kingdom of God!" The disciples were astonished! This saying is direct and without metaphor and precedes the famous "eye of the needle" saying. That the disciples understood the resoluteness of Jesus' radical position is revealed by their question to Jesus, "Who then can be saved?"

If the master's words are true, then how will *any* person ever arrive at the kingdom? Clearly the disciples did not have the idea that some camels will get through a narrow passageway. Jesus replies that a rich man's entry into heaven is possible by God's grace alone. In other words it is so difficult that it is not possible by any human effort. Again, this negates any fudging with tiny ropes and narrow passageways as these could be accomplished through the efforts of men. Jesus is saying a wealthy person may still have a chance by God's grace, but we must consider how few will attain that grace. Jesus did not tell the wealthy man to simply pray for God's grace. He told him to sell everything and give it to the poor.

Why does Jesus take such a hard position? As we recall, the ego is fed by our attachments to the body and the pursuit of making the body comfortable and the mind entertained. Thus, comfortable and entertained, we are distracted from the purpose of life which is to know God. The search for God requires much work and strong intent. The ego defines itself by the outer personality and conditions such as status, wealth, power or the lack of it. It is so tempting to feel a false sense of security, status and power when in the possession of wealth. The ego believes that its wealth is the source of its being. Again Jesus says:

> No man can serve two masters: for either he will hate the one, and love the other; or else he will hold to the one, and despise the other. Ye cannot serve God and mammon. MATTHEW 6:24, KJV

The dictionary defines "mammon" as 1. Riches; wealth. 2. Worldliness; avarice. And then "Mammon" as 1. The personification of riches, avarice, and worldly gain.

Again Jesus advises us:

Sell your possessions and give to the poor. Provide purses for yourselves that will not wear out, a treasure in heaven that will not be exhausted, where no thief comes near and no moth destroys.   LUKE 12:33, NIV

Again the Lord says:

And he said unto them, "Take heed, and beware of covetousness: for a man's life consisteth not in the abundance of the things which he possesseth."   LUKE 12:15, KJV

In the following scripture his position is still radical. Give up *everything*. If we do not, we cannot be the Lord's disciples.

In the same way, any of you who does not give up everything he has cannot be my disciple.   LUKE 14:33, NIV

James wrote another similar commentary on wealth echoing the sentiment of the Lord.

Go to now, ye rich men, weep and howl for your miseries that shall come upon you. Your riches are corrupted, and your garments are moth-eaten. Your gold and silver is cankered; and the rust of them shall be a witness against you, and shall eat your flesh as it were fire. Ye have heaped treasure together for the last days.   JAMES 5:1-3, KJV

Eliminating the ego is the goal, and if circumstances in the world make that difficult then we must "pluck out that eye" (Mark 9:47). Attachment to the world and the objects of the senses is the playground of the ego. This is why the Lord advises separating oneself from worldly attachments.

Do not love the world or anything in the world. If anyone loves the world, the love of the Father is not in him. For everything in the world—the cravings of sinful man, the lust of his eyes and the boasting of what he has and does—comes not from the Father but from the world. The world and its desires pass away, but the man who does the will of God lives forever.
                                                                   1 JOHN 2:15-17, NIV

And in the *Gospel of Thomas*:

> *Jesus said, "Whoever has come to understand the world has found (only) a corpse, and whoever has found a corpse is superior to the world."*
>
> GOSPEL OF THOMAS, NAG HAMMADI LIBRARY, VERSE 56

This means that if we realize the nature of the world, we will find a dead end or a corpse, and if we have come to that realization, we have taken a few steps toward the spiritual path.

It is most important to eliminate the root of these attachments in the mind. If these attachments and worldly expectations are not dealt with we will be distracted from the goal of realizing God. We will be like Lot's wife whose worldly attachments caused her to lose focus as she was fleeing the destruction of Sodom and Gomorrah. Overcome by her attachments to the cities and what the cities represented, she disobeyed her instruction to not look back, and as a result, she became a pillar of salt. So, too, we will habitually continue to embrace our attachments. We will fall again and again into a state of spiritual death and unconsciousness.

It is the ego with its myriad of desires that must be destroyed. We must eliminate the ego. We must stop seeing ourselves as disconnected individuals separated from God. Unless this is accomplished, we will not be able to join Christ in heaven. We must see our positions in life as the characters we play. In this way we would not hesitate to change characters, or if our current character's part came to an end in the scene, we would be just as happy to take up a different part. It would make no difference to us because our sense of identity would not be attached to any of them. We would understand at all times that we were the birthless and deathless I AM and that we had no particular form or identity. We would understand there is no place to call home. Rather, we would realize our eternal nature, which is self-existent as the one I AM, and not separate from any others.

> *Jesus replied, "Foxes have holes and birds of the air have nests, but the Son of Man has no place to lay his head."*
>
> MATTHEW 8:20, NIV

We should know that our nature is pure being, which is empty like space. Realizing this truth is our liberation.

In summary, Satan is the ego or the illusion of separation. The thought of "I" and "mine" hides the reality of our infinite and connected nature in the same way that mud on a lens prevents one from seeing through it. This veiling power of the ego gives birth to evil acts in the world. It is important to understand the nature of the ego in order to surrender it and make spiritual progress. Also, our study of the ego sheds much light on why and how the direct and radical teachings of Jesus could be subverted and bent.

4

Scripture

It is a pity that most people who are in the field of scriptural study pursue intellectual learning without applying what they've learned in their own lives. They think that they have reached the goal, but as far as their actions are concerned, they are no better than a non-believer caught up in the world of likes and dislikes. They are full of ego. They don't know that the words which they have been studying and repeating in their heads have actually created a big wall between them- selves and God. AMMACHI, AWAKEN CHILDREN, VOL. 4

The purpose of this chapter is to instill the possibility in the reader that there may be more to the spiritual path than scripture, and that scripture, though mostly God inspired, is, after all, made of words, and words are limited. Prayer and love may take us to God, but words will never do this because God cannot be con- tained in a box of words. Notwithstanding any errors that have occurred in the translations and copying of scripture through the centuries, scripture is still valuable. Nevertheless, it is important to understand the limitation of scripture. Love is a higher, more reliable revelation of truth than scripture, and it is available to ev- eryone right now.

There is a common orthodox belief that scripture is error free be- cause God has personally guarded every word through all time. Those who suggest that scripture may have errors are accused of being unable to surrender to God.

The infallibility camp reasons that admitting inaccuracy in the scriptures would grant one license to do anything. They explain that if one part of it can be wrong then the whole of it cannot be trusted. If the scriptures have been tweaked and subverted to some degree, then upon what may we depend for spiritual guidance? What can we trust? Paul tells us:

> If I speak in the tongues of men and of angels, but have not love, I am only a resounding gong or a clanging cymbal. If I have the gift of prophecy and can fathom all mysteries and all knowledge, and if I have a faith that can move mountains, but have not love, I am nothing. If I give all I possess to the poor and surrender my body to the flames, but have not love, I gain nothing. 1 CORINTHIANS 13:1-3 NIV

The answer is love. We can always trust love. It is important to remember this as we examine the issue of scriptural infallibility. When we poke the pin of historical truth in our inflatable boat of scripture, we will have a solid ocean liner to rescue us. This ocean liner is love. Love is our primary guide, and scripture is a distant second. And just what is love? God is love (1 John 4:8 & 4:16). What were Jesus' two commandments? Love God and love our neighbor. Love is the operative word. One who has selfless love will not err. One who has scripture but no love is already lost. Paul says:

> The commandments, "Do not commit adultery," "Do not murder," "Do not steal," "Do not covet," and whatever other commandment there may be, are summed up in this one rule: "Love your neighbor as yourself." Love does no harm to its neighbor. Therefore love is the fulfillment of the law. ROMANS 13:9-10, NIV

Even if scripture were the direct unaltered word of God, we would still be lost without love because the ego will interpret the words to suit its own desires and delusions. Any position or belief can be scripturally justified by anyone as a matter of lopsided personal emphasis or interpretation. Militant hate groups quote Jesus overturning the moneychanger's tables as evidence that bombing, maiming, and killing are justified. In the Inquisition, many thousands were hanged or burned at the stake for heresy – all justified by scripture. The Klu Klux Klan regard themselves as soldiers of Christ. All of these groups used scripture to justify their reign of horror and to give their actions the appearance of righteousness. Therefore, it is important that we engage in self-examination to see if we have made any personal investment in the practice of love. If we have not, we must set upon a course of uncovering and cultivating love with the intensity of one fleeing a burning house. Love is the path that Jesus taught.

As we mentioned in the previous chapter, churches, pastors and organizations that do not emphasize the importance of love beyond every other point of dogma or doctrine have not understood Jesus. They are the blind leading the blind. It is astonishing to read through the mountain of Christian literature and find almost nothing addressing the topic of love. It is astounding to review the curriculum of bible colleges and see nothing about the path of love. It is dumbfounding to realize that comparative religion as taught in any university will have nothing to say about love. It is unbelievable that we can sit through hundreds of sermons and not hear a single one on the nature of love and how to become more loving.

Let's examine scripture to see for ourselves whether it is fallible or infallible.

In most every instance where the Greek word "Logos" appears in the New Testament it is translated into English as "word" (e.g. God's word). By reading the English Bible one could assume that when Jesus says "word" he is referring to scripture as in the following:

> But he said, "Yea rather, blessed are they that hear the word of God, and keep it."　　　　　　　　　　LUKE 11:28, KJV

However, in the original Greek, Logos is a much bigger concept than speech or scripture. Logos is the cosmic order or cosmic mind that can only be heard or comprehended in the depths of the ocean of spirit and never in the shallow waters of scripture or speech. Jesus makes this distinction clear in the following passage:

*Why do ye not understand my speech even because ye cannot
hear my word?*   JOHN 8:43, KJV

Jesus was telling the Pharisees in this scripture that they were hearing his speech but they were not capable of understanding what he
meant because they did not comprehend the cosmic picture–the
Logos–the Word. In both of the previous scriptures this meaning is
lost in the English translation. Unless we have dived into the
depths of the Logos, the reading of any scripture will remain shallow. This opens scripture to distortions and biased interpretations.
Thus, scripture can never be the goal, the end or the absolute.
There is a saying, "Before one realizes God, scripture is misunder-
stood. After one realizes God, scripture is unnecessary."

Simply put, scriptures are a road map and not the goal. Studying
scripture to gain knowledge of God is like trying to live in the
blueprint of a house. Trying to glean God from scripture is like
writing the words "Star Spangled Banner" on a piece of paper
and then holding the paper to our ears to hear it.

The Pharisees believed that the keys to heaven were in following
the Law. They had lost the understanding that the key to heaven
is love and that it is the ego that keeps us from love. When the
ego is removed, spontaneous unconditional divine love flows as a
spring of eternal life from our innermost beings. Thus, the meaning of life can never be found in scriptures and can only be found
in life itself. To see it, we need a child's eyes–the eyes of love–not
an adult's eyes.

Any among us who have adopted the position that the Bible has
arrived at the twenty-first century as the perfect, pristine and unaltered word of God will be caught in a cross-fire at the close of
the Bible in The Revelation of Saint John.

> *I warn everyone who hears the words of the prophecy of this
> book: If anyone adds anything to them, God will add to him
> the plagues described in this book. And if anyone takes words
> away from this book of prophecy, God will take away from
> him his share in the tree of life and in the holy city, which are
> described in this book.*   REVELATION 22:18-19, NIV

If the scriptures could not be altered, diluted, changed, mistranslated, removed or falsely added to, then God would not have bothered to impose a penalty for doing that. If God has truly given us free will then we have the free will to alter scripture. If we are not free to alter scripture then God did not really give us free will.

God himself set the precedent for inevitable human error regarding stewardship of the scriptures. God placed Adam and Eve in the Garden of Eden, granted them access to the fruit of good and evil and even allowed the serpent access to the primal couple in order that they might be tempted into the "fall." If God would permit these colossal liberties, then certainly granting man sufficient free will to corrupt the scriptures pales in comparison.

There are several scriptures which are commonly quoted by those who believe in the infallibility of scripture to support their belief.

> *Think not that I am come to destroy the law, or the prophets: I am not come to destroy, but to fulfil. For verily I say unto you, Till heaven and earth pass, one jot or one tittle shall in no wise pass from the law, till all be fulfilled.* MATTHEW 5:17-18, KJV

Many claim this to be Jesus' stamp of approval to the whole of the Old Testament. However, Jesus did not say "scripture" but "law" and we are left with having to determine what he meant by "law." He probably does not mean the 10 commandments or the 613 Mosaic laws, as Jesus himself broke or rebuked a number of these (to be examined later). Rather, he is probably speaking specifically about his mission as the Messiah because he is saying this "law" shall stand until it is "fulfilled." One does not "fulfill" one of the ten commandments or any of the kosher food laws. Regardless of what "law" Jesus is talking about, it is no more than wishful thinking to twist this scripture into proclaiming the infallibility of all scripture.

> *Jesus answered them, "Is it not written in your Law, 'I have said you are gods'? If he called them "gods," to whom the word of God came—and the Scripture cannot be broken—what about the one whom the Father set apart as his very own and sent into the world? Why then do you accuse me of blasphemy because I said, 'I am God's Son'?"* JOHN 10:34-36, NIV

The actual Greek transliteration of "the scripture cannot be broken" is "not able to be abolished." Jesus is about to be stoned to death, and he is pointing out the flaw in *their* thinking. Jesus is not saying that he himself believes the scripture cannot be broken. This scripture does not indicate that Jesus thinks there are no errors in the Old Testament, and his actions indicate the opposite. Jesus certainly "abolished" many pivotal Old Testament scriptures like the Sabbath (one of the 10 commandments), observing kosher food laws, and "an eye for an eye and a tooth for a tooth."

Now we will look at 2 Timothy, 3:16 which is often quoted as proof of infallibility.

> *All scripture is given by inspiration of God, and is profitable for doctrine, for reproof, for correction, for instruction in righteousness:* 2 TIMOTHY 3:16, KJV

This scripture creates the infamous closed-circle-of-proof. My saying I am Napoleon makes me Napoleon, which in turn means that my statement that I am Napoleon is true. This is a closed circle of proof. But what if Paul is wrong about this? Why do we assume Paul's inclusion into the New Testament makes him perfect? He never met Jesus personally. The closed-circle-of-proof is broken when we look at the Old Testament scriptures that Jesus rebuked. These were supposedly Old Testament instructions and commandments given directly from God to Moses and Aaron. If God really did say these things to Moses and Aaron as the Bible states, then why did Jesus say they were wrong?

Another very important point is that God didn't tell the Jews to kill other people and take over their lands. That was the Israelites writing their own history book and attempting to cover ethnic cleansing and base covetousness with a sugar coating of righteousness. Even if it were true that the scripture was originally given by God's inspiration, that does not mean the scriptures have escaped the contortions of the minds of men as the scriptures passed through the long corridor of time. If we are allowed to use the closed-circle-of-proof with this scripture, then we must also be allowed to use it with the Revelation 22:18-19 passage quoted previously. If this Revelation scripture is infallible, then God is telling us scripture *can* be broken.

With regard to Timothy 3:16, it is of further interest to note that most Bible scholars now agree that Paul did not write 1 and 2 Timothy nor Titus. Rather, these books are forgeries and were written after Paul's death by an anonymous author. A brief review of the evidence is discussed further in Appendix A at the end of this book.

Evidence of scriptural tampering is found in Joshua and 2 Samuel.

> *Is not this written in the book of Jasher? So the sun stood still in the midst of heaven, and hasted not to go down about a whole day.*   JOSHUA 10:13, KJV

> *(Also he bade them teach the children of Judah the use of the bow: behold, it is written in the book of Jasher.)*
> 2 SAMUEL 1:18, KJV

If God wrote these two scriptures, and God is referring us to the book of Jasher, then why should anyone have presumed to remove the book of Jasher from the Bible?

There are also unmanageable conflicts in the four gospels. In Matthew 2:11 we read that Jesus was born in a house and not a manger as stated in Luke 2:7. One of these is wrong. Somebody made a mistake, and God did not stop it or correct it.

One need only compare the many English versions of the Bible to see radical differences in fundamental issues. They can't all be correct. Rather, it is reasonable to say all of them contain imperfections and distortions. We can see many deviations in the interpretation of the original Greek version of the New Testament. To follow is a single scripture interpreted first by the King James Version Bible and the second by the New International Version Bible in which Jesus explains an important spiritual principle:

> *The light of the body is the eye: if therefore thine eye be single, thy whole body shall be full of light. But if thine eye be evil, thy*

*whole body shall be full of darkness. If therefore the light that
is in thee be darkness, how great is that darkness!*
MATTHEW 6:22-23, KJV [emphasis added]

The following scripture is the same as the one we just read, but it
is from the New International Version instead of the King James
Version. We will see a dramatic departure in translation.

*"The eye is the lamp of the body. <u>If your eyes are good</u>, your
whole body will be full of light. But if your eyes are bad, your
whole body will be full of darkness. If then the light within you
is darkness, how great is that darkness!*
MATTHEW 6:22-23, NIV [emphasis added]

The New International Version refers to our "eyes being good,"
while the King James Version refers to our "eye being single."
The New International Version scripture is another example of
interpretation that is changed to suit the bias of the interpreters.
They altered the original Greek because they were not able to understand the meaning of it. They changed the scripture to suit
their own understanding.

The direct Greek transliteration reads: *The lamp of the body is the
eye. If therefore is the eye of you single, whole the body of you shining
will be.* The Greek word used where "single" appears (as in "eye
be single") in the transliteration is "haplous," which definitely
means single:

> haplous, *hap-looce'*; probably from Greek 1 (a) (as a par-
> ticle of union) and the base of Greek 4120 (pleko); prop-
> erly *folded together*, i.e. *single* (figurative *clear*) :- single.

The meaning is clear and without ambiguity. The original Greek
says "single eye" and not "good eyes."

The single eye is a very important spiritual principle having to do
with looking at the multiplicity of the world and seeing the unity
of life. Dual-eyed vision is the product of the ego in which the
world and all inhabitants are perceived to be separate from each
other and one's self. How many times has the original message

of the scriptures we know as the Bible been subverted just as we have seen in the previous example?

The scripture below gives us the Biblical version of the value of (Pi, the naturally occurring mathematical value of 3.17 used to calculate the circumference of a circle and other functions). In 1 Kings 7:23 (and also 2 Chronicles 4:2) we read:

> And he made a molten sea, ten cubits from the one brim to the other: it was round all about, and his height was five cubits: and a line of thirty cubits did compass it round about.
>
> 1 KINGS 7:23, KJV

This scripture describes a temple built in the tenth century B.C.E. According to this Old Testament account, the value of Pi is 3 and not 3.17 because the ratio of the circumference to the diameter will equal thirty cubits, which is then divided by ten cubits. To summarize, the men who wrote these scriptures made an error in the dimensions or else it was originally stated correctly but later succumbed to copyist's error or translator's error. The temple could not possibly have had a circumference of thirty cubits if the diameter was ten cubits.

The author has a good friend who, like many others, believes wholeheartedly that the King James Version of the Bible is the only "God certified" version. We must then ask which King James Bible is the true one because the original 1611 King James Bible has the following books that are now missing in the modern King James Bible: Esdras, 2 Esdras, Tobit, Judeth, the rest of Esther, Wisdom, Ecclesiasticus, Baruch with the Epistle of Jeremiah, The song of the three children, The story of Susanna, The idol Bel and the Dragon, The prayer of Manasseh, 1 Maccabees and 2 Maccabees. If we take the position that the current version of the King James Bible is the certified true version, then we must admit it was tampered with in the past or else the additional books could not have found their way into the 1611 Bible. If we take the position that the 1611 version is the certifiable version, then we must admit that the modern version was tampered with when the books were removed.

A casual study of the history of the Bible as revealed in the *Encyclopedia Britannica* will demonstrate beyond a shadow of a doubt that the Bible we have today has been pulled and twisted like a piece of saltwater taffy at the county fair. The earliest Greek translation of the Old Testament is the Septuagint. The name derives from the 72 translators of the work who were sent from Jerusalem to Alexandria by the high priest Eleazar at the request of Ptolemy II Philadelphus (288-247 B.C.E.). The *Encyclopedia Britannica* tells us, "In some books the translators made considerable additions to the original, e.g., those to Daniel, and these became a part of the Septuagint (a.k.a. LXX)." Considerable additions!! The Septuagint had been written for Greek-speaking Jews who had lost the understanding of the Hebrew language. The early Christians generally accepted the Septuagint. Later, after the destruction of the temple in Jerusalem in 70 C.E. there was a movement among Jews to reject the Septuagint because of perceived and disputed discrepancies and inaccuracies. This very same rejected and disputed Septuagint with the very same discrepancies, additions and inaccuracies emerged from this storm of controversy to become what we know today as the Old Testament.

> In the 3rd century C.E., Origen attempted to clear up copyists' errors that had crept into the text of the Septuagint, which by then varied widely from copy to copy. Other scholars also consulted the Hebrew text in order to make the Septuagint text more accurate. But it was the Septuagint, not the original Hebrew, that was the main basis for the Old Latin, Coptic, Ethiopic, Armenian, Georgian, Slavonic, and part of the Arabic translations of the Old Testament. It has never ceased to be the standard version of the Old Testament in the Greek church, and from it Jerome began his translation of the Vulgate Old Testament. ENCYCLOPEDIA BRITANNICA [emphsis added]

If God was absolutely protecting the scriptures from alteration, how could it be possible that the above mentioned copyists' errors appeared, varying widely from copy to copy?

Saint Jerome translated the four gospels from Greek in about 383 C.E., the remaining New Testament somewhat later, then the Old Testament between 390 and 405 C.E. In his Old Testament translation Saint Jerome modified the Septuagint into the Latin Vulgate* version according to the Hebrew originals, and where aspects of the Hebrew originals were missing in the Septuagint, they were added. This in turn became the Roman Catholic Bible of today. Maccabees 3 and 4 and Psalm 151 which appear in the Septuagint were discarded in Saint Jerome's new Bible. Obviously, Saint Jerome did not feel God had written these 3 pieces. If God did not inspire or write them, then who put them there in the first place? God was not steering this chain of events. While the Septuagint and Luther's Bible reject IV Ezra, Saint Jerome thought it appropriate to include it in the Latin Vulgate. Luther's Bible rejects III Ezra as well. Books appearing in Saint Jerome's version but later removed by the Protestant reformers are: I Esdras, II Esdras, Tobit, Judith, Additions to Esther, Wisdom of Solomon, Ecclesiasticus, Baruch, Epistle of Jeremy, Additions to Daniel (Song of the Three Holy Children, History of Susannah, and Bel and the Dragon), Prayer of Manasses, I Maccabees, and II Maccabees. Did God request this wholesale adding and subtracting? If we answer yes then we are faced with the perplexing question of why God did not get it right the first time.

There were many other books that circulated in abundance among Christians for several hundred years after Christ which are either lost or purposefully destroyed. We know of them only by referral in existing writings such as the writings of Origen. Other books have endured or have been rediscovered recently such as the books in the *Nag Hammadi Library,* and we are now free to read them without the censorship imposed in the first 500 years after Christ. The following is a list of Gospels that were rejected by men who may or may not have been guided by the hand of God: *Gospel According to the Egyptians, Protevangel of James, Gospel of Nicodemus, Gospel According to the Hebrews, Gospel of Peter, Gospel of Thomas, Gospel of the Twelve, Gospel of Apeles, Gospel of Barnabus, Gospel of Bartholomew, Gospel of Basilides, Gospel of Cerinthus, Gospel of the Ebionites, Gospel of Eve, Gospel of James the Less, Wisdom of Jesus Christ, Apocryph of John, Gospel of Judas Iscariot, The Living Gospel, Gospel of Marcion, Descent of Mary,*

---

* Common or "market place" Latin, thus, Vulgate or vulgar

Questions of Mary, Gospel of Mary, Gospel of Matthias, Gospel of Perfection, Gospel of Philip, Gospel of Thaddaeus, and Gospel of Truth (source–*Encyclopedia Brittanica*). This is only a list of the gospels. There are also numerous acts, epistles, and apocalypses.

If we take the position that all scripture is ordained by God and directly protected by God to the point that no mistakes or erroneous modifications whatsoever could ever occur, we will be hard pressed to explain the many changes that have occurred to the Bible. For instance, if God ordained the Septuagint and the Latin Vulgate, why did Protestants remove some of the books later?

If the Protestants removed these books because they were not divine, then it throws all of the originals into question. To accept any Protestant Bible as *the* Bible means that in the Septuagint and in the Latin Bible that followed, God allowed non-divine scriptures to become commingled with divine scriptures. Was God asleep when the corrupt scriptures were included with the good? Of course not. God gave man free will, and so we have tampered and bent the scriptures to suit our own view. Because of this, God must return again and again to realign our direction and restore right understanding. God comes; He speaks; we go forth; we make a mess of it. God comes; He speaks; we go forth; we make a mess of it. With the passing of time, God's message is obscured and diluted by men. It has always been this way.

Another interesting contrast is raised when the Jews sent priests and Levites to ask John the Baptist who he was.

> Now this was John's testimony when the Jews of Jerusalem sent priests and Levites to ask him who he was. He did not fail to confess, but confessed freely, "I am not the Christ."
>
> They asked him, "Then who are you? Are you Elijah?"
>
> He said, "I am not."
>
> "Are you the Prophet?"
>
> He answered, "No."   JOHN 1:19-21, NIV

Who are we to believe—the Baptist or Jesus? Is Jesus correct in saying John the Baptist is Elijah (Matthew 11:14), or is John the Baptist correct in saying that he is not? This is a very important issue. The prophecy in Malachi clearly states that Elijah will come as the harbinger of the Messiah. If Elijah is nowhere to be found, then according to the Old Testament, Jesus is not the Messiah. How could John the Baptist, if he really is Elijah, be mistaken about such a pivotal point in the divine drama? How is it possible for him not to know that he is the fulfillment of the prophesied reincarnation of Elijah? The Baptist didn't simply say, "I don't know." He stated flatly that he was *not* Elijah. For biblical literalists this makes quite a bad rub. Those who take every word in the Bible as divine truth will be hard pressed to take the Baptist's statement as being true.

Jesus tells us that John the Baptist is not a perfect being. He is not a Christ. In Matthew 11:11 Jesus says that there are none greater born of women than John the Baptist. This means there are no persons who have been born on this earth who are any more spiritually evolved than John the Baptist. Perhaps some are equal, but none are greater. Jesus goes on to say that the least in the kingdom of heaven is greater than John the Baptist. The flow is this: only a Christ is perfect, and everyone else is still deluded to some degree or another by the ego and is capable of error. This means that every work in the Bible that is written by one who is not a Christ is subject to corruption. An exception to this is possible only if we allow previous prophets to be granted the perfection status of "Christ." However, Elijah was a great one, and in his incarnation as John, he made a large mistake. Another way of looking at this anomaly is to say the occurrence of this scriptural error is perfect. It is God's way of telling us that scripture is not the highest good, nor is it always 100 percent reliable.

The knowledge of our oneness can never be experienced or understood by reading any scripture because words are the product of the mind, and the mind, which is composed of thoughts, is limited. To describe oneness in God to a person who has never personally tasted the sweetness of the experience would be like trying to describe the color blue to someone born blind. No amount of explaining would ever give the blind person knowledge of the color blue. To have knowledge of "blue," one must see it for one's self. In like manner, the truth of our oneness in God is something that can only be known through our own direct personal experience. Scripture may be the finger pointing at the moon, but it is not the moon itself. If we accept that God is eternal and if we accept that thoughts in the mind are limited, then we must conclude that thoughts cannot know, describe or explain God. God is an experience. God *is* experience.

Scriptural law is good to keep those of us who are ego-centered from chaos. Eventually, we will have to transcend law and go directly on-line with love in order to attain the kingdom. The laws are like the bars on a child's crib which keep the child from climbing out and getting into trouble while mother is in the other room. The bars keep us safe, but they are also a prison. Scripture will never give us the experience of direct communion with God. Only love can do that. Love will set us free. Love is something we search for and find within ourselves.

> *If true religion and religious texts can be compared to the surface of the ocean, spirituality is like the pearls and priceless treasures that lie hidden deep beneath the waters. The real treasure lies deep within.*
>
> AMMACHI, AWAKEN CHILDREN, VOL. 7

5

Ego's Home Run with the Bases Loaded

Don't blame them, children. It is extremely difficult to remove egotism and jealousy. These are even seen in advanced sadhaks [spiritual practitioners].

AMMACHI, AWAKEN CHILDREN, VOL. 1 [brackets by author]

Ego was so intent on preventing us from experiencing the truth of our divine unity that he lured many who were in a position of power to remove the idea from Christian scriptures in the formative years of Christianity. Power, wealth and status were the pieces of silver offered for the betrayal of the Truth.

APOSTOLIC SUCCESSION

By the year 200 C.E. these unwitting tools of Ego's plan had organized themselves into a hierarchy of bishops, priests and deacons and claimed, by right of apostolic succession, that we common folk could only get the "truth" from them. The doctrine of "apostolic succession" states that the truth is handed down through time like a baton. It begins with the apostles and is then passed to their direct students and then to their direct students, ad infinitum. And what if we could only get the keys to salvation from these certain individuals? They even claimed to have the power to remove our sins. Common people were not allowed to possess a Bible. How tempting and seductive was Ego's proposal to this "anointed" hierarchy of "special" ones. Ego was desperate–Jesus had exposed him, and Ego had to find a way to hide. Jesus did not approve of such a master-slave relationship even among his own disciples.

In the Gospel of Mark, both James and John privately asked Jesus to grant them their desire. Jesus asks what he could do for them. They reply that they desire for one of them to sit at Jesus' left hand and the other to sit at his right hand. When the other ten disciples got wind of their request they were upset with the two usurpers. James and John were asking to be elevated above the others.

> *Jesus called them together and said, "You know that those who are regarded as rulers of the Gentiles lord it over them, and their high officials exercise authority over them. Not so with you. Instead, whoever wants to become great among you must be your servant, and whoever wants to be first must be slave of all."*
>
> MARK 10:42-44, NIV

Jesus tells them that they shall not exercise lordship one over the others like the Gentiles. In another instance the same issue comes up again. The disciples are disputing who should be the boss.

> *They came to Capernaum. When he was in the house, he asked them, "What were you arguing about on the road?" But they kept quiet because on the way they had argued about who was the greatest. Sitting down, Jesus called the Twelve and said, "If anyone wants to be first, he must be the very last, and the servant of all."*
>
> MARK 9:33-35, NIV

The bishops, priests and deacons' claim to authority had been handed down, according to them, from Peter and his appointment to the position of the "rock." This is indicated in the next scripture.

> *When Jesus came into the coasts of Caesarea Philippi, he asked his disciples, saying, "Whom do men say that I the Son of man am?"*
>
> *And they said, "Some say that thou art John the Baptist: some, Elias; and others, Jeremias, or one of the prophets."*
>
> *He saith unto them, "But whom say ye that I am?"*
>
> *And Simon Peter answered and said, "Thou art the Christ, the Son of the living God."*

And Jesus answered and said unto him, "Blessed art thou, Simon Barjona: for flesh and blood hath not revealed it unto thee, but my Father which is in heaven. And I say also unto thee, That thou art Peter, and upon this rock I will build my church; and the gates of hell shall not prevail against it."

MATTHEW 16:13-18, KJV

However, Thomas, the brother of Jesus, tells the story differently.

Jesus said to his disciples, "Compare me to someone and tell me whom I am like."

Simon Peter said to him, "You are like a righteous angel."

Matthew said to him, "You are like a wise philosopher."

Thomas said to him, "Master, my mouth is wholly incapable of saying whom your are like."

Jesus said, "I am not your master. Because you have drunk, you have become drunk from the bubbling stream which I have measured out."

THE GOSPEL OF THOMAS, THE NAG HAMMADI LIBRARY*, VERSE 13

The above scripture elevates the disciple Thomas above Peter and Matthew. This negated the authority of the apostolic succession that holds Peter, the first pope, at the beginning of the lineage. Of course, these ideas could not fit with the hierarchy's plan to control the gate and sell tickets to the living fountain of life which is Christ. In the latter scripture two interesting things occur. First, Jesus is not denying being the Messiah but rather proclaims Thomas to be one with him. Secondly, Peter is found to be lacking in understanding and remains at a station below Thomas. Thomas has transcended the limitations of the mind in his understanding and can find no words to say who or what Jesus is. Jesus is saying that in Thomas' transcendent revelation, that they are no longer master and disciple but are merged as one.

---

* Early Christian texts rediscovered in a cave near Nag Hammadi, Egypt in 1946

Scriptures like this had to be eliminated if the mechanism for preserving the authority of the hierarchy were to be preserved. Ego appealed to the hierarchy as the desire for status and power. In addition, the early church very nearly split in two with much rancorous and volatile discussion as to who or what Jesus is. Essentially there were two camps. Simply put, the argument revolved around whether Jesus was a man who became God or whether Jesus was God who came as a man. Thomas took the position that he was wholly incapable of saying who Jesus is, and this did not sit well with entrenched opinions. Because the ego is by nature insecure, it wants to categorize, label and compartmentalize Jesus.

In these "Gnostic" scriptures, which the hierarchy condemned and sought to destroy, we should not be surprised to find more references to the idea that the Kingdom of God is within us. If God can be found within our own selves, then the usefulness of a bishop or priest may be questioned. For them it would be like trying to sell air to breathe when there is air all around us. Jesus said:

> *Beware that no one lead you astray, saying, "Lo here!" or "Lo there!" For the Son of Man is within you. Follow after him! Those who seek him will find him.* THE GOSPEL OF MARY
> (MAGDALENE), 8:15, THE NAG HAMMADI LIBRARY

> *Jesus said, "If those who lead you say to you, 'See, the kingdom is in the sky,' then the birds of the sky will precede you. If they say to you, 'It is in the sea,' then the fish will precede you. Rather, the kingdom of God is inside of you, and it is outside of you. When you come to know yourselves, then you will become known, and you will realize that it is you who are the sons of the living father. But if you will not know yourselves, you dwell in poverty and it is you who are that poverty."*
> THE GOSPEL OF THOMAS, THE NAG HAMMADI LIBRARY, VERSE 3

After the Roman emperor Constantine converted to Christianity and came to power in 323 C.E., these bishops, priests and deacons were granted the use of the Roman police force. Ego rounded third base and headed for home plate. The penalty for disagreeing with the stated views of these bishops, priests and deacons on the meaning of Christ and who is allowed to be a Christian took a nasty turn. As one might expect, all books which contradicted the hierarchy's hold on power were destroyed. As part of this, the largest library in the world, the Library of Alexandria, was burned to the ground in 640 C.E. Hundreds of thousands of scrolls and manuscripts were lost forever. For hundreds of years Ego's Inquisition through the vehicle of the church would terrify Europe in a murderous rampage that belongs in the infamy hall of fame along with Hitler and Stalin. On February the 17th, in the year 1600, a Dominican monk, Father Giordan Bruno, was burned alive at the stake because he held the belief that God was in all things and all things were God and that the universe was infinite and filled with an infinite number of worlds. In 1632 Galileo published *Dialago dei due massimi sistemi del mondo,* which supported Copernicus' heretical hypothesis that the earth was not the center of the universe but revolved around the sun. Galileo, after inventing the telescope, had proved Copernicus to be right and was ready to demonstrate it to anyone willing to look. Galileo spent the rest of his life sequestered in a condition of house arrest imposed upon him by the judges of the Inquisition. He avoided a fiery death by recanting his position, while Father Bruno refused to compromise his views, believing a martyr's death to be the better option. Father Bruno took Copernicus a step further by stating that even the sun was not the center of the universe because the universe was infinite and had no center. The ego is the antithesis of Father Bruno's no-center. The ego, by its very nature, is destined to imagine that it is the center of the universe, and by extension, everything associated with it must also be the center.

Ego's campaign of horror lasted 600 years, from 1237 until 1834, when the Inquisition was officially abolished. It is ironic that the church would be the Ego's own vehicle of persecution and intolerance. The Inquisition occurred because the same Pharisaic mindset had found a new set of identities. They called themselves Christians, and they continued to crucify the Lord. If caught, the "heretics" would be murdered just like Jesus with burning and hanging replacing the wooden cross. The idea that God or Christ could be arrived at within oneself would seriously compromise the power of these bishops, deacons and priests. If God or Christ could be found within our own selves, then we would not be quite so dependent on the hierarchy. Finding God within our own

selves was a direct contradiction to the idea that we should be obligated to receive the truth from a select few via the conduit of apostolic succession. Ego was afraid of losing power, and it was
ready to commit murder to defend its fragile existence.

THE GNOSTICS - THE COMPETITION

Prior to Constantine's conversion, there was another broad-based
camp which believed that Christ's message was to experience God
or Christ *directly*. They affirmed this to be the path to the mysteries
of our existence in Christ. The Christians who held this view were
called Gnostic Christians from the Greek word "gnosis," meaning
to know or to have knowledge. The antagonism that existed between the hierarchy and the Gnostics is well documented. When
Gnostics met for church, they drew lots to see who would assume
the various roles. Elaine Pagels writes in her book *The Gnostic Gospels*:

> *How did members of this circle of "pneumatics" [the Gnostics]*
> *(literally, "those who are spiritual") conduct their meetings?*
> *Irenaeus [Bishop of Lyons] tells us that when they met, all the*
> *members first participated in drawing lots. Whoever received a*
> *certain lot apparently was designated to take the role of priest;*
> *another was to offer the sacrament, as bishop; another would*
> *read the Scriptures for worship, and others would address the*
> *group as a prophet, offering extemporaneous spiritual instruc-*
> *tion. The next time the group met, they would throw lots again*
> *so that the persons taking each role changed continually.*

> *This practice effectively created a very different structure of au-*
> *thority. At a time when the orthodox Christians increasingly*
> *discriminated between clergy and laity, this group of Gnostic*
> *Christians demonstrated that, among themselves, they refused*
> *to acknowledge such distinction. Instead of ranking their mem-*
> *bers into superior and inferior "orders" within a hierarchy, they*
> *followed the principle of strict equality. All initiates, men and*
> *women alike, participated equally in the drawing; anyone*
> *might be selected to serve as priest, bishop, or prophet. Further-*
> *more, because they cast lots at each meeting, even the distinc-*
> *tions established by lot could never become permanent "ranks."*
> *Finally—most important—they intended, through this practice,*

to remove the element of human choice. A twentieth-century
observer might assume that the Gnostics left these matters to
random chance, but the Gnostics saw it differently. They be-
lieved that since God directs everything in the universe, the way
the lots fell expressed his choice.

Such practices prompted Tertullian to attack "the behavior of the heretics:"

> *How frivolous, how worldly, how merely human it is, without*
> *seriousness, without authority, without discipline, as fits their*
> *faith! To begin with, it is uncertain who is a catechumen, and*
> *who a believer: they all have access equally, they listen equally,*
> *they pray equally, even pagans, if any happen to come... They*
> *also share the kiss of peace with all who come, for they do not*
> *care how differently they treat topics, if they meet together to*
> *storm the citadel of the one only truth... All of them are*
> *arrogant...all offer you gnosis!*
>
> THE GNOSTIC GOSPELS, ELAINE PAGELS [brackets by author]

When the book burning was ordered, some Gnostic Christians hid existing scriptures in burial urns, hoping that God would one day return them to the world. Many of these lost scriptures resurfaced on October 4, 1946, when a sheepherder discovered them. The scrolls were found buried in a three-foot tall clay urn in a cave near Nag Hammadi, Egypt. Since then these scriptures have been called the *Nag Hammadi Library*, and they are now available to anyone who cares to go exploring.

This discussion is not intended to be an indictment of the Roman Catholic Church but rather an indictment of the ego. In a world that is utterly dominated by the viewpoint of the ego, how can we expect events to be otherwise? The ego has used religion to its own end for thousands of years, as we see the same dark activities reoccurring throughout history and in all religions.

In summary, it is the nature of the ego to desire power and control. A fledgling Christianity was subverted by this dark influence. The scriptures were bent and doctrines fabricated to preserve the ego's grip on humanity.

6

Salvation is Grace and Hard Work

*God will not simply give anything to anyone without their
working for it. Self-effort and grace are interdependent. If tapas
(spiritual discipline) is performed sincerely, you can then see
God's Grace flowing into you. Sitting behind the closed doors of
a room saying, "The sun is not giving me any light" is silly.
Open the door and light will come in. Likewise, open the doors
of your heart by removing the obstacles of egotistic thoughts and
by developing qualities such as love, humility, etc. That takes
effort. Prepare your mind to become a suitable instrument of
God's Grace which flows in a never ending stream.*

AMMACHI, AWAKEN CHILDREN, VOL. 1

Grace and hard work are like two wings on the same bird – the
bird of salvation. Many believe that because Jesus died for our sins
he has already paid the price of admission to the kingdom of God
for each and every one of us. Therefore, all that is left for us to secure our place in the kingdom is to confess our belief in Jesus
Christ. The following scripture is often raised as evidence of this.

*Jesus said to her, "I am the resurrection and the life. He who
believes in me will live, even though he dies; and whoever lives
and believes in me will never die. Do you believe this?"*

JOHN 11:25-26, NIV

The idea that all we have to do is say, "I believe in Jesus" and then
sink into the soft comfortable sofa of business-as-usual, making no
effort to remove our own selfishness or to practice the Master's

commandments, is nothing more than pure laziness. Such a belief is as seductive and misleading as it is convenient. Prepaid resurrection fits the consumerist disposition of our culture along with instant coffee and drive-through banking. It is a powerful tool for ministers who wish to fill up their church pews and collection plates. Weak-kneed preachers are going to tell us that it's "easy." This occurs in all religions. In this way, our church attendance becomes a spiritual insurance policy. The reasoning goes like this: "If I confess my belief in Jesus and go to church on Sundays, I will get my ticket to heaven." We go about our business oblivious of the many things Jesus said we must do, and so we make no progress toward the kingdom. We do nothing to become loving people. We do nothing to reclaim our lost innocence. The idea of prepaid resurrection and instant faith is misleading and painfully wrong because of the harm it does to the faithful or those of us who would like to be faithful. If the belief in prepaid resurrection fell to an understanding that we must make many sacrifices and undergo hardships to gain the kingdom, the church pews would gather dust, and the collection plates would be circulated in vain. However, Jesus was always fearless in his ability to be direct and explicit.

In the preceding scripture, "He who believes in me will live, even though he dies" does not mean the physical body will be immortalized. It means we will have eternal life even though our bodies die. We are spirit and not flesh. It means the soul will cease to be identified with the body and will become identified with the Christ within. It will realize its own inherent immortal being–the I AM. Bodies may come and go, but the soul is unaffected. It lives even though the body dies.

"..and whoever lives and believes in me will never die." This line contains the fly in the ointment for those who subscribe to instant belief and prepaid resurrection. Christ is saying we must not only believe in him, but we must *live* in him. And what does it mean to live in him? It means to be merged in God and Christ. In the following scripture Jesus expresses the reality of this merging:

> *On that day you will realize that I am in my Father, and you are in me, and I am in you.*　　　JOHN 14:20, NIV

Salvation is Grace and Hard Work 93

This passage by Jesus concerning our fundamental unity and what it means "to live in him," is echoed by Ammachi:

> You are the "I" which is in me and I am the "you" which is in you. The feeling of difference is due to the blindness of ignorance. In truth, nothing is separate.
>
> AMMACHI - OMKARA DIVYA PORULE, PART 1

There are those who propose the following scripture as proof that belief alone is all that is required of us.

> But as many as received him, to them gave he power to become the sons of God, even to them that believe on his name:
>
> JOHN 1:12, KJV

This passage is often quoted in the little brochures found beneath our windshield wipers after visiting the local mall – the brochures with titles such as, "Where Will You Spend Eternity?" First of all, Jesus didn't say this. This is John's opinion. Secondly, giving us the power to do something does not mean we can or will do it. It simply means it is available to us. Thirdly, we are all sons and daughters of God now, but we have lost the understanding of this truth.

Let's see what the Master says about this. In the following scripture it appears at first glance that salvation is a simple matter.

> I tell you the truth, whoever hears my word and believes him who sent me has eternal life and will not be condemned; he has crossed over from death to life.   JOHN 5:24, NIV

In John 5:24 the original Greek text for the "word" of Jesus as in, "...hears my word..." is *logos*. The *Encyclopedia Britannica Dictionary* defines *logos* as follows:

> **Log-os** (log'os) *n.* 1 In classical Greek and neo-Platonic philosophy, the cosmic reason giving order, purpose, and intelligibility to the world. 2 The creative Word of God, the second person of the Trinity, incarnate as Jesus Christ, identified with the cosmic reason.

This is not mere audio transmission of sound waves causing an eardrum to vibrate. Greek for that kind of "word" as in ordinary speech is *rheomati*. For instance *rheomati* is the original Greek text for the "word" in the following scripture in Matthew:

> But he answered and said, It is written, Man shall not live by bread alone, but by every **word** that proceedeth out of the mouth of God.　　　MATTHEW 4:4, KJV [emphasis added]

In John 5:24 Jesus says we must hear his *logos*. We must come to a profound realization or revelation that is experienced in the deepest place of the heart. It is not merely passing the eyeballs across a passage in our family Bible or listening to a pair of lips part company with words at the Sunday pulpit. The "Word" that Jesus says we must hear is something far beyond mere talk. It is an error for the translators of the Bible to translate the *logos* as simply "word." In the following scripture the Greek word *logos* is again translated as "word," but we see the context is cosmically oriented, and "word" has been capitalized in an effort to correctly show that the "Word" is not merely human speech.

> In the beginning was the Word, and the Word was with God, and the Word was God.　　　JOHN 1:1, NIV

What does it gain a person to mouth the words, "I believe in Jesus," and still have no understanding of what it means to love God with all of our hearts and all of our minds and to love our neighbors as our selves? To "hear" the word or *logos* of Jesus is to feel what the Master meant when He said that what we do to the least of persons we do to Him (Matthew 25:24). It is to understand that our love must be given equally and unconditionally to all in the same way that God's rain falls on the just and the unjust (Matthew 5:45). It is to understand that God or Christ is the true nature of every human being.

We may mouth the words, "I believe in Jesus," but can we really say we believe in Jesus if we have no love for others? If heaven could be attained without rolling up one's shirt sleeves and doing the hard work, then Jesus would not have bothered to give us such detailed instructions such as following the last six of the ten commandments, giving our money to the poor, becoming the servant of all, loving everyone equally and becoming as a little child in our spirit. He would have told us to forget about any of these commandments and simply profess our belief.

> *If you love me, you will obey what I command.*
>
> JOHN 14:15, NIV

> *Why do you call me, "Lord, Lord," and do not do what I say?*
>
> LUKE 6:46, NIV

And again:

> *Therefore go and make disciples of all nations, baptizing them in the name of the Father and of the Son and of the Holy Spirit, and teaching them to obey everything I have commanded you. And surely I am with you always, to the very end of the age.*
>
> MATTHEW 28:19-20, NIV [emphsis added]

If salvation were as simple as professing a belief in Christ then every single Christian would be going to heaven. Jesus tells us that not all Christians are going to heaven.

> *Not everyone who says to me, "Lord, Lord," will enter the kingdom of heaven, but only he who does the will of my Father who is in heaven. Many will say to me on that day, "Lord, Lord, did we not prophesy in your name, and in your name drive out demons and perform many miracles?" Then I will tell them plainly, "I never knew you. Away from me, you evildoers!"*
>
> MATTHEW 7:21-23, NIV

Christians can be evildoers? Jesus is saying that not everyone who calls him "Lord" is going to heaven. We may assume that anyone who calls to Jesus, "Lord, Lord," has professed a belief in Jesus and has defined him or herself as a Christian. Not only have these people professed their belief in Jesus, they are actively doing works *in the name of Jesus.* They are not simply benchwarmers. The problem lies in the fact that these same people made no effort to eliminate the ego, and so they never knew Christ. They did not keep their lamps filled with the oil of innocence and pure selfless love.

They did not trim their wicks with humility as the process of intro-spection and fearless self-examination. The fire of divine love can never burn in the presence of the ego.

And again Jesus points out the difference between talking-the-talk and walking-the-walk:

> *You hypocrites! Isaiah was right when he prophesied about you: These people honor me with their lips, but their hearts are far from me.* MATTHEW 15:7-9, NIV

It is the ego which prevents our knowing God directly, and only a few have any knowledge or awareness of the ego. Of these per-sons only a few will have any understanding that giving up the ego is not only desirable but the most vital aspect of the path to Christ. Of the ones who have this understanding only a few will have the necessary detachment to surrender their ego to God.

> *Enter through the narrow gate. For wide is the gate and broad is the road that leads to destruction, and many enter through it. But small is the gate and narrow the road that leads to life, and only a few find it.* MATTHEW 7:13-14, NIV

Again:

> *For many are called, but few are chosen.* MATTHEW 22:14, KJV

If salvation were as simple as professing belief in Jesus, then all Christians would go to heaven. But Jesus says few will be chosen. Many are called, but out of these *only a few* will make it. This should be sobering. Only a few are going to heaven. There are some who believe only their specific church congregation is go-ing to heaven. In their analysis not even the other churches be-longing to the same sect are going to heaven. We might question the selective process, but the numbers may not be far off.

Salvation has little to do with what we say. It has little to do with whether or not we show up for church every Sunday. It requires strong faith in the eternal Christ that burns like a million suns at the core of our being. It has to do with living our lives as though we understood that we were all brothers and sisters eternally bound by the shining river of God's infinite love. It has to do with becoming innocent like a little child.

We are saved by grace alone, but it is our faith and diligent effort that invites God's grace. God helps those who help themselves. However, can we say that we have true faith if we do not keep the commandments of the Lord? Failing to follow the Lord's instructions shows that we do not have faith in him. Failing to follow his instructions with the utmost intensity shows that we do not take him seriously. Therefore, our works are the gauge of our faith. This is the meaning of the scripture saying faith without works is dead. It is not possible to have love without compassion because compassion is the expression of love. In the same way it is not possible to have faith without works because works are the expression of our faith.

Jesus says that we must walk the narrow way. He tells us quite clearly that a humble, loving and childlike nature is what is needed. A contentious, arrogant, self-centered nature is like hard rock which the nourishing rain of divine grace will not penetrate, and religious pride (my-way-is-the-only-way) is the hardest rock of all. Grace is always here and now. It is a golden divine light that perpetually falls on the just and the unjust equally. However, to receive that grace, we must plow the ground of our minds, transforming the hard rock of the ego into the fertile soil of self-surrender. Only then will grace be able to penetrate our souls, lifting us into the kingdom of God's infinite being.

James says:

> What good is it, my brothers, if a man claims to have faith but has no deeds? Can such faith save him?　JAMES 2:14, NIV

> You foolish man, do you want evidence that faith without deeds is useless?　　　　　　　　　JAMES 2:20, NIV

> You see that a person is justified by what he does and not by faith alone.　　　　　　　　　JAMES 2:24, NIV

As the body without the spirit is dead, so faith without deeds is dead. JAMES 2:26, NIV

But Paul says:

Not by works of righteousness which we have done, but according to his mercy he saved us, by the washing of regeneration, and renewing of the Holy Ghost; TITUS 3:5, KJV

Paul is correct in saying we are saved by grace alone, and James is correct in saying faith and good works are inseparable. Our efforts and "works" are required in order to receive God's grace, but it is the grace, not the works, that saves us. It should be obvious to anyone that Jesus and the Old Testament provide ample proof that we cannot act any way we want and expect to receive grace. After forgiving her, Jesus told the adulteress to go and sin no more (John 8:11). However, most of us live in corruption, that is to say our eye is not single, and our minds still give safe harbor to the devil which is the ego. We must take up the battle against the ego by confronting the hordes of our past selfish actions. In the end, like asking a thief to catch itself, the ego can do nothing, and we are left with no choice but to surrender to God. God will save us by his grace if we are humble, sincere and intense in the prosecution of our own delusions.

With regard to salvation, it is equally important what goes on in our minds and our thoughts. We work hard to purify the mind in order to receive grace.

For as he thinketh in his heart, so is he. PROVERBS 23:7, KJV

But I say unto you, That whosoever looketh on a woman to lust after her hath committed adultery with her already in his heart. MATTHEW 5:28, KJV

It is not possible for us to lust after another in our minds and also hold the vision that we are all one. Lust turns the other person into an object. Lust, gluttony, vanity, envy, jealousy, and covetousness all spring from the I-am-the-body idea. Physical adultery or

covetousness = greed.

mental adultery are both the same because they enhance the I-am-the-body idea.

Heaven, God, Christ, hell, Satan and the ego are all to be found within ourselves. It must be made clear that "within" in this context does not stop six inches behind the eyebrows. There is the appearance that the physical body is all there is to us. If we point our finger at the twinkling stars of the midnight sky which gleam and sparkle from the vast inky depths of interstellar space, we can get a sense of the depth of space. The inner direction is just as deep and vast. As we move inward, we begin to unify and merge with other aspects of the subconscious worlds of other humans. As we go beyond that, we begin to experience wholeness with aspects or archetypes of the Divine. As we go beyond that, we approach the center of being which is God or Christ. At this point we realize that we are all truly brothers and sisters. No one is excluded. All of us have this as our origin. It is this central core which is the bubbling fountain of life that flows eternally from the center of each one of us.

In order to receive God's grace, we must become warriors and take up arms on the battlefield of our own minds. We will assess, sublimate, subdue and integrate the subsurface layer of our awareness, the subconscious, which is the realm of the ego. As a first step, we avoid actions that reinforce self-centered delusions that arise from a mistaken identification with the body. Attachment to sexual pleasure, the taste of food, as well as mental attachments which give rise to mental afflictions such as stealing, gossiping and murdering all reinforce the "I thought" in the same way that steel cabling reinforces The Golden Gate Bridge. Removing these self-centered activities is the hard work that is required. Salvation does not come without effort on our part, but it is grace, in the end, that carries us to the goal. It is our hard work and sincere intention that is the most potent prayer for God's grace.

Seven deadly sins
Pride   Gluttony
Envy   Lust
Anger
Avarice
sadness / pride

7

Who is Jesus?

The mind should disappear. You should become "no-mind." A person who is in the state of "no-mind" might dwell in the world of diversity, but in reality, he is in God. You might see him act or speak, but he does neither. He is actionless and has no speech; he is still and silent in all circumstances. But your mind will impose a mind on him. Your mind will impose a body, speech and action onto him. You yourself are divided; therefore you will try to make him divided also. Yet, try your whole lifetime, put forth all your effort and call the whole world to help you, and still you cannot divide him. You will become exhausted and collapse trying to do the impossible.

AMMACHI, AWAKEN CHILDREN VOL. 4, P302

It is not possible for us to know the true nature of Jesus unless we, ourselves, become like Jesus. If our Christian fathers had known this, much trouble could have been avoided. In 325 C.E. Roman Emperor Constantine convened the first ecumenical council, which is now referred to as the Council of Nicaea. His main purpose in calling the council was to make an attempt at resolving the rancorous and heated debate that had arisen over the correct understanding of the nature of Jesus. The main body of Christianity was in great danger of fragmenting like a watermelon sitting on a stick of dynamite. The question as to the nature of Jesus had become a seething volcano of dissention that threatened to erupt with an irrevocable destructive force. The entire fourth century was consumed by this controversy.

If God is the infinite and immutable monad of existence, how could such a One be contained wholly in the fleshly package we know as Jesus who had a mortal birth, grew, changed and was mortally killed? The doctrine of Arianism stated that if God is immutable then the Son who is mutable (shown in the scriptures as subject to growth and change) cannot be God.

> *"The incarnate Lord who was born, wept, suffered, and died could not be one with the transcendent first cause of creation who is beyond all suffering."*
>
> ENCYCLOPEDIA BRITANNICA, RE: ARIUS.

This point of view was made popular by the Alexandrian presbyter Arius, and it arose out of his intent to establish the unity and simplicity of the eternal God. The antagonists of this view at the other extreme were the monophysites who stated that Jesus was absolutely one and the same as the eternal God. In between was the Nestorian doctrine which stated that Jesus had two natures which were, in effect, cohabitating as the appearance of Jesus on earth. In truth, such discussion is futile as the true nature of Jesus, or any other incarnation of God, is beyond the mind.

JOHN 14:6

Jesus is one of the ways, but he is not the only way. Did Jesus really mean that only through him we can enter the kingdom of God? John 14:6 is the most often quoted scripture to be offered as proof that Jesus is the only way. This statement appears in John but not in the other three gospels.

> *Jesus saith unto him, I am the way, the truth, and the life: no man cometh unto the Father, but by **me**.*
>
> JOHN 14:6, KJV [emphsis added]

In the last word of this scripture we must understand who it is that is the "me." No man comes to the father except by *me*. Because we see through the eye of ignorance we imagine Jesus to be like us. He appeared to be a physical person like us, but there was a significant difference. In Jesus there was no individual. There was no ego. There was no "I" and "mine." He was in the state of "no mind" as described at the beginning of this chapter by Ammachi. There was only God, and one who is one with God we call a Christ. When we speak of God universally we say the "father," and when we speak of God appearing in a human form we say it is "Christ." When most of us think of Jesus, we see and know only the flesh and imagine him to have an ego or a set of identities, attachments and desires like we do. We are incapable, in our present state of dualistic thinking, to comprehend the nature of Jesus.

Jesus was the Christ, but the Christ is much more than what we see as Jesus. The body of Jesus had a beginning in the womb of Mary, but the Christ exists eternally–long before the body of Jesus came into being. The Christ is never born and, therefore, never dies. There is only one Christ in all eternity. Our confusion over the nature of Jesus stems from our inability to see the body as nothing more than a garment. Jesus knew he was the Christ and not the perishable body. We, on the other hand, see bodies only, and therefore, we are not capable of understanding who Jesus is. Jesus clarified the distinction between the Christ and what we perceive to be the man Jesus.

> *A certain ruler asked him, "Good teacher, what must I do to inherit eternal life?"*
>
> *"Why do you call me good?" Jesus answered. "No one is good–except God alone."* LUKE 18:18-19, NIV
>
> *Don't you believe that I am in the Father, and that the Father is in me? The words I say to you are not just my own. Rather, it is the Father, living in me, who is doing his work.*
> JOHN 14:10, NIV
>
> *You heard me say, "I am going away and I am coming back to you." If you loved me, you would be glad that I am going to the Father, for the Father is greater than I.* JOHN 14:28, NIV
>
> *Then Jesus cried out, "When a man believes in me, he does not believe in me only, but in the one who sent me. When he looks at me, he sees the one who sent me."* JOHN 12:44-45, NIV

By myself I can do nothing.   JOHN 5:30, NIV

Jesus says that it is the father that dwells in him and as him that
does the works. He is saying that the father is greater than the
fleshly appearance of the man Jesus. Jesus says that if we believe
in him we are believing in God only and not in Jesus. Jesus says
that of his own self he can do nothing. Jesus is telling us we are
making an error if we point our finger to Jesus and proclaim that
Jesus is the doer, the cause, or the maker of these good things.
That is because Jesus is not a "self" like you and I imagine ourselves to be, but rather a Self – the I AM – God. Jesus is in the
state of "no mind." Jesus regarded himself as being empty like
space or transparent like the sky with God being the only doer.
Paul expresses his understanding of this emptiness or no-
thingness in the following passage:

> *Your attitude should be the same as that of Christ Jesus: Who,*
> *being in very nature God, did not consider equality with God*
> *something to be grasped, but made himself nothing, taking the*
> *very nature of a servant, being made in human likeness.*
>   PHILIPPIANS. 2:5-7, NIV

Lord Krishna counsels his friend Arjuna on the truth of acting
without being the doer:

> *The disciplined man, who knows the underlying principle of*
> *reality, thinks: "I really don't do anything at all," certain that*
> *whether seeing, hearing, touching, smelling, eating, walking,*
> *sleeping, breathing, talking, excreting, grasping, opening or*
> *shutting the eyes, it is merely the senses acting on the objects of*
> *sense. The man who acts, having rendered his actions to Brah-*
> *man and abandoned attachment, is untainted by evil, in the*
> *same way that a lotus leaf is untainted by water.*
>   BHAGAVAD GITA, CHAPTER 5, TRANSLATED BY W.J. JOHNSON
>   OXFORD UNIVERSITY PRESS

The apparent contradiction between Jesus saying that except by
him we cannot enter the kingdom of God and also saying that of
his own self he can do nothing is very important. It is the eternal
Christ that is necessary for entering the kingdom. It is the eternal

Christ making the statement in John 14:6. This is the Christ that existed before the body of Jesus came into being. This is the Christ that is the only begotten son of the father. If we think that the Christ is limited to the body of Jesus then we are mistaken. Jesus does not want us to make this error, and so he tells us that it is not he that does these things, and we should not "call him good." Ammachi explains further the state of being a Christ.

> *Once the ego is removed, you are no more a person. You become consciousness. You become formless. The ego is the material which gives name and form. Once the ego is destroyed, name and form are gone. You may give a name to the saint and you may attribute a form to him, but he is neither. He becomes like the wind. He becomes space.*
>
> AMMACHI, AWAKEN CHILDREN, VOL. 5

Imagine there is a lake in which we fish and from which we receive our daily sustenance. After some time we are grateful to the lake, and we offer thanks and praise to the lake. The lake answers back and says that it is not he (the lake) that provides the sustenance, but rather it is the water that is within the lake that provides for us. The water is the same in every lake. Because there are many lakes, all filled with the same water, we may say that the lake is water, but we cannot say that water is limited to any specific lake. In the same way we may say that Jesus is the Christ, but we cannot say the Christ is only Jesus in an exclusive sense. Ammachi comments on this:

> *Children, no great soul will say "Only through me you will be saved." Has Sri Ramakrishna said, "Follow me alone, otherwise there is no hope." Has Ramana Maharshi said so? Did any of the great saints and sages of the past make statements like that? No. A real knower of the Self will not say that. What they say is to move forward according to your chosen path, having firm faith in it. That is what is said by the founders of all the religions.*
>
> *But after their demise, the followers interpret it in a different way. Doctrines like, "Have faith only in our religion," or "Only through our path," etc. are spread by the followers who*

have no visalata (broadmindedness). Do you know what a
Mahatma [a Christ] means when he says, "Believe in me"?
The "I" they talk about is not the small "I" which concerns the
individual. It is that "I" which is the Supreme Principle. As
far as a great soul is concerned, "In me" means "In God."
Taking this and interpreting it as caste, religion, etc., the fol-
lowers think in a narrow-minded way. Sri Krishna told
Arjuna, "Have faith in Me," that "I" which is the Supreme
Principle. But now, some Hindus say that you will get Libera-
tion only if you believe in Krishna, some others say that Shiva
alone is the Liberator and so on. This is not correct. What we
(the Sanatana Dharma) say is, whether it is Krishna or
Christ or Nabi, they all help us to attain the Supreme.
Whether you come through the southern side or northern side
or from the east, you can reach the ashram. Those who say
"Only our religion is true," are mistaken. Real Mahatmas will
never be bound by an institution. They will go forward keep-
ing the Supreme Truth alone as the ideal.

AMMACHI, AWAKEN CHILDREN, VOL. 1 [brackets by author]

That Jesus was speaking as the universal I AM in John 14:6–as the
water and not the lake–is further reinforced by examining the passage in Jesus' original language, which was Aramaic. The following is a quote from the book *The Hidden Gospel* by Dr. Neil
Douglas-Klotz, Ph.D. (published by Quest Books). This book is a
delightfully enlightening discussion of the translation of the four
gospels from Aramaic. The translations are from the Bible of Eastern Christians, which is written in Western Aramaic. The earliest
manuscript copy of this Bible dates to the fourth century C.E. as
does the earliest copy of the Greek version of the four gospels. Aramaic Christians of various denominations claim this Bible to be
the most accurate presentation of the Master's teachings. Dr. Douglas-Klotz begins his discussion of John 14:6 with a review of the
first two words which are "I am" (as in "I am the way..."). The Aramaic bible does not simply say "I" in John 14:6. It could, but it
doesn't, and that distinction is revealing.

In the Aramaic version, we find the construction "I am" repre-
sented by the word "I" repeated: ena ena, as in "I-I." This has
several possible interpretations: an intensive form of "I," the es-

sence of individuality, the "I" inside the "I," or something like "the 'I am.'" Again, in a culture where the word for God means Unity, the sense of the individual cannot be ultimately separated from the divine. Only one "I Am" exists, which is Alaha.
THE HIDDEN GOSPEL BY DR. NEIL DOUGLAS-KLOTZ , PH.D.

Because the scripture says "I-I" and not just "I," it underscores the understanding that it is more than the person of Jesus talking in an exclusive way. It is the eternal "I AM," the Christ that dwells within each one of us. It is THAT which existed "before Abraham" that says, "I am the way."

Jesus said, "It is I who am the light which is above them all. It is I who am the all. From me did the all come forth, and unto me did the all extend. Split a piece of wood, and I am there. Lift up the stone, and you will find me there."
GOSPEL OF THOMAS, NAG HAMMADI LIBRARY, VERSE 77

This is the same I AM talking that existed before Abraham. Jesus clearly reveals that it is not the persona of the man Jesus talking as he advises us that he exists in all things (in the wood and under the stone). The physical body of Jesus would not be found in the wood or under the stone.

To further illustrate, we can see a wave on the ocean, but we cannot say the wave is separate from the ocean. Likewise, we can say there is an individual soul, but we cannot say it is separate from God. Jesus sees the body, but he is not attached to it. Rather he identifies with the ocean and not the wave. The wave, like our bodies, is something that comes and goes. The opposite perception is true for us. We see only the small wave of our own bodies and have no awareness of the ocean of being. Thus, we are attached to the wave and suffer as a result of it. In truth, we are, right now, like Jesus because our true nature has always been the pure ocean of being. The difference is that he knew his divinity, and we do not know ours. One may point out that he worked many miracles, whereas we cannot, indicating we are not divine in the same way as Jesus. The Master tells us that the faith of a mustard seed can move a mountain. Jesus had this faith–that knowing or gnosis–but we do not. We are simply not aware of our divine nature.

> *He replied, "Because you have so little faith. I tell you the truth, if you have faith as small as a mustard seed, you can say to this mountain, 'Move from here to there' and it will move. Nothing will be impossible for you."* MATTHEW 17:20, NIV

Becoming aware of our divine nature is the beginning of the end for the ego and all selfishness. There will be no reason to covet and every reason to love. Then we become as Christ because we will realize perfection—that Christ is our true Self and not the body and the ego. In the following scripture Jesus tells us we can also be a Christ.

> *The disciple is not above his master: but every one that is perfect shall be as his master.* LUKE 6:40, KJV

We will realize the truth of our oneness in Christ and be set free because of it.

> *Then you will know the truth, and the truth will set you free.* JOHN 8:32, NIV

In the above scripture Jesus does not say that it is he who will set us free but the truth that will set us free.

There are further interesting considerations regarding the Jesus-is-the-only-way scripture quoted at the beginning of this chapter.

> *Jesus answered, "I am the way and the truth and the life. No one <u>comes</u> to the Father except through me."* JOHN 14:6, NIV [emphasis added]

In the original Greek text, the word "comes," *erchetai*, is in the present tense. This means that Jesus was referring to his physical presence in the context of those individuals to whom he was speaking at that time. It cannot be interpreted as "will come" or "has come" but only as "now comes." This very-present-tense view of the scripture is further exonerated by the next two sentences that clearly indicate Jesus was referring to his audience seeing and experiencing him then and there. By seeing Jesus personally then and there, they had seen the Absolute as well. The idea of exclusivity in which Jesus is the only occurrence of God manifesting as a physical incarnation for all time is simply not in this scripture.

In the following commentary on this passage Dr. Douglas-Klotz reinforces the present tense meaning of the Greek word for "comes" as it appears in John 14:6.

> *In this sense, the person of Jesus, whom his disciples see and who walks, talks, and eats with them, provides a doorway between the realities. Through his presence they can find a personal relationship with abwoon, the breathing life of all. Through attunement to Jesus' breathing, atmosphere, and way of prayer, they will be led to experience what he experiences. Focusing on the teacher as a doorway to the divine is a spiritual practice that still exists today in Jewish and Islamic mysticism.*
> THE HIDDEN GOSPEL BY DR. NEIL DOUGLAS-KLOTZ , PH.D.

By reviewing the Aramaic, two revelations appear. 1) When John 14:6 was translated from Aramaic to Greek, the translators understood that Jesus was speaking specifically about his presence then and there in the context of a group of specific listeners. The Greek translators used a present tense "comes" because that is the meaning they properly derived from the original Aramaic. Modern translators have mistakenly expanded the narrow present tense time reference to mean for all time. 2) Ultimately it is the I AM THAT I AM that begins John 14:6 and is not exclusive to Jesus. It is the ocean talking and not the wave. "Why do you call me good?" In Luke 18:18 Jesus is asking why we think it is the wave (a specific personal Jesus) that does these things.

Dr. Douglas-Klotz continues with a detailed explanation of each word in John 14:6 as it appears in Aramaic, but we have not included it here. He follows by offering this complete translation of John 14:6 from the Aramaic Bible.

> *The "I Am" is the path, the sense of right direction and the life force to travel it. Simple presence illuminates what's ahead, frees our choices, and connects us to nature's power. No one comes into rhythm with the breathing life of all, the sound*

*and atmosphere that created the cosmos, except through the
breathing, sound and atmosphere, of another embodied "I"
connected to the ultimate "I Am."*
THE HIDDEN GOSPEL BY DR. NEIL DOUGLAS-KLOTZ , PH.D.

Let's move to another angle of consideration. Jesus states in John
that all others who have come before him are thieves and robbers.

*All who ever came before me were thieves and robbers, but the
sheep did not listen to them.* JOHN 10:8, NIV

Does this mean that Abraham, Moses, and Elijah were all thieves
and robbers? If this scripture is true, then why is the Old Testament included in the Bible? If we take John 14:6 literally then we
are duty bound to take John 10:8 literally. If we take John 10:8 literally then the entire Old Testament must be thrown out as a bo-
gus work because the prophets were all thieves and robbers. We
can refute the idea that Jesus meant Moses and Elijah were robbers and thieves because the Lord talked to them in the transfigu-
ration in Matthew 17:3. In the same way we can refute the idea
that Jesus is the "only way" by the many references to attaining
the kingdom in which he did not include himself as part of the
formula. It goes without saying that no one comes to the Father
except by the Christ, but the Christ existed before the body of
Jesus, and it is the same Christ that was Krishna, Buddha,
Mohammed and others.

In the following scripture Jesus gives direct instructions for attaining the kingdom, and he does not include himself or any necessary belief in him in those instructions.

*On one occasion an expert in the law stood up to test Jesus.
"Teacher," he asked, "what must I do to inherit eternal life?"*

*"What is written in the Law?" he [Jesus] replied. "How do you
read it?"*

*He [the expert] answered: "Love the Lord your God with all
your heart and with all your soul and with all your strength
and with all your mind; and, Love your neighbor as yourself."*

"You have answered correctly," Jesus replied. "Do this and you will live." Luke 10:25-28, NIV (brackets by author)

Jesus clearly tells the man that loving God intensely and loving your neighbor as yourself are all that is necessary to attain eternal life. He did not add that it was necessary to believe in Jesus only or that it was even necessary to follow him. Jesus would be guilty of lying to the man if it were true that belief in Jesus only was an absolute prerequisite for attaining eternal life. When confronted with this scripture, some will attempt to maintain that Jesus is the only way by saying that loving God automatically implies loving Jesus because God and Jesus are one. However, this rationale will backfire when we swing the sword in the other direction. If Jesus is God then *any* love of God will qualify us for heaven even if we are not followers of Jesus or have never heard of Jesus.

John underscores Jesus' statement that love is all that is necessary to arrive at the goal:

Dear friends, let us love one another, for love comes from God. Everyone who loves has been born of God and knows God.
1 John 4:7, NIV

Jesus' most famous speech was the Sermon on the Mount in which he delivered a cornucopia of spiritual wisdom, including the Beatitudes, to a multitude of people. If entry into heaven were conditioned solely on belief in Jesus alone, he would certainly have revealed this pivotal fact to the multitudes. If belief in Jesus alone were the single most important factor for getting into heaven, why did the Lord fail to mention it here? In the Beatitudes Jesus describes several conditions or types of people who will attain the kingdom. Not once does Jesus say, "Blessed are those who believe in me for they shall attain the kingdom of God."

Blessed are the poor in spirit, for theirs is the kingdom of heaven.
Blessed are the pure in heart, for they will see God.
Blessed are the peacemakers, for they will be called sons of God.
Blessed are those who are persecuted because of righteousness, for theirs is the kingdom of heaven. Matthew 5:3, 8-10, NIV

So Jesus tells us that those who have surrendered totally to God will have the kingdom of God. If our hearts are pure we will see God. And what is a pure heart? A pure heart is an innocent heart full of selfless love. A child has a pure heart even if he/she knows nothing of religion or Jesus.

In summary, only by experiencing the eternal Christ directly will we know the nature of Jesus.

8

Other Christs

Some forms are products of devotees' imaginations. Yet other forms are of Divine Personalities who actually lived in the past like Sri Rama or Sri Krishna. They are not simply imaginary forms meant only for concentration. As you know, Lord Buddha, Chaitanya Mahaprabhu and Jesus Christ were great souls who lived at one time. Likewise, Sri Rama and Sri Krishna were Divine Incarnations who lived on this earth. They were not mere mythical heroes.

AMMACHI, AWAKEN CHILDREN, VOL. 2

The Christ is universal and timeless and has been appearing before humanity in a fleshly form since the dawn of the world.

The common orthodox view is that Jesus proved his superiority over other spiritual leaders like Buddha or Krishna because he accepted the ultimate sacrifice of the crucifixion, and the other spiritual leaders did not do this. The idea here is that Jesus sacrificed his body so that we might be relieved of our sins. A common analogy is to refer to Jesus as a sacrificial lamb, and therefore, we have been saved by the "blood of the lamb."

> Sacrifice – 1. to offer as a sacrifice 2. to suffer loss of, give up, renounce, injure, or destroy esp. for an ideal, belief, or end 3. to sell at a loss.   *Webster's Collegiate Dictionary*

Only if we give up something that is important to us can we say it is a sacrifice. If we donate our old discarded clothes to charity, it is not a sacrifice. Great masters like Jesus do not consider their bodies, and subsequently all the pleasures the body can buy, to be desirable. For an incarnation of God, the greatest sacrifice is *having* a body. To these great ones, the body is a prison which they willingly inhabit for the sole purpose of relieving the suffering of the world and restoring righteousness. For them, the sacrifice is to be in this world away from their true abode which is heaven. It is like allowing oneself to be locked in a prison to help and serve the prisoners. It is a relief to get out of the prison, in this case the physical body, when the task is completed. For us the death of the body appears to be a sacrifice because our egos depend on it. We desire the pleasures the body can give us, and we mistakenly project this point of view onto Jesus. But for Jesus, who had no ego and did not need a body to substantiate an ego, getting rid of the body was a blessing. Jesus revealed that he preferred to move on to the next world as he was dragging his cross through the street on the way to be crucified:

> *A large number of people followed him, including women who mourned and wailed for him. Jesus turned and said to them, "Daughters of Jerusalem, do not weep for me; weep for yourselves and for your children."*　　　Luke 23:27-28, NIV

Jesus is telling the weeping women that it is worse to be in the world than to be leaving it. That would be the logical conclusion of one who is leaving this world and all of its sorrows and going to paradise. Jesus reveals his sublime destination to one of the criminals who is being crucified along with him:

> *Then he said, "Jesus, remember me when you come into your kingdom."*

> *Jesus answered him, "I tell you the truth, today you will be with me in paradise."*　　　Luke 23:42-43, NIV

The Buddha is called *The Compassionate One* because he agreed to remain in the body and teach mankind instead of entering into nirvana (heaven) at the point of his supreme enlightenment. Thus, we can make the point that the Buddha's sacrifice was as great as Jesus' because he agreed to stay in the prison of the body for the benefit of suffering humanity. Ammachi sits for 10 or 12 hours a day with no break, hugging all that come to see her. Often the crowds in India number ten to twenty thousand in a single day. She hugs each one into the late morning hours and will not leave until the last person is hugged. Here is a present day Christ who is the very embodiment of love and compassion. We could not imagine ourselves even lifting our arms twenty thousand times in a day to deliver the hugs. And day after day, year after year, for twenty years her life has been a supreme sacrifice of the body and the ego.

The most important aspect of Jesus' life was that he championed love as the path to salvation. According to Jesus, it is the amount of love we have mustered in the course of our lives that grants or denies entry into heaven and not the crucifixion. It is love and not the crucifixion that destroys sin.

In truth, there is one Only Begotten Son, the Christ, who has appeared as all of the incarnations throughout all time. Each incarnation brings the same essential message but stated in a different way to suit the times and the various cultures. To say that one is greater than any of the others because some act was performed that the others did not perform is simply ignorance.

MELCHIZEDEK

Paul tells us in Hebrews of another Christ named Melchizedek who appeared in Genesis 14:18 to bless Abraham. Abraham was so impressed with Melchizedek that he gave him ten percent of his possessions based entirely on one brief encounter when Abraham was returning from rescuing his nephew, Lot. Melchizedek is mentioned again in Psalms 110:4. Melchizedek was not a Jew but a pagan. He could not have been a Jew because Paul says he was a high priest outside of the tribe of Levi, and according to Jewish law, only a Levite could be a priest. In fact Levi, the father of that tribe, had not even been born. It would be another 1,800 years before Moses would appear with the Ten Commandments.

Paul says:

> During the days of Jesus' life on earth, he offered up prayers
> and petitions with loud cries and tears to the one who could

save him from death, and he was heard because of his reverent
submission. Although he was a son, he learned obedience from
what he suffered and, once made perfect, he became the source
of eternal salvation for all who obey him and was designated
by God to be high priest in the order of Melchizedek.

HEBREWS 5:7-10, NIV

This is very interesting. First of all, Paul is saying that Jesus was
not always perfect but was made perfect at some point as the result of his own strenuous effort. Not only that, but upon being
made perfect he was granted the right by God to be high priest in
Melchizedek's order! If Jesus is Christ then who is Melchizedek
that God would make Jesus a priest in Melchizedek's order? This
places Melchizedek above or at the least equal to Jesus in a hierarchy of priests.

We have this hope as an anchor for the soul, firm and secure.
It enters the inner sanctuary behind the curtain, where Jesus,
who went before us, has entered on our behalf. He has become
a high priest forever, in the order of Melchizedek. This
Melchizedek was king of Salem and priest of God Most High.
He met Abraham returning from the defeat of the kings and
blessed him, and Abraham gave him a tenth of everything.
First, his name means "king of righteousness;" then also,
"king of Salem" means "king of peace." Without father or
mother, without genealogy, without beginning of days or end
of life, like the Son of God he remains a priest forever. Just
think how great he was: Even the patriarch Abraham gave
him a tenth of the plunder!   HEBREWS 6:19-7:4, NIV

In this passage Paul again tells us that Jesus has become a high
priest forever in the order of Melchizedek. In Genesis,
Melchizedek is referred to as the king of Salem. Salem is an old
testament name for Jerusalem, but Paul tells us that in this case
"king of Salem" means "king of peace," meaning that
Melchizedek was not the king of a physical location. Melchizedek
did not have a father or mother nor any ancestors nor was he ever
born nor will he ever die. Wow! God incarnated as Melchizedek
by materializing a fully-grown physical body that Melchizedek

could de-materialize at any time. Thus, he had no birth from a womb, no mother or father, no ancestors and no death. Paul goes on to say that like the Son of God–in other words, like Jesus–he remains a priest forever. Paul is saying Melchizedek is like Jesus. They are both incarnations of God. If Paul is correct then Melchizedek is a more direct and more powerful incarnation of Christ than Jesus because Jesus did not materialize a body but had to come through the birth canal of Mary. According to Paul, Jesus labored to attain perfection, implying that there was a previous state of imperfection, but can we say that one who was able to materialize a body at will came so imperfectly? Rather, Melchizedek was eternally perfect. Therefore, Jesus was admitted to Melchizedek's order and not vice versa.

> Jesus said, "When you see one who was not born of woman, prostrate yourselves on your faces and worship him. That one is your father."
> GOSPEL OF THOMAS, NAG HAMMADI LIBRARY, VERSE 15

If the preceeding verse is correct, then Melchizedek is God incarnate, and according to Jesus, we should worship Him.

> One might even say that Levi, who collects the tenth, paid the tenth through Abraham, because when Melchizedek met Abraham, Levi was still in the body of his ancestor. If perfection could have been attained through the Levitical priesthood (for on the basis of it the law was given to the people), why was there still need for another priest to come–one in the order of Melchizedek, not in the order of Aaron? HEBREWS 7:9-11, NIV

According to Jewish law, only the Levites descended from Aaron could be priests. Paul says that God disagreed and, contrary to the law, sent Jesus who was of a different order–the order of Melchizedek.

> For it is clear that our Lord descended from Judah, and in regard to that tribe Moses said nothing about priests. And what we have said is even more clear if another priest like Melchizedek appears, one who has become a priest not on the basis of a regulation as to his ancestry but on the basis of the

power of an indestructible life. For it is declared: "You are a priest forever, in the order of Melchizedek."
HEBREWS 7:14-17, NIV

Paul continues to refer to Jesus as a priest who is *like* Melchizedek. It is clear that Paul considers Melchizedek to be the equal of Jesus if not greater. If Melchizedek is equal with Jesus then Melchizedek is a Christ–an incarnation of God–and he was not of the nation of Israel because the nation of Israel had not yet been born. He was a pagan.

KRISHNA

Many Hindus would consider the *Bhagavad Gita* (Song of God) to be one of the central scriptural references for their faith. In it, Sri (pronounced "shree"–meaning lord) Krishna reveals the "way" to his disciple Arjuna, and in this regard the "Gita" resembles the four gospels which are the record of what Christ said. Krishna was a man, a Christ, who walked the earth as Jesus did. He was an incarnation of God. He was a Christ. In the following scripture Sri Krishna declares his purpose:

> *When goodness grows weak, when evil increases, I make myself a body. In every age I come back to deliver the holy, to destroy the sin of the sinner; to establish righteousness.*
> THE SONG OF GOD; BHAGAVAD GITA – TRANSLATED BY
CHRISTOPHER ISHERWOOD & SWAMI PRABHAVANANDA

Sri Krishna also echoes Jesus' affirmation of oneness with God.

> *I am the birthless, the deathless,*
> *Lord of all that breathes.*
> *I seem to be born:*
> *It is only seeming,*
> *Only my maya.*
> *I am still master*
> *Of my prakriti*
> *The power that makes me.*

He who knows the nature
Of my task and my holy birth
Is not reborn
When he leaves this body:
He comes to me.

THE SONG OF GOD; BHAGAVAD GITA – TRANSLATED BY
CHRISTOPHER ISHERWOOD & SWAMI PRABHAVANANDA

Here Sri Krishna says that he is one with the "father" (God) who is birthless and deathless. Only God is birthless and deathless. Krishna states flatly that he is the Lord of all that breathes. His fleshly body is only an appearance and does not in itself hold or reveal the Christ, which is beyond any particular body. Thus, Krishna tells us that his being born in a body is only an appearance. Maya is the appearance of the ego which gives rise to the notion of duality or a world that is separate from ourselves. This duality is created by God as a dream or as a play. Suffering arises by mistaking the shadow (the world, the ego) for the flame (God). Thus, Krishna's birth and body are only part of the illusion or the dream. He says that he is the master of his prakriti, which is the total of the forces of nature used to bring his body and the entire physical universe into being. Because of this, and like Jesus, Krishna was able to perform countless miracles in his lifetime. Krishna says that he is master of all of that. Further, in the same way that Jesus states that those who understand him shall be granted eternal life, Krishna states that any who know his (Krishna's) nature will not be reborn but will be granted eternity. In the Hindu and Buddhist view, we are born again and again as long as the ego and its desires persist. Births are created from our desires. Thus, the goal is to end the succession of dying again and again and again (the death that Adam and Eve were promised for eating the fruit of the knowledge of good and evil), and so Krishna promises that if we can understand him, we will not be reborn but will have eternal life. Eternal life is life that is unbroken by the cycling wheel of birth and death.

And again Lord Krishna affirms his divinity:

I am the goal of the wise man, and I am the way. I am the end
of the path, the witness, the Lord, the sustainer. I am the place

of abode, the beginning, the friend and the refuge. Fools pass
blindly by the place of my dwelling here in the human form;
and of my majesty they know nothing at all, who am the Lord,
their soul. Fill your heart and mind with me, adore me, make
all your acts an offering to me, bow down to me in self-surren-
der. If you set your heart upon me thus, and take me for your
ideal above all others, you will come into my Being.

THE SONG OF GOD; BHAGAVAD GITA—TRANSLATED BY
CHRISTOPHER ISHERWOOD & SWAMI PRABHAVANANDA

BUDDHA

Lord Buddha appeared approximately 500 years before Jesus. He
was a prince who left his wife and baby to find the answer to suffering, disease, old age and death. He spent six years in the forest as
an ascetic doing austere spiritual practices such as fasting to the
point of death. The idea of the ascetics is that one must be dis-
tanced from the body as much as possible by denying the senses.
This phase ended when he sat on the banks of a river and watched
a boat go by. In that boat a person was playing a stringed instrument. It occurred to the Lord that if the string is stretched too tight
it breaks, and if it is too loose it makes no music. Abandoning his
ascetic practices, he spent another long period of time meditating
in the forest. At the end of this he resolved to sit under a bodhi tree
until he either attained enlightenment or died trying. For forty days
and nights he sat. Mara the tempter came in several forms, attempting to seduce the Lord, offering him lordship over countries,
nymphs for his pleasure, etc. Mara attempted to lure him away
from his victory, but he was beyond that. He was seeing through
form, and so He attained enlightenment or nirvana. The celestial
beings were concerned that he would not stay on earth to help others resolve their own salvation, and so they appealed to Him. As an
act of extreme sacrifice, he agreed to stay and teach. Because of
this, he is called the Compassionate One. Compassion toward all
beings and dissolution of the ego are central pillars in the teaching
of the Buddha. The following is one of His quotes.

You are my children, I am your father; through me you have
been released from your sufferings. I myself having reached the

other shore, help others to cross the stream; I myself having attained salvation, am a savior of others; being comforted, I comfort others and lead them to the place of refuge. My thoughts are always in the truth. For lo! my self has become the truth. Whosoever comprehends the truth will see the Blessed One.

There have been many Christs appearing to the world. They all have the same message.

9

Jesus and the Old Testament

Unfortunately most religions are led by intellectuals. The heart alone can guide a person, but the heart has been forgotten. Only a true Master who dwells within the heart can throw light on the path of religion. Such a person alone can unite the people; he alone can make people understand the true import of religion and religious principles.

AMMACHI, AWAKEN CHILDREN, VOL. 7

In the final analysis, only Love is wholly reliable. This chapter will explore the possibility that some of the Old Testament and some interpretations of the Old Testament might be the product of men and their egos and not God. We will establish a beachhead for discarding or re-interpreting some of the Old Testament by exploring what Jesus taught. Jesus himself sets the precedent for such an examination.

We know that Jesus directly disputes the fourth of the Ten Commandments, which has to do with keeping the Sabbath. In the following scripture, the Pharisees try to catch Jesus violating the commandment of keeping the Sabbath, but Jesus flatly rejects it.

> He said to them, "If any of you has a sheep and it falls into a pit on the Sabbath, will you not take hold of it and lift it out? How much more valuable is a man than a sheep! Therefore it is lawful to do good on the Sabbath." MATTHEW 12:11-12, NIV

Jesus says it is all right to do any good thing on the Sabbath. It is fortunate that Jesus does not list the keeping of the Sabbath as necessary for attaining eternal life, or we would be in maximum trouble according to the following scripture from Exodus. Take special note of the put-to-death part.

> *Observe the Sabbath, because it is holy to you. Anyone who desecrates it must be put to death; whoever does any work on that day must be cut off from his people.* EXODUS 31:14, NIV

The Old Testament book of Leviticus contains detailed laws including what foods to avoid and other detailed instructions such as to how to perform ritual sacrifices for the atonement of sins. Also included are prohibitions concerning incest, bestiality, prostitution, consorting with wizards, putting tattoos on the body, homosexuality, sex out of wedlock and making of idols or graven images. We are also told that we must keep the Sabbath and observe specific religious holidays and feast days. The Sabbath is not just resting on the seventh day of the week but applies to a broad range of cyclic activities such as planting a field for six years and resting it for a year. In Numbers 13:32-36 a man is caught gathering firewood on the Sabbath, and from there things go rather badly for him.

> *While the Israelites were in the desert, a man was found gathering wood on the Sabbath day. Those who found him gathering wood brought him to Moses and Aaron and the whole assembly, and they kept him in custody, because it was not clear what should be done to him. Then the Lord said to Moses, "The man must die. The whole assembly must stone him outside the camp." So the assembly took him outside the camp and stoned him to death, as the Lord commanded Moses.*
> NUMBERS 15:32-36, NIV

The poor man's wife had probably complained, "Thomas, the children and I are freezing, and little Johnny is getting sick. Would you sneak out and get a little wood?" Does our salvation really depend on avoiding work on the Sabbath, or does it depend on how much we are able to love and express compassion? Did God really have that man stoned to death? Only someone who does not know God would think that God had this man stoned to death. Our choices are as follows: 1. God is an evil schmuck; 2. Moses was not always perfectly in tune with God; 3. Moses never said God told him to stone the man to death; or 4. We play the God's-Mysteries-are-unexplainable wild card and walk away. If we believe that everything in the Old and New Testament is the absolute word of God then choice number 4 is our only option. However, if we are wrong the consequences are horrendous because we will base our conception of God on a lie. Jesus clearly disagreed with the Old Testament on this account. He threw out the death penalty for working on the Sabbath. He said doing any good work on the Sabbath is acceptable. Which position, Jesus or the Old Testament, is the true word of God? We may think that God changed his mind, but in Malachi 3:6 God says that he does *not* change. Again, we must either play wild card #4 and walk away, or we must consider that God never said that anyone should die for working on the Sabbath much less picking up a little firewood.

There are accounts in the Old Testament in which God tells the Israelites to slay men, women and children of other tribes. How are we to reconcile God's advice to kill innocent women and children with God's commandment, "Thou shalt not kill?" How can this possibly reconcile with Jesus' commandment to love our enemies (Matt. 5:44)?

> When the Lord your God brings you into the land you are entering to possess and drives out before you many nations—the Hittites, Girgashites, Amorites, Canaanites, Perizzites, Hivites and Jebusites, seven nations larger and stronger than you—and when the Lord your God has delivered them over to you and you have defeated them, then you must destroy them totally. Make no treaty with them, and show them no mercy. Do not intermarry with them. Do not give your daughters to their sons or take their daughters for your sons, for they will turn your sons away from following me to serve other gods, and the Lord's anger will burn against you and will quickly destroy you. This is what you are to do to them: Break down their altars, smash their sacred stones, cut down their Asherah poles and burn their idols in the fire. For you are a people holy to the Lord your God. The Lord your God has chosen you out of all the peoples on the face of the earth to be his people, his treasured possession.   DEUTERONOMY, 7:1-6, NIV

God did not write the above scripture. It was written by an Israeli historian putting his own self-righteous spin on a dark moment in Israeli history. The following quote from Jesus reveals a radically different approach:

> They came to Capernaum. When he was in the house, he asked them, "What were you arguing about on the road?" But they kept quiet because on the way they had argued about who was the greatest. Sitting down, Jesus called the Twelve and said, "If anyone wants to be first, he must be the very last, and the servant of all." MARK 9:33-35, NIV

Did the Israelites see themselves as the servants of the Hittites, Girgashites, Amorites, Canaanites, Perizzites, Hivites and Jebusites, as the Israelites drove them from their land, claiming God told them they could have it to graze their own herds? According to Jesus, being "chosen" means being the servant of all. The attitude of "servant of all" never slips even a glimmer through these autobiographical chronicles of conquest, covetousness, and ethnic cleansing. It should be noted that the inhabitants of the United States who were descended from European stock did exactly the same thing to the Native Americans. The atrocities were horrendous. Few nations and tribes can claim exemption from this (perhaps the Swiss and the Hopi Indians). This only serves to illustrate the wide-ranging and relentless grip of the ego in this world.

The idea that God had chosen the Israelites above all other people is solely the work of Israeli historians. God loves all people equally. Every person is God's chosen person. Those who are first will be last, and those who are last will be first (Luke 13:30). This is similar to the Taoist saying, "An empty glass must be made full and a full glass must be made empty." These sayings are commentaries on the power of humility. The last sentence in Deuteronomy 7:6 was spoken by Ego and not by God. It is always Ego that says, "I am special. I am chosen." The greatest among us are those who regard themselves as the servants of all. There are no exceptions to this.

> The greatest among you will be your servant. For whoever exalts himself will be humbled, and whoever humbles himself will be exalted. MATTHEW 23:11-12, NIV

Ammachi says the same.

> *Children, just the thought, "I am spiritual, I am spiritually advanced," or "I am a renunciate," can be a big stumbling block to your spiritual progress. Such thoughts are also part of the ego, but a more subtle form of ego. You may think, "I am great because I have renounced everything. Look at all those worldly people out there who are still immersed in the quagmire of materialism. They are so ignorant!" You may feel that those who live in the world are far beneath you. If you cherish such thoughts, it only shows that you are mentally immature. It means that you are ignorant. Those who live in the world may be ignorant, but they are not on the spiritual path; whereas, you are supposed to be on the spiritual path and yet you are still spiritually ignorant. Such thoughts are of the ego and need to be uprooted.* AMMACHI, AWAKEN CHILDREN, VOL. 7

Were these campaigns of horror enacted because God was concerned about contaminating the Israelites, or were the priests concerned with competitors who threatened their authority? Was it an act of covetousness in which the Israelites were consumed with desire for grazing lands occupied by others? These unfortunate activities have been going on everywhere since the dawn of recorded history. Eventually the Israelites went on to the Promised Land. With Moses out of the way, God (the priests) escalated His (their) thirst for blood. In these post-Moses scriptures God orders the Israelites not simply to conquer a people but to slay every man, woman and child. A blatant rape of the fifth commandment, "Thou shalt not murder," follows:

> *Now go, attack the Amalekites and totally destroy everything that belongs to them. Do not spare them; put to death men and women, children and infants, cattle and sheep, camels and donkeys.* 1 SAMUEL 15:3, NIV

Some contend that our pitiless and merciless God "took no prisoners" to keep the Israelites pure and undefiled by the filth of other religions. Was God so paranoid that he was compelled to ask the Israelites to kill every man, woman and child to protect the Israelites from the dirt of other religions? Was God so paranoid that he commanded them to go on a murderous rampage, breaking the fifth commandment in the bleakest possible way? God wept as spears and swords plunged into the tender breasts of little, innocent babies. He wept even more for the compassionless brutality that had conquered the hearts of the perpetrators of this blood feast. God wept as he saw that the true motivation for this unspeakable carnage was covetousness, lust for power, greed and ego, ego, ego masquerading as moral pious superiority. No doubt many of the murderers soothed their burning consciences by reminding themselves that it is not possible to understand God's mysterious ways. No doubt many of Hitler's henchmen comforted themselves by thinking, "It is not possible to understand Der Fuehrer's mysterious ways," as they opened the valves of death in the gas chambers of Auschwitz.

In the following scripture Jesus offers a marked contrast. Ego was whispering the same things in the ears of John and James that he had whispered to the Israelites when he convinced them to slay the Amalekites. In this instance, Jesus was traveling to Jerusalem with the disciples when a Samaritan village refused to let them stay the night. The attitude that Jesus takes here is very different from slaying every man, woman and suckling infant.

> *And when his disciples James and John saw this, they said, "Lord, wilt thou that we command fire to come down from heaven, and consume them, even as Elias did?"*
>
> *But he turned, and rebuked them, and said, "Ye know not what manner of spirit ye are of. For the Son of man is not come to destroy men's lives, but to save them." And they went to another village.*
>
> LUKE 9:54-56, KJV

A dominant and reoccurring theme in the Old Testament is the smiting of enemies.

> *You will pursue your enemies, and they will fall by the sword before you.* LEVITICUS 26:7, NIV

Jesus says that point of view is wrong.

"But I tell you who hear me: Love your enemies, do good to those who hate you, bless those who curse you, pray for those who mistreat you." LUKE 6:27-28, NIV

What are we to think about these horrific murderous deeds in the Old Testament perpetrated for the expressed purpose of cleansing the earth of other religions and cultures? The concept of loving your enemies cannot be reconciled with the murdering rampages in the Old Testament.

When Jesus appears in the world, among the same Israelites and surrounded by many "other religions," he fails to offer even a hint of advice concerning the possibility of defilement from these other religions, idols or gods. Jesus never mentions the dangers of idolatry. He is obviously not concerned about it. Contrarily, He states that if they are not against us, they are for us (Mark 9:40 and Luke 9:50). The stark and glaring contrast of these two extremes is astounding. We are compelled to consider that God did not tell the Israelites to slay anybody. Ego told them to do the killing, and Ego told them they were the "chosen ones." Ego convinced them that they were racially and spiritually superior to everyone else. That our brothers and sisters the Israelites could have gotten so far away from the truth as to murder every man, woman, and suckling infant should cause us all to weep with compassion.

To maintain perspective, we should remember we are talking about a few historical instances in the Old Testament, which overall is a sublime and inspired scripture. There is no nation, tribe, or race that can claim innocence when it comes to moral and spiritual self-righteousness. When the Europeans began to visit China, the Chinese regarded them as crude barbarians. When the Europeans settled the Americas, the natives were seen as sub-human savages, and every manner of contemptible abuse and exploitation was heaped upon them. Adolph Hitler also had this attitude. The Aryan race was morally superior, and it was Mr. Hitler's divine calling to put things aright. In his book *Mein Kampf*, Hitler makes his case:

Every manifestation of human culture, every product of art,
science and technical skill, which we see before our eyes today,
is almost exclusively the product of the Aryan creative power.
This very fact full justifies the conclusion that it was the Aryan
alone who founded a superior type of humanity; therefore he
represents the archetype of what we understand by the term:
M A N. He is the Prometheus of mankind, from whose shin-
ing brow the divine spark of genius has at all times flashed
forth, always kindling anew that fire which, in the form of
knowledge, illuminated the dark night by drawing aside the
veil of mystery and thus showing man how to rise and become
master over all the other beings on the earth. Should he be
forced to disappear, a profound darkness will descend on the
earth: within a few thousand years human culture will vanish
and the world will become a desert.
ADOLPH HITLER, MEIN KAMPF, CHAPTER 11 –
RACE AND PEOPLE, TRANSLATION BY JAMES MURPHY

It is clear that Hitler regarded *his* race as the chosen people. And
as with all such egoistic delusions, there must be a reviled race to
serve as the backdrop for clarification and contrast.

He will stop at nothing. His utterly low-down conduct is so
appalling that one really cannot be surprised if in the imagi-
nation of our people the Jew is pictured as the incarnation of
Satan and the symbol of evil.
ADOLPH HITLER, MEIN KAMPF, CHAPTER 11–
RACE AND PEOPLE, TRANSLATION BY JAMES MURPHY

The black-haired Jewish youth lies in wait for hours on end,
satanically glaring at and spying on the unsuspicious girl
whom he plans to seduce, adulterating her blood and remov-
ing her from the bosom of her own people.
ADOLPH HITLER, MEIN KAMPF, CHAPTER 11 –
RACE AND PEOPLE, TRANSLATION BY JAMES MURPHY

Hitler regarded intermarrying of the Aryan race with inferior
races as a travesty of cosmic proportions, just as the Israelites did
in the Old Testament. And like the Israelites, he would go so far
as to commit genocide to defend that position.

If Nature does not wish that weaker individuals should mate with the stronger, she wishes even less that a superior race should intermingle with an inferior one; because in such a case all her efforts, throughout hundreds of thousands of years, to establish an evolutionary higher stage of being, may thus be rendered futile.

History furnishes us with innumerable instances that prove this law. It shows, with a startling clarity, that whenever Aryans have mingled their blood with that of an inferior race the result has been the downfall of the people who were the standard-bearers of a higher culture.

ADOLPH HITLER, MEIN KAMPF, CHAPTER 11 –
RACE AND PEOPLE, TRANSLATION BY JAMES MURPHY

In Hitler's opinion he was obligated by a just and moral duty to rid the world of those peoples who were a defilement to the rest of the world. It was just this attitude that motivated the Israelites to slay the Amalekites—every man, woman, child and infant. In the 1990's we have again witnessed the same horror of ethnic cleansing in Europe and Africa, all accompanied by the same rhetoric. It is as if the same person keeps making the same racist speech over and over again from ancient times until now.

As long as Satan persists as the ego in all of us, we will have the desire to be "chosen" and "special." We are all blind, and these holocausts perpetrated by collective national psychotic episodes of narcissistic grandiosity fueled by the attitude of being special, chosen, or morally superior have been going on since the dawn of the ego. In fact being "special" is a favorite food for the ego along with "special's" twin, "wretched miserable sinner."

We see the same sectarian elitism in the Christian world. Many sects believe they alone are in possession of the true interpretation of the scriptures and that all other Christian sects are going to hell. Most sects proclaim that being a Christian is the only way to salvation. Without a doubt, there are many Christians today who would support a world war if they thought it would convert everyone else to their way of believing. They would reason that the others are lost to hell anyway unless a forceful intervention is made at gunpoint. They would consider it their moral duty to save the pagans from themselves.

We must consider that it is the nature of the ego to sanctify our actions even when they are evil. Throughout history, we read these justifications in the archives of every country. No country will war against another with the idea that it is wrong to initiate the war. Everyone wants to believe that God is on his/her side and so it is common for historians to record the murderous and covetous acts of their own nation as being commanded by God. Even today, many younger Japanese are not aware that Japan bombed Pearl Harbor and was the initial aggressor in bringing the United States into World War II. This is because the act has been purposefully left out of Japanese history books.

The Klu Klux Klan's main web page title says, "Proclaiming a Message of hope and deliverance for White Christian America! *If my people which are called by my name will humble themselves and pray and seek my face and turn from their wicked ways; Then will I hear from heaven, will forgive their sins, and will heal their land.* II Chronicles 7:14" The leader of the KKK is shown as *Pastor* Thomas Robb. Their propaganda is saturated with references to God, Jesus, Old Time Religion and the impression that the KKK is thoroughly rooted in Christian principles. It is their idea that the white race is the only pure race.

The attitude of moral and spiritual superiority leading to the justification of murder still persists in all religions. In our times we have seen fundamentalist Islamic forces call for Jihad (holy war) after Jihad. "Martyrs" with bombs strapped to their bodies detonate the explosives in public areas, killing and maiming innocent victims. Suicidal terrorists plotted for two years to hijack and then crash jetliners into the World Trade Center buildings. The clergy promise heaven and 70 virgins to those who cooperate. A similar promise of reward in the afterlife was made to World War II Japanese Kamakaze pilots who crashed their bomb-laden airplanes into enemy ships. We see this same ignorance not only in large matters (large collective egos) such as world wars but also in situations involving only one or two people. The following clip is from the Saturday, November 06, 1999 edition of *The Daily Oklahoman.*

Suspect 'Obeying' God Redding, Calif. – One of two brothers accused of killing a gay couple in July told a newspaper he shot the men because he believed their homosexuality violated God's law.

"I'm not guilty of murder, I'm guilty of obeying the laws of the Creator," Benjamin Matthew Williams, 31, told The Sacramento Bee in a jailhouse interview Thursday.

Williams said he didn't belong to any organized hate groups but he hoped his violence would incite more killings, the newspaper said.

The Williams brothers were probably inspired by the following Old Testament scripture:

> *If a man lies with a man as one lies with a woman, both of them have done what is detestable. They must be put to death; their blood will be on their own heads.* LEVITICUS 20:13, NIV

If the Williams brothers had asked Jesus first, he would have no doubt said, "If either of you is without sin let him fire the first bullet." Of course this is a reference to John 8:7 where Jesus saves an adulterous woman from being stoned to death and thereby takes issue once again with the Old Testament. In the Old Testament God allegedly told Moses and Aaron that adultery and homosexuality were equal offences, both being punishable by death along with a long list of other offenses.

The following is an interesting tongue-in-cheek open letter addressed to a popular radio talk show host that came drifting through the author's river of email:

> *Dear Dr. Laura,*
> *Thank you for doing so much to educate people regarding God's law. I have learned a great deal from you, and I try to share that knowledge with as many people as I can. When someone tries to defend the homosexual lifestyle, for example, I simply remind him that Leviticus 18:22 clearly states it to be an abomination. End of debate. I do need some advice from*

you, however, regarding some of the specific laws and how to best follow them.

When I burn a bull on the altar as a sacrifice, I know it creates a pleasing odor for the Lord (Lev. 1:9). The problem is my neighbors. They claim the odor is not pleasing to them. How should I deal with this?

I would like to sell my daughter into slavery, as it suggests in Exodus 21:7. In this day and age, what do you think would be a fair price for her?

I know that I am allowed no contact with a woman while she is in her period of menstrual uncleanliness (Lev. 15:19-24). The problem is, how do I tell? I have tried asking, but most women take offense.

Lev. 25:44 states that I may indeed possess slaves, both male and female, provided they are purchased from neighboring nations. A friend of mine claims that this applies to Mexicans but not Canadians. Can you clarify?

I have a neighbor who insists on working on the Sabbath. Exodus 35:2 clearly states he should be put to death. Am I morally obligated to kill him myself?

A friend of mine feels that even though eating a shellfish is an abomination (Lev. 10:10), it is a lesser abomination than homosexuality. I don't agree. Can you settle this?

Lev. 20:20 states that I may not approach the altar of God if I have a defect in my sight. I have to admit that I wear reading glasses. Does my vision have to be 20/20, or is there some wiggle room here?

Most of my male friends get their hair trimmed, including hair around the temples, even though this is expressly forbidden by Lev. 19:27. How should they die?

I know from Lev. 11:6-8 that touching the skin of a dead pig makes me unclean, but may I still play football if I wear gloves?

My uncle has a farm. He violates Lev. 19:19 by planting two different crops in the same field, as does his wife by wearing garments made of two different kinds of thread (cotton/polyester blend). He also tends to curse and blaspheme a lot. Is it really necessary that we go to all the trouble of getting the whole town together to stone them as it says to do in Lev. 24:10-16? Couldn't we just burn them to death at a private family affair like we do with people who sleep with their in-laws? (Lev. 20:14)

I know you have studied these things extensively, so I am confident you can help. Thank you again for reminding us that God's word is eternal and unchanging.

Your devoted fan, Jim

LAWS OF DEATH

One must be put to death for the following offenses listed in Leviticus, Numbers and Deuteronomy: Giving your children to Molek (chief deity of the Ammonites), cursing your father and mother, sleeping with another's wife or husband (both adulterer and adulteress are to die), a man sleeping with father's wife or daughter-in-law (both parties die), man sleeping with man, woman sleeping with woman, sex with an animal (both perpetrator and animal must die), being a medium of spirits, blaspheming the name of the Lord (stoning by entire community), murder, anyone other than a Levite who goes near the tabernacle when it is being torn down or put up, anyone other than a Levite approaching the sanctuary, worshipping Baal of Peor (a Moabitish deity), showing contempt for a judge or priest and being a false prophet. Also if you are a girl who marries, and it is claimed by your new husband that he found you not to be a virgin, and if your parents are unable to prove you are a virgin, then you must be stoned to death in front of your parent's house.

Those among us who have raised or know of any troublesome children will find the following scripture morbidly amusing.

If a man has a stubborn and rebellious son who does not obey his father and mother and will not listen to them when they discipline him, his father and mother shall take hold of him and bring him to the elders at the gate of his town. They shall say to the elders, "This son of ours is stubborn and rebellious. He will not obey us. He is a profligate and a drunkard." Then all the men of his town shall stone him to death. You must purge the evil from among you. All Israel will hear of it and be afraid. DEUTERONOMY 21:18-21, NIV

If we know anyone (like the Williams brothers) who reads these laws and says, "Well, the world wouldn't be in the predicament we're in today if we did it like God told Moses!" we should pray for them. What is missing in the world today is love and compassion. When love and compassion wane, law and order wax.

The death laws quoted above and the other laws concerning daily affairs are all reported by the Bible to be direct communication from God to Moses and Aaron. For example:

The Lord said to Moses and Aaron, "Say to the Israelites: Of all the animals that live on land, these are the ones you may eat: You may eat any animal that has a split hoof completely divided and that chews the cud." LEVITICUS 11:1-3, NIV

There follows in Leviticus a long list of animals that we may or may not eat. Of all the edible animals in the water, we may eat only those with scales and fins. We may not eat oysters, shrimp or catfish. Did God really tell us to follow these commandments as stated in the Bible? If God said it, why are not all Christians obeying his commandments?

Fortunately for the twentieth-century restaurant business, Jesus cancels the voluminous scriptural injunctions about what to eat and how to cook in one fell swoop.

What goes into a man's mouth does not make him "unclean," but what comes out of his mouth, that is what makes him "unclean." MATTHEW 15:11, NIV

Who is right about the food laws, the Old Testament or Jesus? Did God change his mind, or did God really say it to begin with? As an aside, we can easily admit that many of these laws are rooted in common sense if not the divine revelation of the creator. However, as stated earlier, according to Malachi 3:6 God does not change. If God does not change, then either Jesus is wrong, or the Old Testament is wrong. If God did change his mind then Malachi is wrong.

Jesus pointedly disagrees with the following scriptural law from Leviticus. Bear in mind, according to the Bible, God is communicating these laws directly to Moses and Aaron.

> *If anyone injures his neighbor, whatever he has done must be done to him: fracture for fracture, eye for eye, tooth for tooth. As he has injured the other, so he is to be injured.*
> LEVITICUS 24:19-20, NIV

Jesus says this is not right. Is Jesus denying Moses' authority and authenticity as God's spokesperson?

> *You have heard that it was said, "Eye for eye, and tooth for tooth." But I tell you, "Do not resist an evil person. If someone strikes you on the right cheek, turn to him the other also."*
> MATTHEW 5:38-39, NIV

The least we can make of this is that Jesus discarded some of the Mosaic law. Of the Ten Commandments, he discarded the first four and kept the last six (Matt. 19:18). If God is Jesus and Jesus is God, then either God didn't say some of those things, or Moses was in error, or God changed his mind later. If God didn't say it or if Moses was wrong then we would have to admit that scripture is not always true, or it might have once been true but is not necessarily true now due to the dilution of translations and the passing of time. If we sweep Malachi 3:6 under the rug we can take the position that God changed the rules. That would clear the way for God to remove the first four of the Ten Commandments. Graven images would go the way of keeping the Sabbath, eating pork and exchanging eyes and teeth as a vehicle of retribution. The only other way out is to say that Jesus was not the Messiah, and therefore, these Mosaic laws are still in effect and that the Williams brothers did the will of God when they executed the gay couple.

The Judaism we are left with today is the Judaism of the Pharisees. At the time of Jesus there were other sects, such as the Essenes, whose teachings succumbed to obscurity at the hands of the Pharisees. The Pharisees did not include any doctrine in the Old Testament which contradicted their view, just as the early Christian church "purged" the Bible of unacceptable books, delivering to us the filtered view we know today as the New Testament. In the following scripture the disciples understood that the Master was warning them about the teachings of the Pharisees and the Sadducees:

> *Then they understood that he was not telling them to guard against the yeast used in bread, but against the teaching of the Pharisees and Sadducees.*   MATTHEW 16:12, NIV

To explain the inconsistencies between Jesus and the Old Testament, theologians have devised the concept of a "new covenant," meaning that God has changed the Old Testament rules by sending Jesus with a new set of teachings. This is no more than a doctrinal invention to patch the gaping crack that exists between Jesus and the Old Testament. The truth of the matter is Jesus felt some teachings in the Old Testament were wrong from the beginning. There was never a time when they were right. It should be noted that Jesus never says he brought any sort of new covenant. He never apologizes or rationalizes with the Old Testament scriptures with which he is at odds. He simply disagrees with them. Jesus mentions the word "covenant" only at the Last Supper regarding the act of communion with bread and wine.

Ironically, if we attempt to justify these differences by saying God can change the rules, then we open the door to accepting other religions. If God can change the rules according to time, then God can change the rules according to space. If God's commandments and word can change from one time to another then we must be prepared to admit that God can change his commandments according to geography, culture or any other modes of division. God's instruction and method of worship for one part of the world can be different from another part of the world to suit the culture and inclination of the local inhabitants. Nonetheless, the essentials will be the same.

God came as Jesus to restore that which had been lost in a super-ficial observance of laws and rules. Love had been lost, and Jesus had come to restore the deeper understanding. If a law did not have anything to do with one's ability to love God or one's neighbor then it was of no lasting consequence.

> *One of them, an expert in the law, tested him with this question: "Teacher, which is the greatest commandment in the Law?"*
>
> *Jesus replied: "Love the Lord your God with all your heart and with all your soul and with all your mind. This is the first and greatest commandment. And the second is like it: Love your neighbor as yourself. All the Law and the Prophets hang on these two commandments."*   MATTHEW 22:35-40, NIV

Jesus is saying that all 613 of the Jewish laws and all of the Proph-ets, their lives, utterances and what they might have meant by anything whatsoever are subservient to love. Paul agrees.

> *Let no debt remain outstanding, except the continuing debt to love one another, for he who loves his fellowman has fulfilled the law. The commandments, "Do not commit adultery," "Do not murder," "Do not steal," "Do not covet," and whatever other commandment there may be, are summed up in this one rule: "Love your neighbor as yourself." Love does no harm to its neighbor. Therefore love is the fulfillment of the law.*
>   ROMANS 13:8-10, NIV

In summary, we can consider that some of what we read in the Old Testament did not come from God but from the ego. God is not covetous, jealous and vengeful. Rather, God is nothing short of love itself. Wherever love is expressed, there we are seeing or experiencing God. Understanding this will help us to reach out to God with affection and a deep heart-felt longing. Also, God never condemned other religions. This was the work of jealous and cov-etous priests. The best yardsticks for measuring the validity of the scriptures are love, compassion, kindness and mercy.

10

All Religions are Paths to God

The reality of religion is something far beyond people's concept about it. The so-called intellectuals of all religions have taught people about a religion that they themselves have created; a religion corresponding to their own ideas, which has little to do with true religion and its essential principles. They fool the people by making them follow only the external aspect of religion, and never the internal. If the internal oneness of religions were to be revealed, their own importance would be greatly diminished and they wouldn't be given any more attention. This is the reason why they highlight only the external differences. Otherwise their egos will starve, which would be unbearable to them. Also, since they, themselves, are stuck in their own intellects, they cannot assimilate the real principles of spirituality; and if they have not imbibed those principles, how can they teach anyone about spirituality?

AMMACHI, AWAKEN CHILDREN, VOL. 7

In this chapter we will reflect on the truth that all of the world's major religions are paths to God. Let us pause to refresh our philosophical foundation by reflecting for a moment on our true nature and the nature of the ego. The afflictive emotions such as jealousy, greed and hatred are products of the ego, and the ego is an illusory mental fabrication composed of I-am-this and I-am-that. This is in contrast to the plain and simple primal being of I AM. Therefore, the "anti-God" or "anti Christ" is the ego and its delusional attachment to the external projections of I-am-this and I-am-that. By mistakenly assuming I-am-this and I-am-that, we form attractions and aversions to specific things, and these attractions and aversions we call our body of desires. The sum total of these attachments are our own personal egos. For example, the belief that we are physical bodies will prompt us to amplify our indulgence in sensual pleasure. If we believe that we are Christians, then we may be compelled to diminish or even destroy anything which is not Christian because our existence is threatened by these other religions. Bodies, religions and political parties are changing and impermanent like clouds drifting in the sky. Only our true nature, the I AM, is permanent and unchanging.

It is more than probable that the Old Testament prohibition regarding other religions was an attempt to cement the authority and power of the priests. Of course, this would be an entirely understandable and common act of human covetousness and jealousy on their part. This sort of activity has been going on since the birth of the ego. The ego is as prone to such short sightedness as it is for night to follow day. It would be hard to imagine the priests being so pure that they did not have these emotions, especially if their power and authority were challenged by competitors. It is easy to imagine that they could insert their diversionary tactics into the scriptures in the form of "the word of God" and to impose the death penalty for any disobedience. It is possible that all along it was not God who was vengeful, wrathful and jealous but the priests.

The first of the Ten Commandments states, "You shall have no other Gods before me." Many have mistakenly interpreted that to mean, "You shall have no other religions before me."

> The very words "nation" and "religion" imply division and diversity. This diversity may seem to create an obstacle in fostering peace in the world, yet in reality it is this diversity that brings richness and beauty to the world and human life. Just as a bouquet having flowers of different colors is more beautiful than a bouquet of flowers of the same color, there is one truth that shines through the rivers and mountains, flowers, the sun, moon and stars and you and I. All are expressions of this One Reality. It is by assimilating this truth in life that we can discover the inherent beauty in this diversity. When we work together as a global family, not belonging to a particu-

*lar race or nation, peace and happiness will once again pre-
vail on this earth.*
AMMACHI, ADDRESS TO THE UNITED NATIONS, AUGUST 29, 2000

By exploring other faiths, we begin to see what is common to all
paths: love, tolerance, innocence, compassion, devotion to God,
forgiveness and service to others. As these essential aspects are
clarified and reinforced by their appearance again and again in
the major faiths of the world, we begin to find acceptance and tolerance toward other faiths.

Hinduism, Buddhism, Taoism and many other religions that thrive
in the world today existed before Jesus came to this earth. Since the
spirit of Christ is our oneness in Christ and since what opposes the
Christ is the ego and the absence of love, how could it profit the
devil to create religions that teach us how to love God, to be selfless
and to abandon our egocentric way of seeing things? That would be
counter productive to the devil, who wants us to be selfish, to hate
others and to forget about love, compassion and mercy.

> *But when the Pharisees heard this, they said, "It is only by
> Beelzebub, the prince of demons, that this fellow drives out
> demons."*
>
> *Jesus knew their thoughts and said to them, "Every kingdom
> divided against itself will be ruined, and every city or house-
> hold divided against itself will not stand. If Satan drives out
> Satan, he is divided against himself. How then can his king-
> dom stand?"* MATTHEW 12:24-26, NIV

How could it profit Satan (ego) to offer the same teachings that
Jesus offered? As in the scripture above, Satan would be divided
against himself. Satan doesn't tell us to become innocent like
children and to love God and to love one another as all major religions do. Satan doesn't tell us to forgive others and to give to the
poor. Satan doesn't tell us to abandon selfishness. Satan doesn't
tell us to pray to God. Satan wants us to have thoughts like,
"What's in it for me?" or "Get the other guy before he gets you,"
or "There is no God," or "The purpose of your life is to be comfortable and enjoy all the pleasure you can get."

There is ample evidence in the New Testament and Old Testament that God approved of other religions, and so it will be profitable to explore some of these.

THE MAGI

> *After Jesus was born in Bethlehem in Judea, during the time of King Herod, Magi from the east came to Jerusalem and asked, "Where is the one who has been born king of the Jews? We saw his star in the east and have come to worship him."*
> MATTHEW 2:1-2, NIV

In this scripture the word "Magi" comes from the Greek word **magos**, *mag'-os*; of foreign origin; a *Magian*, i.e. Oriental *scientist*, by implication a *magician*: sorcerer, wise man. The word "star" comes from the Greek word **aster**, *as-tare'*; (stronnumi); a *star* (as *strown* over the sky), literal or figurative - star. The word "east" comes form the Greek word **anatole**, *an-at-ol-ay'*; (anatello); a *rising* of light, i.e. *dawn* (figurative); by implication the *east* (also in plural): dayspring, east, rising.

These "Magi" were from a foreign land and were pagans. They were magicians and sorcerers according to the Greek word "magos." Most likely they were from the circle of magician-priests of Babylon who practiced the divine arts of divination, prophecy, reading of dreams, healing and astrology. The esoteric activities of these enlightened Babylonian seers are well documented.

In the previous scripture, The Greek words translated as "star" and "east" (as in seeing a star in the east) can be taken literally or figuratively. Figuratively is the best choice because no one else had seen the star. In those days there were no city lights to obscure the display of stars in the velvet, black night canopy. Such a brilliant guiding star would have been visible to many and for many days. Secretly wishing to kill the Christ child, Herod called the sorcerers to him to find out when the star had appeared. If it had been an obvious physical apparition, many others could have told Herod the answer. Also, the Magi were from the East, which would have placed a physical star to their west–over Jesus. The scripture would then need to read that the Magi saw the star in the west. The only other explanation for the star is to say that it was either an astrological event that required a sorcerer adept in the science and art of divination through astrology to interpret, or the star appeared to the inner sight of the Magi as a vision. The star was most likely an inner vision because it moved and led the Magi to the Christ child after their visit with Herod. It was a guiding light that only their talents as magicians and sorcerers allowed them to see. To others, its appearance was veiled. The Magi were also adept at dream interpretation because that is how they learned not to have anything further to do with Herod and to return home by another route (Matthew 2:12). They no doubt divined that they were in danger of being stoned to death for being magicians, seers and sorcerers. Such a death would be required according to the Mosaic commandments in Numbers and Deuteronomy. The Magi were so close to God that they were able to travel a long distance and find God's incarnation using only the roadmap of inner divination and revelation. The first to find, recognize and worship Jesus, the incarnation of God, were from another religion.

BALAAM

Beginning in Numbers 22:5 the story of Balaam, son of Beor, unfolds. Balaam was also a pagan sorcerer. God had given him the power to bless and curse others. The Israelites were near the end of the forty years of wandering and had taken up residence on the plains of Moab. Balak, the king of Moab, became alarmed at the prospect of sharing precious resources, such as grazing land, and sent for Balaam to curse the Israelites. The elders of Moab find Balaam and, with fee in hand, ask him to perform his magic curse. Balaam asks the elders to spend the night so that he can talk to God about the situation.

God came to Balaam and asked, "Who are these men with you?"

Balaam said to God, "Balak son of Zippor, king of Moab, sent me this message: 'A people that has come out of Egypt covers the

face of the land. Now come and put a curse on them for me.
Perhaps then I will be able to fight them and drive them away.'"

But God said to Balaam, "Do not go with them. You must not
put a curse on those people, because they are blessed."

NUMBERS 22:9-12, NIV

The Moabs return to the king without their sorcerer, but the king
sends them back to Balaam offering even more money. Once
more Balaam asks Balak's representatives to spend the night, and
again Balaam talks with God. God tells Balaam to go back with
the men but do only as He says. On the way, Balaam's donkey
talks to him, and an angel appears to Balaam because God opens
his eyes. Balaam has audience with Balak and instructs Balak in
the preparation of seven special ritual altars (bear in mind these
are pagan ritual altars—Balaam was a pagan sorcerer). Balaam has
several more intimate conversations with God. God puts words in
Balaam's mouth (referred to as an oracle, Num. 23:7), and
Balaam blesses the Israelites. Balaam was an oracle, a man capable of casting spells or curses, and a pagan, yet he talks with
God and seeks to do God's will. God also talks to and instructs
Balaam. Balaam is obviously in favor with God, is a servant of
God and is from "another religion."

MELCHIZEDEK

Melchizedek is yet another example of one who is in favor with
God but not a Jew. There are few characters in the Bible that
evoke the feeling of any underlying mystery in the way that
Melchizedek does. In Genesis, Abraham is returning from defeat-
ing Chedorlaomer and rescuing Lot when Melchizedek intercepts
Abraham. The meeting is said to have taken place just south of
the City of David at a spring called En Rogel.

Then Melchizedek king of Salem brought out bread and wine.
He was priest of God Most High, and he blessed Abram, say-
ing, "Blessed be Abram by God Most High, Creator of heaven
and earth. And blessed be God Most High, who delivered your

> *enemies into your hand." Then Abram gave him a tenth of*
> *everything.* GENESIS 14:18-20, NIV

Melchizedek was a priest of God but was of another culture and another religion. In fact he was not just a priest. He was an astounding God Man: a Christ. Melchizedek managed to impress Abraham with such intensity that Abraham immediately gave him a tenth of everything he owned. He did this after only one unexpected encounter!

JESUS AND OTHER RELIGIONS

Religions are road maps to the Self (I AM) or God, which lies within us. Passing through the wilderness of the ego, which lies hidden from most of us just below the surface of our conscious awareness, we encounter pitfalls and wrong turns. Religions are road maps through the subconscious. Arriving at the center, we merge with God and, like the prodigal son, reclaim our lost immortality. To put it another way, we realize that our true original nature is immortality, and we stop dreaming that we are separate egos that are trapped in a seemingly endless cycle of birth, death and rebirth. Religion and scripture are not the goal. God is the goal, and spirituality is the practice of walking the path to God. Spirituality has to do with experiencing God intimately and directly. Without this direct experience there is no salvation, no getting to heaven, no being born again, no enlightenment, no nirvana, no liberation and no end to suffering.

Nowhere in the four gospels does Jesus say that other religions are bad. If other religions were the handiwork of Satan then surely Jesus would have been compelled to warn us about such a heinous pitfall.

> *And John answered and said, "Master, we saw one casting out devils in thy name; and we forbad him, because he followeth not with us."*

> *And Jesus said unto him, Forbid him not: for he that is not against us is for us.* LUKE 9:49-50, KJV [emphsis added]

In all four gospels, Jesus did not once warn us about other religions. In fact he reverses the issue of religiophobia by stating flatly that those who are not against him are for him! If we take Luke 9:50 literally then the implication is very broad indeed. One could argue that the person casting out devils was doing so in Jesus' name, and therefore, Luke 9:50 grants religious tolerance only to other factions who do their works in the name of Jesus. Even this much tolerance among various Christian sects would be a vast improvement! However, Jesus did not limit or qualify his statement on religious tolerance. He did not say, *"If they do works in my name* and they are not against us then they are for us."* What Jesus did say is, "...he that is not against us is for us." This is a very broad and sweeping statement and consistent with his overall policy of love, tolerance, and acceptance. It means that a Hindu who is not against Jesus is for Jesus. It means that a Buddhist who is not against Jesus is for Jesus.

If we accept the orthodox hypothesis of "one life then heaven or hell" and that gaining heaven would be impossible without accepting Jesus Christ as our personal savior, then it would have been *extremely* important for the Lord to have warned us about other religions. We would have only one life to get it right, and if we are absorbed in another religion, we most likely would not have accepted Jesus as our personal savior. Other religions would be the very worst of pitfalls. If this were true about other religions, and a good shepherd guides his sheep, then why didn't Jesus warn us? If Jesus is the "only way" then there would be no greater threat to our salvation than the lure of other religions. These religions could have only one purpose and that would be to siphon away the faithful from their solitary chance at salvation. It would be unthinkable that the Lord himself would fail to warn us about the deadliest of all pitfalls.

At the time of Christ, a handful of Christians were eclipsed by millions of followers of many diverse religions worldwide. The Vedas, which are the sacred scriptures of Hinduism, are the oldest known literary work in human history, dating back at least 5,000 years, and some say 10,000, based on certain astronomical references contained in the work.

If one reads the various religious works such as the *Bhagavad Gita* from Hinduism, the *Dhamapada* from Buddhism, the *Koran* from Islam and the *Tao Te Ching* from Taoism, one is immediately impressed by the stark similarities. Love God, practice kindness and compassion towards others, strive to eliminate selfishness as the ego and other key principles arise again and again as if the same person had written them. They vary somewhat in exterior trappings, but the important points are all there. By studying these religions, it is easy to see that Christ has not come once but many times and addressed the truth of our oneness to suit other cultures in their own language and the vernacular of the times. Would not a compassionate God do so? Our own father would show us repeatedly how to tie our shoe laces. In the same way, God would come to teach us again and again. He would come as many times as it took to lead each of us to salvation.

The revelations of God's truth through these Eastern religions was and is so deep and profound that the Holy Spirit saw no reason for Paul and his companions to travel there.

> *Paul and his companions traveled throughout the region of Phrygia and Galatia, having been kept by the Holy Spirit from preaching the word in the province of Asia.*   ACTS 16:6, NIV

Some may argue that the Holy Spirit stopped them from traveling to Asia because the religions in Asia were too evil to deserve the benefit of Paul's preaching. That would imply that God did not love the Asian people and that he had no interest in their salvation. That would be unthinkable in light of Jesus telling us to love all people in the same way that God's rain falls on the just and the unjust (Matthew 5:45). If Asia was that evil then all the more reason for Paul to go there. The truth is these religions were not in need of Paul's preaching.

United we stand; divided we fall. In this way Ego takes us away from love by encouraging us to possess a judgmental and divisive attitude. Ego will divide our vision and rob us of the truth that we are all spiritual brothers and sisters. We are divine siblings not because of what we believe but because of who we are. We are united not because of dogmatic belief but because we all originate from the same I AM. Ego has been so successful at veiling this truth that we have killed one another thinking we have done God's will.

Jesus says that he has other sheep in other folds, (other religions in other cultures) and that he himself has the power to appear again in another body. "One fold and one shepherd," is a reference to our universal brotherhood and sisterhood in which we are emanations of the I AM. There is only one Christ appearing as (but not limited to) Jesus, Buddha, Mohammed or Krishna.

> *I am the good shepherd; I know my sheep and my sheep know me—just as the Father knows me and I know the Father—and I lay down my life for the sheep. I have other sheep that are not of this sheep pen. I must bring them also. They too will listen to my voice, and there shall be one flock and one shepherd. The reason my Father loves me is that I lay down my life—only to take it up again. No one takes it from me, but I lay it down of my own accord. I have authority to lay it down and authority to take it up again. This command I received from my Father.*
> JOHN 10:14-18, NIV

I have the power to take it up again... and again and again and again. Gautama the Buddha, Krishna the Avatar, and Jesus the Christ are all ONE. They were all appearances of the one Christ.

FALSE PROPHETS

Most who may be described as false prophets are wholly ego-driven. They may even have supernatural powers and speak powerfully and convincingly. They may display any of the seven gifts of the Holy Spirit. The Indian Puranas (stories) are full of men who practiced severe penance and austerities to gain powers which they used for malevolent ego-driven purposes. God-realized souls and especially incarnations can also have supernatural powers, so the presence or absence of these powers is not an indicator. However, a false prophet will display these powers publicly like a circus performer out of the desire to attract followers, whereas a true prophet will not display them unless it is necessary and only for a selfless purpose. A true prophet has no desire or need to attract anyone. A true prophet is motivated by love alone, whereas a false prophet is motivated by the ego. A true prophet expects nothing in return, whereas a false prophet expects something in return. Jesus expresses this idea in the following scripture.

> *I am the good shepherd. The good shepherd lays down his life for the sheep. The hired hand is not the shepherd who owns the sheep. So when he sees the wolf coming, he abandons the sheep and runs away. Then the wolf attacks the flock and scatters it. The man runs away because he is a hired hand and cares nothing for the sheep.* JOHN 10:11-13, NIV

A false prophet is the hired hand. He claims to be a spiritual leader, but he is in it for the wages of money or fulfillment of an ego-centered point of view. Because holy men or prophets are esteemed and honored by others, egos will be attracted to playing that role like chickens are attracted to grasshoppers. Therefore, false prophets will always be in abundance, while few true prophets appear on the pages of human history.

It is difficult to know who is a false teacher because s/he may say the right things. Jesus tells us that we may examine his/her actions (fruits) to be able to tell a false prophet from a real one.

> *Watch out for false prophets. They come to you in sheep's clothing, but inwardly they are ferocious wolves. By their fruit you will recognize them. Do people pick grapes from thornbushes, or figs from thistles? Likewise every good tree bears good fruit, but a bad tree bears bad fruit. A good tree cannot bear bad fruit, and a bad tree cannot bear good fruit. Every tree that does not bear good fruit is cut down and thrown into the fire. Thus, by their fruit you will recognize them.* MATTHEW 7:15-20, NIV

This scripture implies that there are other true prophets that would appear on this earth at a later time. Otherwise, Jesus would not have bothered to give us instruction as to how to identify them. He would have simply said that he was the only true prophet and that we should not bother with examining the fruits of any others.

In other words, do not pay much attention to the particular beliefs, doctrines and dogmas, but rather see how they live their lives and observe what they inspire others to do. Jesus is saying the important measuring stick is how people act—their fruits—and not what they believe. Therefore, it is not important whether we follow Jesus or Buddha or whether we dunk or sprinkle to baptize or whether we believe Jesus was God who became a man or a man who became God. Rather, is a person compassionate? Is a person humble, or does s/he advertise his/her divinity with much pomp and circumstance? Does a person give freely with nothing required in return, or does s/he want you to pay money for services or require you to pledge allegiance to him/her? A true prophet cares nothing for money or fame. Does a person make arrangements to care for the poor and the downtrodden? Is s/he innocent like a child? Does a person openly display miracles or ramble on about supernormal experiences, thus betraying a hidden agenda of attracting others? A true prophet is full and complete and has no need of attracting anyone or anything. S/he sees all others as part of his/her self, and the sheep are attracted to him/her naturally without advertisements just as honeybees are attracted to nectarous flowers. In other words, a false prophet is one who sounds good but is still the slave of his own ego.

To identify other legitimate prophets, we can begin our search by looking to those Great Ones whose lives and teachings have endured through the ages. If we look at the millions who follow their teachings today, we realize that their fruit is enormous. For example, after journeying 3000 years through the corridors of time, the teachings of Lord Krishna in the *Bhagavad Gita* (Song of God) are still as vibrant and poignant as ever. This is because these beings were incarnations of God, and the words they speak and the actions they performed have tremendous power. Jesus said that heaven and earth may pass away, but his words would not. By closely studying their lives and teachings, we come to the realization that they are all operating from the same point of view. They were all one with God. They were one with the Self. There was absolutely no sense of separateness about them at all. From this arises their tremendous love and compassion.

All of the world's major religions are paths to God. They have passed the test of time.

11

Graven Images

Just as we remember our father when we see his portrait, we are reminded of God, the Creator of the world, when we see the idol. When a devotee of Krishna sees the idol of Sri Krishna, he remembers the real Lord Krishna and not the stone image. Temples and idols are needed for those of us who are drowned in ignorance.   AMMACHI, AWAKEN CHILDREN, VOL. 1

In our search for unity and peace among the religions of the world, we will take up the issue of graven images—especially if we are Christian, Muslim or Jewish. We will demonstrate that icons or images are good for spiritual practice. Meditating on God with a form will take us to God with no form.

In the chapter *Jesus and the Old Testament*, we explored the precedent set by Jesus in looking past some aspects of the Old Testament laws, and we will apply that precedent to the question of graven images. The prohibition against worshipping false idols appears in the Ten Commandments in Exodus and then again in several other Old Testament scriptures.

> *You shall not make for yourself an idol in the form of anything in heaven above or on the earth beneath or in the waters below. You shall not bow down to them or worship them; for I, the Lord your God, am a jealous God, punishing the children for the sin of the fathers to the third and fourth generation of those who hate me, but showing love to a thousand generations of those who love me and keep my commandments.*
> EXODUS 20:4-5, NIV

Do not make idols or set up an image or a sacred stone for your-
selves, and do not place a carved stone in your land to bow
down before it. I am the Lord your God.   LEVITICUS 26:1, NIV

The mind imagines that happiness arises from being a separate
individual. This individuality is continuously inflamed by thinking we will gain happiness from relationships, cars, houses,
clothes, money, status, control of others, sex, drugs or other
worldly bounty. These things are merely reflections of the ALL,
and since they are impermanent, they can never provide lasting
happiness. True and lasting happiness can only come from God,
who must be searched for and experienced within ourselves.
When we try to find happiness in the objects of the senses mentioned above, we are really searching for God but in all the wrong
places. By thinking these things bring happiness, we are really
worshipping our own ego and the presumed objects of happiness. This is true idolatry.

In the New International Version of the New Testament the word
"idolatry" appears four times–three by Paul and one by Peter.

> *Therefore, my dear friends, flee from idolatry.*
>   1 CORINTHIANS. 10:14, NIV

> *The acts of the sinful nature are obvious: sexual immorality,*
> *impurity and debauchery; idolatry and witchcraft; hatred, dis-*
> *cord, jealousy, fits of rage, selfish ambition, dissensions, fac-*
> *tions and envy; drunkenness, orgies, and the like. I warn you,*
> *as I did before, that those who live like this will not inherit the*
> *kingdom of God.*   GALATIANS 5:19-21, NIV

> *Put to death, therefore, whatever belongs to your earthly na-*
> *ture: sexual immorality, impurity, lust, evil desires and greed,*
> *which is idolatry.*   COLOSSIANS. 3:5, NIV

> *For the time past of our life may suffice us to have wrought the*
> *will of the Gentiles, when we walked in lasciviousness, lusts, ex-*
> *cess of wine, revellings, banquetings, and abominable idolatries.*
>   1 PETER 4:3, NIV

In Paul's "idolatry" scriptures, the word "idolater" appears twice, both written by Paul. Again, the second example clearly indicates that Paul defines an idolater as one who is intoxicated with immoral acts, greed and impurities of the mind, as opposed to bowing to statues. The Greek word from which "idolatry" was translated can mean worship of idols either literally or figuratively. Figuratively fits with the context of the rest of the scripture and especially in the preceding quote by Paul in which he states flatly that the acts of immorality, lust and impurity *are* idolatry. The idea here is that an idolater is one who lives his/her life for the purpose of pursuing bodily pleasures and other worldly desires. In effect, such a person worships these things and not God. This is true idolatry and has nothing to do with bowing to statues.

> *But now I am writing you that you must not associate with anyone who calls himself a brother but is sexually immoral or greedy, an idolater or a slanderer, a drunkard or a swindler. With such a man do not even eat.*   1 CORINTHIANS, 5:11, NIV

> *For of this you can be sure: No immoral, impure or greedy person—such a man is an idolater—has any inheritance in the kingdom of Christ and of God.*   EPHESIANS, 5:5, NIV

It is interesting to note that Jesus does not address the subject of graven images or idol worship anywhere in the four gospels. The words "idol," "idolatry" and "idolater" were never spoken by Jesus. In the following scripture Jesus clearly discards the Old Testament commandment prohibiting graven images.

> *Now a man came up to Jesus and asked, "Teacher, what good thing must I do to get eternal life?"*

> *"Why do you ask me about what is good?" Jesus replied. "There is only One who is good. If you want to enter life, obey the commandments."*

> *"Which ones?" the man inquired.*

> *Jesus replied, "Do not murder, do not commit adultery, do not steal, do not give false testimony, honor your father and mother, and love your neighbor as yourself."*   MATTHEW 19:16-19, NIV

The story of the rich man who wanted to follow Jesus is worthy of examination because Jesus tells the man to follow the commandments, and the man asks Jesus, "Which ones?" Being aware of the commandments, the man wants to know specifically which ones he must follow to enter the kingdom. Jesus lists only the last six of the Ten Commandments, leaving four of the commandments conspicuously missing. Loving our neighbor as our own selves was not one of the Ten Commandments and was inserted here by Jesus instead of the tenth commandment which tells us not to covet our neighbor's things. Jesus has omitted the first four of the Ten Commandments (Exodus 20:3-17) which are: 1. Have no other gods before me, 2. Make no graven images, 3. Do not misuse the Lord's name and, 4. Keep the Sabbath holy. The last six commandments are 5. Honor your father and mother, 6. Do not commit murder, 7. Do not commit adultery, 8. Do not steal, 9. Do not give false testimony against your neighbor, 10. Do not covet what belongs to your neighbor.

One may argue that Jesus omitted the first four because the man was already keeping them and only needed to be told to keep the last six. This argument is discounted by the man's reply that he had kept all of these commandments.

Jesus did not list the first four commandments to the man as being necessary for attaining eternal life. He did not list them because they were not necessary for attaining eternal life. The first three commandments have to do with how we approach our relationship with God while the fourth is a doctrinal/cultural issue. By contrast, the six commandments listed by Jesus as necessary for attaining eternal life all have to do with how we relate to each other. It appears from Jesus' discussion with the wealthy man that Jesus is content to let us pursue God in our own ways. Let us continue to consider the second commandment from a logical point of view.

Graven (gra'-ven) adj. Carved or cut.

A graven image is simply a statue or idol. An image is a representation of something. An image is a symbol that is used to aid the mind in focusing on what the image represents. Mathematics is an entire language of symbols. In the absolute sense, God is beyond any description or form because God is infinite and without limits. Descriptions and forms are an attempt by the human mind to place limitations on the infinite. However, it is very difficult to have a relationship with God as pure formless being, and so it is helpful to have some symbol of God that the mind can hold on to as an aid to loving God. In this understanding of idols and images, the printed word "God" that we see on this very page is no different than a statue of God. Both serve the same purpose. When we see the word "God" it is a symbol that invokes something that is quite beyond the printed word. We all understand that the printed word "God" that we see on this page is not actually and specifically the one living God.

There are some who have realized that printing the word "God" is a graven image and so they have taken to writing "G_d" as an attempt to remain in compliance. However, this is futile because we all know what they mean by "G_d," and they have simply replaced one image with another. By extending the reasoning for writing "G_d," we must also admit that verbally speaking the word "God" is yet another image or icon that abstractly represents the real thing. Therefore, we would have to avoid actually saying the word "God" to remain in compliance. After all, the written word is nothing more than an extension of the spoken word. We can take this further by understanding that any thought of God cannot possibly be God since God is infinite and beyond the limitations of mental concepts. Therefore, any thought or concept we may use to define or "capture" God will have to be regarded as a graven image. Just as written words are the extension of spoken words, so too are spoken words the extension of thoughts. To remain fully in compliance we will have to stop writing "God," talking about "God," or even thinking about "God"! It goes without saying that for anyone who has taken up the practice of writing "G_d," keeping a crucifix or any portraits of Jesus in the house would be absolutely forbidden.

In this country it is common to pause before a sporting event to watch Old Glory, the flag of the United States of America, be raised slowly while the national anthem is sung. We all understand that the flag is not the actual United States, but nonetheless, we may experience deep feelings of patriotism as we hold our right hands over our hearts, saluting Old Glory as it slowly ascends the flag pole. Our eyes may even well up with tears as we consider all that the flag stands for. Before an assembly in school begins, all persons may be asked to rise to face the flag and recite the Pledge of Allegiance. The pledge starts out, "I pledge my allegiance to the *flag* of the United States of America." Why shouldn't it say, "I pledge my allegiance to the United States of America" instead of the flag? The flag is a graven image. We take this symbol seriously enough to be offended if someone desecrates it or defiles it.

If we are Christian, and we have not yet considered writing "God" as "G_d," we may allow ourselves to keep a crucifix hanging in our house. We may even bow to it or make offerings to it such as incense or lighted candles. The crucifix is a graven image. However, we all know that we are not actually offering anything to the crucifix, but rather we are making an offering to Jesus or acknowledging Jesus or praying to Jesus. The presence of the crucifix helps our minds to remember the Lord and the compassion that was expressed in the great sacrifice of his crucifixion. It helps us to get concentration on God. It helps us to stay focused in our daily life and remember the teachings of the Lord.

The concept of idols or images representing God is like any other symbol such as a printed word, a spoken word, a flag or a crucifix. If we can accept the usefulness of these images and idols then the only question remaining would be which images to use.

All this being said about idolatry, God still does not require that our love for Him come from perfect understanding. God does not require that our concept of Him be perfect. Who among us can claim to have the perfect understanding of God? God accepts our love no matter how imperfect our conception of Him may be. In the same way, a father will not push away his two-year-old child if the child fails to chant "father" in a perfectly pitched pentatonic musical scale. The father accepts his young child's love fully and completely even though the child can only utter "Dada." Worshipping God as any image even without the understanding of the common source of these images is like "Dada." This is why Jesus did not feel it necessary to warn us about worshipping graven im-

ages and pointedly omitted it in his list of necessary commandments when the wealthy man asked, "Which ones?" For Jesus, it
was love and not the form that was most important.

POLYNOMIAL MONOTHEISM

Hinduism has something for everyone. At one end of the spectrum is absolute non-duality in which God is utterly transcendent
being and beyond the mind, beyond all names and forms. At the
other end we have polynomial monotheism which means one indescribable God appearing as many names and forms. The first is
God the transcendent (God is beyond everything), and the second
is God the immanent (God *is* everything). Those who practice the
latter form of Hinduism know there is only one God, and realizing that our one God cannot fit into any single name or form,
they are ready to assign an infinite number of names and forms
to the one indefinable God. Both points of view really come to the
same end—it is not possible to corral God with the mind. Both
points of view are really expressing the same infinite reality. The
first is saying there is no form that is God, and the second is saying all forms *are* God. The mistake is made when we claim that
any particular form is true to the exclusion of other forms. God is
content to be the *Everything* or the *Nothing* but never only partly
"this" to the exclusion of "that."

The Christian doctrine of the Holy Trinity is like the concept of
gods and goddesses in other religions. The Hindu religion is the
undisputed champion for creating images of God. At last count
the number was around 300,000, whereas the Holy Trinity has
the Godhead divided into three aspects, which are the Father, the
Son and the Holy Spirit. The fact that Hindus worship only one
God, of which the 300,000 gods and goddesses are but aspects,
also qualifies them under the first commandment, "Thou shalt
have no other Gods before me." As mentioned earlier, Hindus
call this one pure, unspeakable and formless God "Brahman."
The *Upanishads* are a body of scriptures that are part of the *Vedas*,
which were mentioned previously. The following *Upanishad* titled
Isha opens with a short statement:

Filled with Brahman are the things we see.
Filled with Brahman are the things we see not.
From out of Brahman flows all that is:
From Brahman all – yet is he still the same.
Om...Peace–peace–peace

THE UPANISHADS, TRANSLATED BY SWAMI PRABHAVANANDA
AND FREDERICK MANCHESTER

Brahman (God) cannot be defined as any specific form and yet is the support of all that is. Being no specific form, Brahman is that eternal radiant intelligence which animates and informs all individual beings. Brahman is beyond the mind and the senses, and yet Brahman is the very Self of our selves upon which the dance of the mind and the play of the senses revolve in their endless theater of existence. Simultaneously transcendent and immanent, Brahman can only be known by diving into the depths of our own beings. The Self is the transcendent nature of creation, and creation is the immanent nature of the Self. The body of the scripture for the Upanishad *Isha* continues:

In the heart of all things, of whatever there is in the universe, dwells the Lord. He alone is the reality. Wherefore, renouncing vain appearances, rejoice in him. Covet no man's wealth.

Well may he be content to live a hundred years who acts without attachment—who works his work with earnestness, but without desire, not yearning for its fruits—he, and he alone.

Worlds there are without suns, covered up with darkness. To these after death go the ignorant, slayers of the Self.

The Self is one. Unmoving, it moves swifter than thought. The senses do not overtake it, for always it goes before. Remaining still, it outstrips all that run. Without the Self, there is no life.

To the ignorant the Self appears to move—yet it moves not. From the ignorant it is far distant—yet it is near. It is within all, and it is without all.

He who sees all beings in the Self, and the Self in all beings, hates none.

To the illumined soul, the Self is all. For him who sees every-where oneness, how can there be delusion or grief?

The Self is everywhere. Bright is he, bodiless, without scar of imperfection, without bone, without flesh, pure, untouched by evil. The Seer, the Thinker, the One who is above all, the Self-Existent—he it is that has established perfect order among ob-jects and beings from beginningless time.

THE UPANISHADS, TRANSLATED BY SWAMI PRABHAVANANDA
AND FREDERICK MANCHESTER

If God or Self or Brahman is the diamond, then the various gods and goddesses are the facets on the diamond. To simplify, we might refer to the facets as wisdom, love, patience, creation and dissolution. To use another analogy, we may liken God to fire. Then qualities such as heat, light and gas would be like the gods and goddesses are to Brahman. These gods and goddesses are ac-tually archetypes that we all share in common as we travel toward the center of our beings (the kingdom of God is within us, Luke 17:21). As we approach the very center, all various archetypes are distilled into fewer and more broadly encompassing archetypes. In Taoism, all diversity may be eventually distilled into two primal powers called *yin* and *yang*, which are complimentary opposites and are seen in the world of form as male and female, hard and soft, hot and cold, sun and moon and so on. Complimentary op-posites means that each defines the other. Yin and yang arise out of the undifferentiated Absolute or Tao which is also the same as Brahman in concept. In Hinduism the same concept takes a threefold expression known as the three *gunas*. They are *tamas*, dark and inert; *rajas*, active and energetic; and *sattva*, harmonious equilibrium.

In the Jewish Kabbalah, this primal one Being is called the Einsoph. Einsoph manifests in the world of form as the ten Sephiroth. The directionalized will of the Einsoph manifests as the first or crown Sephira, called Keter. From Keter are formed the primal duality of Cochmah, the *Great Father*, and Binah, the *Great Mother*. From the interaction of this trinity, the other seven Sephiroth are formed. They are Mercy, Strength, Grace, Victory, Honor, Foundation and Kingdom.

As mentioned previously, Hinduism also has another prevalent facet, and that is the path of non-duality or *advaita* (a Sanskrit word meaning "not two"). This path goes to the opposite end of the spectrum from gods and goddesses. It assumes no forms for God at all. It does not admit any "others" but only the one luminous Self (as in I AM). It is not at all accurate to say that Hinduism is involved exclusively with worshipping gods and goddesses.

The Old Testament also portrays God as multiple gods.

> *Then God said, "Let <u>us</u> make man in <u>our</u> image after <u>our</u> likeness..."* GENESIS 1:26, NIV [emphasis added]

> *And the Lord God said, "The man has now become like one of <u>us</u>, knowing good and evil."* GENESIS 3:22, NIV [emphasis added]

The "us" and "our" in the previous two scriptures is often loosely translated as God and angels. "Let us make man..." is very curious because it indicates that God was not the only creator. There were other co-creators. The Jewish Kabbalah explains that there are seven diverse powers or beings called Elohim that are the first emanations of form from out of the formless Einsoph. It is the Elohim that are doing all of the creating (*The Encyclopedic Outline of Masonic, Hermetic, Qabbalistic and Rosicrucian Philosophy* by Manly P. Hall). The word Elohim is used many times in the Old Testament as well as Yahweh (Jehovah) and numerous other names. All of them were simply translated as God in the English version. In the first sentence of the Old Testament, the Hebrew word for God is Elohim:

> *In the beginning God created the heavens and the earth.*
> GENESIS 1:1, NIV

This explains the mysterious occurrences of God as a plurality in the previous scriptures and unmistakably reveals the idea of God as a multiplicity peeking from behind the pillars and curtains in the Old Testament.

Genesis also reveals God to be a plurality of male and female:

So God created man in his own image, in the image of God he created him; male and female he created them.

GENESIS 1:27, NIV

This scripture clearly indicates that the nature of God is both male and female because the first man, the mirror image of God, was both male and female.*

All of the diverse gods and goddesses emanate from the center of being, which is God. It would be a mistake to imagine these gods and goddesses as abstract. They are intelligent and conscious beings. If God can think and act as a human being, then God can also think and act in the form of gods and goddesses. They may be approached, supplicated and prayed to, and in so doing we are actually praying to the One. These gods and goddesses are forms through which we may communicate with the Supreme Being until we develop sufficiently to commune with God without forms. By approaching any facet or archetype in the diamond that is God, we will be led to God by the path of that facet. A person may choose a facet according to his or her nature.

To aid in understanding the nature of the various facets of God, the Hindu sages of antiquity personified them as the various gods and goddesses using the language of symbols to reveal the great diversity of the Divine Form. To study and understand the gods and goddesses is to understand the subconscious. They are a map of the subconscious, and so worshipping God with a form is a helpful stepping stone. In the end, the ego dissolves, and the revelation remains that all forms are merged in or have their existence in a seamless unity.

Statues constructed to represent an aspect of God can actually become a focus of God's presence in much the same way that a mag-

---

* Genesis has two complete and independent creation stories with the first in chapter 1 and the second, featuring Adam and Eve, in chapter 2. The scripture referenced here, Genesis 1:27, has man and woman being created at the same time as opposed to Genesis 2:22 which has man being created first and woman to follow as an afterthought created from the rib of man. Most biblical scholars believe these contradictory accounts are actually two separate creation stories that were eventually merged in Genesis. The first account indicates that men and women have equal status in the eyes of God.

nifying lens may be used to focus sunlight and bring a piece of paper to flames. To use another analogy, a blowtorch may be held to a piece of iron until it begins to glow red-hot. The metal will become activated with the heat of the blowtorch, and it will continue to glow as long as the blowtorch is applied to it every 20 or 30 seconds. By approaching the red-hot iron metal, we can warm our cold hands. The heat that originated from the blowtorch will be transferred to our hands via the piece of red-hot iron. In the same way, a statue or deity may begin to radiate God's spiritual energy if it has been "heated" by the prayers, worship and offerings of many devotees, or if it was installed with the resolve of a Perfect Master. Such a statue or idol is of great benefit, warming the heart and the soul with God's peace, love and compassion.

God is both impersonal and personal. To say otherwise is to presume to limit God. Therefore, God may be seen as monotheistic, pantheistic and polytheistic. There is only one God (monotheism). If there is only one God, then there can be nothing else simply because everything that exists must arise from and be made out of God. There can be nothing that is independent from God; otherwise, there is more than one God. Therefore, God sustains and is one with all of creation and all beings (pantheism). Every aspect of the creation is a revelation of the creator. We worship and adore God's various aspects, seeing God as mountain, rivers, wind, sun, compassion, patience, tolerance, forbearance, love, the cornucopia of life, the creator of the universe, the maintainer of the universe and the dissolver of the universe. To each of these aspects we give a name, and we may worship one of them individually (polytheism), knowing that we are really worshipping the one indescribable whole. To recap, there is one singular God (monotheism) who inhabits or informs all of creation (pantheism) and whose countless divine qualities are worthy of worship (polytheism).

Is Judaism also a polynomial monotheism (one God with many names or attributes) like Hinduism? According to the Kabbalah it is. Jewish Kabbalistic doctrine explains that in the beginning there was the EIN, or the vacuum of pure spirit. This is identical in concept to Buddha Nature in Buddhism and Brahman in Hinduism. Buddhists are quick to point out that Buddha Nature (inherent emptiness) is not "nothing," and Hindus are quick to point out that

Brahman is not a "something." These are simply two attempts to describe the same "indescribable." Continuing with Kabbalistic doctrine, the EIN SOPH, the limitless and boundless, arises from the EIN. Limitless and boundless are conditions. The unconditioned now has conditions. This is followed by EIN SOPH AUR, or limitless light, which is additional limitation or form. These progressive limitations are seen by the Kabbalah as progressive concentrations toward the individuation of the Supreme Essence, or in other words, God personalized. The Zohar says:

> "When the concealed of the Concealed wished to reveal Himself He first made a single point: the Infinite was entirely unknown and diffused no light before this luminous point violently broke through into vision."

The name of this point is I AM, which in the Hebrew language is *Eheieh*. This dot is the Kether or the crown Sephira. From this emanates 39 additional sheaths or spheres of vibration, with each becoming progressively dense and limited.

The various aspects of formless Einsoph are addressed thusly: *Eheieh*, meaning pure I AM THAT I AM; *Jehovah*, meaning Essence of Being; *Jehovah Elohim*, meaning God of Gods; *El*, meaning the Creator; *Elohim Gibor*, meaning God the Potent; *Eloah Vadaath*, meaning God the Strong; *Jehovah Tzaboath*, meaning God of Hosts; *Elohim Tzabaoth*, meaning Lord God of Hosts; *Shaddai El Chai*, meaning Omniportent and last but not least *Adonai Melekh*, which means God. When we as Christians pray to God, do we mean *Eheieh* (I AM), *Yahweh* (Jehova) or *Elohim*? All of these names and many more are in the Old Testament. God doesn't care about the name or the form we address; He only wants our love.

Then come ten reflections of the Sephiroth and then the ten hierarchies. One of these hierarchies, called the *Ten Hierarchies of Beings*, is especially interesting, so we will list them here. They are the *Hierarchy of the Cherubim the Holy Animals*, the *Hierarchy of the Cherubim the Wheels*, the *Hierarchy of the Thrones the Mighty Ones*, the *Hierarchy of the Dominations the Brilliant Ones*, the *Hierarchy of the Seraphim the Flaming Serpents*, the *Hierarchy of the Virtues the Kings*, the *Hierarchy of the Principalities the Gods*, the *Hierarchy of the Arch-*

angels *the Sons of God,* the *Hierarchy of the Angels the Seat of the Sons,* and the *Hierarchy of Humanity the Souls of Just Men.*

BAAL

The most common reference to idols in the Old Testament is Baal. Baal is a Semitic word meaning lord or owner and is applied as a general term to deities of various tribes. The various Baals were typically nature gods and goddesses, usually having to do with some aspect of the agricultural cycle. Not understanding the unity behind all such aspects, the worshippers of these Baals frequently came into competition with each other. Some cults such as the Baal Peor (Numbers 25:3) were characterized by gross sensuality and licentiousness. However, this was not universally true of the Baal cults. Baalism was also part of the ancient Semitic culture. It is not clear, historically, whether the idol worship condemned by the Old Testament prophets was the treatment of Yahweh (God of Israel) as a local nature god with rites; or whether Baalism was recognized to be distinct from Yahweh from the start. The slaughter of the priests of Baal perpetrated by Elijah in 1 Kings 18:40 was born of his antagonism for a specific rival deity.

Thus, with the Baals, the monotheistic view was lost, and there was only pantheism. At the writing of this book, we see that the pendulum has swung the other way. Monotheism has degenerated into an individually personified God who has forfeited his participation in the theater of life. He has retreated into the "beyond," leaving us bereft of any direct personal contact with Him in our world. The current orthodox monotheistic concept of God assumes that God is a distinctly separate individual like you or me residing in a kingdom far, far away. However, monotheism and the individuation of God are mutually exclusive of one another. If God is one (monotheism) then God *must* be everywhere and in everyone. If God is one then God must be omnipresent (everywhere). The proper view is that God is both transcendent (monotheism) and immanent (pantheism) with polytheism being the expression of worship in pantheism. Only by understanding that God is the I AM in every being and every atom can we see

God is both monotheistic (an absolute singularity) and pantheistic (within everything).

> Go beyond the worship of deities and merge in the Supreme
> Being. Realizing the basic Source of all souls, be that Reality
> Itself. The soul that plays the discordant note falls down. Unless you give up the sense of multiplicity, you cannot escape
> pain. When the True Form of the individual soul is known to
> be Pure Consciousness, then there is nowhere to go and no
> place from where to come. Nor is there any difference between
> oneself and others. Then everything becomes One Equality.
> However, until one sheds the sense of individuality one must
> worship the Lord and meditate on the Divine Form that one
> likes realizing that Form to be one's own Self.
>
> AMMACHI, OMKARA DIVYA PORULE

12

Reincarnation

GOD WILL GIVE US ANOTHER CHANCE

All creatures of this world are evolving. Before the end of a particular lifetime each creature evolves and reaches a certain level. In some cases, downfall will also occur. The next birth, whether it will be a higher birth or a lower birth, is determined by the evolution or degeneration of that particular soul. It all depends on the mental, physical and intellectual actions which one performs. AMMACHI, AWAKEN CHILDREN, VOL. 3

Reincarnation is a central theme in both Hindu and Buddhist philosophy. It also peeps through the pages of the Old and New Testament. Many early Christian fathers embraced reincarnation, as does current Jewish Kabbalistic doctrine. In this chapter we will explore the concept of rebirth as we continue to unify the major religions of the world.

First the bad news. As we begin to see, getting to heaven is perhaps not as easy as we would like it to be. There is only "one way," and that is the surrender of the "I" or ego, and love is the path for removing it. Let's recap briefly some of the scriptures we have reviewed in this book. Jesus tells us we are not getting into heaven if we do not become as little children. He says it will be extremely difficult if we are rich (most everyone in the United States is rich in comparison to the rest of the world). He tells us that many are chosen, but few will make it. We not only must guard our actions but now we must also guard our very thoughts. He tells us that whatever we do (or fail to do) to any person whatsoever, no matter who s/he is, we do to him. Have any of us treated Jesus badly lately? He tells us we must love everyone equally, in the same way that the sun shines on the just and the unjust. Jesus tells us that simply accepting him as our lord and savior will not be enough. He says that many will come to him saying that they healed in his name and cast out demons in his name, and he will say that he does not know them. We wish salvation were easy like pouring cereal out of a box. But it is not easy. There must be a deep and fundamental change in our perceptions of ourselves and others.

Now the good news. If we don't get it right before we die, God is going to give us another chance because God knows it is not possible to accomplish all of Jesus' commandments in one lifetime. In fact, God is going to give us as many opportunities as it takes. Success is built into the plan. No one would expect a six-year old to master calculus after one day in the first grade. He or she must go back to the classroom again and again for what seems, in the mind of the child, to be a very long time. In the same way, God is going to send us to school innumerable times, with each lifetime being one day in God's school. What are we studying? We are learning to be like our Father. We are learning to be perfect even as our Father is perfect (Matthew 5:48). In this chapter we will look at Old and New Testament scripture and the writings of the early church fathers to support the idea of reincarnation.

KARMA

We are reborn because of our desires and for the fulfillment of our karmas. As the common saying has it, "What goes around comes around." Karma is referred to as the law of cause and effect. Isaac Newton's third law of motion states that for every action there is an opposite and equal reaction. Albert Einstein demonstrated mathematically that the universe is curved. In fact, if we were to shoot an arrow with infinite energy, and if it did not strike any object in its journey, it would eventually hit us in the back. Paul says we will reap what we sow (Galatians 6:7). If we are out-of-touch and dysfunctional as a human being, we will suffer. If we are cruel to others or to animals, cruelty will return to us in some form. If we steal then we will experience unexpected loss in some way. We can put off going to God, but the consequence will be our own self-created suffering.

In Hinduism and Buddhism, the concept of reaping what we sow is called karma. God is not seen as vengeful and punishing but rather compassionate and merciful, waiting to respond to our slightest whimper and call. The jealous tyrannical god who is perpetually punishing, smiting and casting the naughty into the sulphurous flames of eternal damnation is simply a projection from the minds of humans who are themselves jealous, cruel and punishing. It is we ourselves who create our own misery. If we put our fingers to a hot stove after being warned not to do so, can we say God has punished us for our disobedience? If we spit up into the air, we will receive spit in the face. Can we say that it was God's punishment or vengeance if we ignore the law of gravity and receive spittle in the eye? God is love. God is compassionate and watches our suffering with sadness, not anger or contempt. He does not even go so far as to say, "I told you so," because that would defy God's eternal spirit of love. God loves us intensely. He has only care and concern that we are ignorant and suffer because of our ignorance. It is a mistake to say that God angrily metes out punishment to sinners. Only egos do that.

Karma brings us to the issue of reincarnation. When we are born into another body, we inherit circumstances that are the result of our past actions. Some think it disrespectful to say that one is born with an affliction because s/he is reaping the fruit of his/her previous actions. But if we are not responsible, then that makes God responsible for the affliction. Also, if we do not take responsibility for our own suffering, we will blame others and become bitter.

Why would God create innocent humans from scratch and put some in ideal conditions, such as a loving family, while God assigns another person to an impoverished single mother who is addicted to heroin and is an atheist? If we accept that God is love, then such a thing could not happen.

If we look at an afflicted person and express no compassion, then we have erred again. We are all part of each other. God's compassion and mercy extend to all who suffer. We should do the same.

By serving others who are less fortunate, we become participants in God's mercy.

A PARODY

The Creator of the universe was absorbed one night in his fantasies of cruelty, for the Creator lived and dreamed for that purpose only. He had no love or compassion. His bony hand rested thoughtfully under his gaunt, angular chin. Suddenly his eyes widened with eagerness as the ultimate plan for his ever-evolving Sport of Cruelty dawned in his dark, perverted mind. The Creator had conceived of the most vile act ever perpetrated in the annals of eternity! His pride knew no bounds. Rubbing his hands with eager anticipation, he ran to his laboratory to enact his foul scheme.

Up until this point there were no humans on the earth. Now he would create humans with the ability to be self-conscious – something he had overlooked in animals. He would convince the little darlings that they had free will to choose heaven or hell as the goal of their pitiful short life. Ironically, these poor little ones would have no choice as to whether or not they would be born into his macabre charade. None of them would have the opportunity to choose to be or not to be part of his dance of endless torture. That is something the Creator would be delighted to force upon them. He would create two possible and final endings for their lives. One is beautiful, and that he would call heaven. The other would be a state-of-the-art showcase of torment and horror. It would be the cherry on his ice cream soda of wickedness, and he would call it hell. He had to have heaven as the dangling carrot, or the little darlings would give up and not play. However, the creator would make darn sure that very few ever got in. What fun is that? It would be much better to watch the suffering and torment of the little darlings in hell. The Creator nearly swooned with delight, imagining the music of their piteous cries and screams. He had arranged hell so that it would be for all eternity, and there could be no pardons for any reason whatsoever. He made the rules. No mercy!

As mentioned above, there had to be some sport in it, so heaven was created as the bait. However, actually getting in would be like hitting the multi-state Power Ball lottery. The game was rigged; most would only pay. The Creator set up a very difficult obstacle. It was a gauntlet of powerful temptations that each human would have to pass through to get to heaven. Further, he would create Satan, "the tempter," a being of vastly superior intelligence and cunning, to tempt the little darlings in every way possible, thus assuring that most ended up as his victims in the fires of hell. To put the final seal of success on this wicked plot, the Creator issued a mandate in which each little darling human only got one chance to get it right. Make a mistake? Oh, too bad. The Creator set his plan in motion and retired to his bedchamber to rest from his labors. With a deep sense of satisfaction, he slithered in between the covers and closed his eyes, deeply content and satisfied. After all, he had conceived the perfect evil.

The above story is a parody of the current orthodox view of heaven and hell. What grotesque and macabre foolishness is it to imagine that God would create humans from his canister of primal matter, throw them into a world seething with all manner of temptations and give them only one chance to get it right? And if they failed they would be tortured for all eternity–that's forever and ever. If God were to implement this absurd and cruel scenario, then who would want to go to heaven and live with such a monster? It would be better to go to hell where one might at least have the opportunity to comfort the suffering. If God allowed, much less created, such an evil plan, he wouldn't be God. Those who say God created such a plan for innocent humans, who didn't ask to be created in the first place, do not know God at all. Not a tiny bit. At the least, a compassionate God would return the failed humans to "scratch" from whence they were made. Then there would be no eternal suffering. However, if you were part of the hierarchy of bishops, priests and deacons in the formative years of Christendom, and if you were claiming the sole right to dispense Christ, then a one-life-eternal-hell story would work rather well to corral the allegiance of the masses. Fear and guilt make strong ropes.

The church hierarchy wanted to control all access to God with themselves as the gatekeepers. They wanted us to believe that God had only given us one chance, and they were holding our tickets. The idea that we might get another chance would be damaging to their ability to posses and control us. Reincarnation holds that we are born and die again and again until the final day of liberation (resurrection) when one enters into God permanently. Judgement happens continuously. Merging with God stops the round of births and deaths. Of course, "endless hell" would not be compatible with reincarnation, although it should be noted both Hinduism and Buddhism state that we go to heaven worlds or hell worlds in between births according to the merits of our life on earth.

There are some who propose that Hebrews 9:27-28 refutes the idea of reincarnation. Paul says:

> *Just as man is destined to die once, and after that to face judgment, so Christ was sacrificed once to take away the sins of many people; and he will appear a second time, not to bear sin, but to bring salvation to those who are waiting for him.*
> HEBREWS 9:27-28, NIV

Let us examine the first sentence of the scripture and especially the words "destined," "after," and "judgement" in the original Greek. "Destined" is **apokeimai**, *ap-ok'-i-mahee*; from (apo) and (keimai); to *be reserved*; figurative to *await*. "After" is **meta**, *met-ah'*; a primary preposition (often used adverb); properly denoting *accompaniment; amid* (local or causal). "Judgement" is **krisis**, *kree'-sis; decision* (subject or object, for or against).

An examination of the Greek could also lend a translation of, "Just as man is destined to die once, and after that to face judgment," as follows: "And in as much as a man awaits the single death [the final death of the ego] which accompanies the decision..." (brackets by author) The word "face" as in "face judgement" does not exist in the original Greek and is added by the translators to amplify their own view.

As long as the ego persists, we will be drawn continuously from one birth to the next in order to satisfy the desires of the ego. It is our own desires that perpetuate this condition. These births and these deaths are of the body only. Only the body is born and dies.

We are not the body, and so we are really not born, and we really do not die. Because of our attachment to the body, it seems that we are dying and being reborn as if in a dream. The ego and its accumulated tendencies pass from one life to the next. At the point of liberation, the ego is extinguished once and for all, stopping the round of births and deaths, and the soul merges with God, thus enjoying the unbroken bliss of eternity.

In this context there is only one death, and that is the death of the ego. This death comes when we make the decision of the final "letting go" or surrender. The crucifixion represents the death of the ego. Jesus died on the cross as an example of selflessness and surrender. By willingly giving up his body, he demonstrated to us that we are not the perishable body but imperishable spirit.

Let us paraphrase Hebrews 9:27, applying what we have learned from the actual Greek words:

> *Christ surrendered himself to be crucified in order to correct the sin of our ignorance. Likewise everyone awaits the final death as the crucifixion of the ego which is the fruit of the decision to surrender to God. Then comes salvation as Christ is revealed for the second time in that self-existent luminous I AM bubbling up as the fountain of eternal life from the center of our own being.*

With the understanding that writers of the scriptures may be divinely inspired but not necessarily divinely perfect, we can re-examine Paul's declaration in Hebrews that man is appointed to die but once. If we are not able to accept a metaphorical explanation of this scripture, then at least we must accept the possibility that Paul could be wrong at any time about any thing, especially if Paul's opinion contradicts the apparent acceptance of the doctrine of reincarnation by Jesus. In the chapter titled "Scripture" we explored the idea that John the Baptist was mistaken when he claimed not to be Elijah. If the Baptist can make a mistake then Paul is also capable of error. We will read later in this chapter that many early church fathers believed in reincarnation.

On more than one occasion, the disciples openly proposed reincarnation in their questions and answers to Jesus. The Master had multiple opportunities to tell us that reincarnation was false, but he did not. In fact, he responds and moves harmoniously with their questions as though nothing at all were strange or out of place. Let's look at some of them.

THE BLIND MAN

> *As he went along, he saw a man blind from birth. His disciples asked him, "Rabbi, who sinned, this man or his parents, that he was born blind?"* JOHN 9:1-2, NIV

The disciples wanted to know the reason for the man's blindness. They offered two possibilities to Jesus. Either the man was blind because of the sins of his parents, or he was blind because he was reaping the fruit of his own sins (karma). If our souls do not exist prior to this birth and if the man was born blind, then when or where could he have committed the sins that caused his blindness? His soul would have existed prior to that birth, and he would have been engaged in a corporeal setting with other people to commit sins against or with. In other words, the blind man had a previous life. This indicates that the pre-existence of the soul was a prevalent idea among the disciples; otherwise, how could they have asked such an unusual question? Neither does Jesus ask them where they got such a strange idea. He does not marvel that they have presented him with such a foolish concept. Where did they get this idea? As we have seen in the "blind man" scripture and other scriptures, the concept of reincarnation was understood by Jesus and the disciples. They employed the concept in these discussions in a matter-of-fact way.

ELIJAH'S RETURN

Elijah the prophet is believed to have lived in the ninth century B.C.E. At the point of his death a fiery chariot with horses of fire took him in a whirlwind to heaven, and he was seen no more (II Kings 2:11). Four hundred years later, Malachi closed the last lines of the Old Testament with a prophecy from God, stating that God would send Elijah before the "great and terrible day of the Lord" comes (Malachi 4:5). The Jewish people were expecting Elijah to return as the necessary preface to signal the coming of the Messiah.

The disciples all felt that Jesus was the Messiah, but they were puzzled. Where is Elijah? The disciples asked the Master about this, and he told them that Elijah had already returned as John the Baptist. The first discussion of this is in Matthew, chapter 11.

> I tell you the truth: Among those born of women there has not risen anyone greater than John the Baptist; yet he who is least in the kingdom of heaven is greater than he. From the days of John the Baptist until now, the kingdom of heaven has been forcefully advancing, and forceful men lay hold of it. For all the Prophets and the Law prophesied until John. And if you are willing to accept it, he is the Elijah who was to come. He who has ears, let him hear.   MATTHEW 11:11-15, NIV

> The disciples asked him, "Why then do the teachers of the law say that Elijah must come first?"

> Jesus replied, "To be sure, Elijah comes and will restore all things. But I tell you, Elijah has already come, and they did not recognize him, but have done to him everything they wished. In the same way the Son of Man is going to suffer at their hands." Then the disciples understood that he was talking to them about John the Baptist.   MATTHEW 17:10-13, NIV

These scriptures indicate that the disciples and Jesus believed in reincarnation. John the Baptist was the reincarnation of Elijah. In an attempt to fit these scriptures into the orthodox view of *one-life-only*, some believe that Elijah never died as we know it because he went up in a chariot of fire, thus discounting John the Baptist as an instance of reincarnation. Their thinking is that Elijah did inhabit John the Baptist, but it was not rebirth because Elijah had never died. For this "discounting" to really work, the Baptist would need to have returned in the same fiery chariot as a grown man. However, he was clearly placed in the womb of a human mother, after which he had a very mortal and common birth.

Jesus said he was "born of woman," and in Luke 1:13-17, an angel tells John's father, Zacharias, that John will be born to his wife Elizabeth, "And he will go before him in the spirit and power of Elijah." Others use this last line to say that John the Baptist was under the power of Elijah but was not the incarnation of Elijah. However, Jesus says in no uncertain terms that John *is* Elijah and not simply an ambassador of Elijah's power, *"This is Elijah... He who has ears to hear let him hear"* (Matthew 11:14-15). Also, Malachi does not say that Elijah will appear by proxy but that Elijah himself will return.

WHO IS THE SON OF MAN?

Yet another discussion between Jesus and the disciples underscores their belief in reincarnation.

> *When Jesus came to the region of Caesarea Philippi, he asked his disciples, "Who do people say the Son of Man is?"*
>
> *They replied, "Some say John the Baptist; others say Elijah; and still others, Jeremiah or one of the prophets."*
>
> *"But what about you?" he asked. "Who do you say I am?"*
>
> *Simon Peter answered, "You are the Christ, the Son of the living God."*   MATTHEW 16:15-16

The flow here seems to be that if a prophet were to appear, he must be the incarnation of one of the prophets from the past, and so Jesus is asking the disciples who the people think has incarnated as Jesus. The idea of the reincarnation of the prophets is taken for granted, and the sole point of the question is to find out who the multitudes believe him to be. These scriptures indicate that, at least to Jesus and the disciples, the concept of reincarnation was common fare. Herod also heard that others were saying one of the prophets of long ago had reincarnated. This again indicates that such a belief in reincarnation was common at that time.

> *Now Herod the tetrarch heard about all that was going on. And he was perplexed, because some were saying that John*

had been raised from the dead, others that Elijah had ap-
peared, and still others that one of the prophets of long ago
had come back to life. LUKE 9:7-8, NIV

JUDAISM AND REBIRTH

The following Old Testament scriptures prohibit talking to the dead. While this is not a direct endorsement of rebirth, it none-theless indicates that the soul can be functioning quite well with-out a body; otherwise, there could be no conversing with them. It also indicates that after they die, these souls are somewhere. Can they be in heaven or hell without first having an orthodox final judgement day? Or perhaps they are now in heaven or hell be-cause there is no "final" judgement day when all souls are judged and assigned permanently to either region. Or, if there is a final judgement day, from what place are they now, prior to the judge-ment, able to converse with the living? Reincarnation would have them in various after-worlds that can be generally grouped as heaven or hell, each with multiple levels of enjoyment or severity.

The following two scriptures assert the life of the soul after the body falls away:

> *Let no one be found among you who...is a medium or spiritist*
> *or who consults the dead.* DEUTERONOMY. 18:10-11, NIV

> *Do not turn to mediums or seek out spiritists, for you will be*
> *defiled by them. I am the Lord your God.* LEVITICUS 19:31, NIV

The next scripture clearly asserts the existence of at least this soul prior to being placed in the womb.

> *The word of the Lord came to me, saying, "Before I formed*
> *you in the womb I knew you, before you were born I set you*
> *apart; I appointed you as a prophet to the nations."*
> JEREMIAH 1:4-5, NIV

Solomon tells us in the following passage that if we do evil deeds in this life, we will have to reap the effects in our next incarna-tion. It is clear in this passage that Solomon believed in reincarnation. Having forsaken the law, these ungodly men will be re-born in another life to inherit their curse.

> *Woe be unto you, ungodly men, which have forsaken the law of the most high God: for if you increase it shall be to your destruction. And if you be born, you shall be born to a curse...*
> ECCLESIASTICUS 41:8-9, KJV, 1611 EDITION, APOCRYPHA

Flavius Josephus, 37 C.E. to 93 C.E., is the most well know Jewish historian. He was a Pharisee, born Joseph ben Matthias, who served as a commander in Galilee in the Jewish revolt against Rome in 66 C.E. His *Jewish Antiquities*, written about 93 C.E., describes the history of the Jews from the Creation onward with a particularly full account of the Maccabees and the dynasty of Herod. Reincarnation runs through his works like salt through a salt shaker. He talks of rebirth in such a matter-of-fact way that one must assume it was an accepted way of thinking which was so common at the time that it did not merit any further explanation. Many historians believe the previously mentioned discussions between Jesus and the disciples involving rebirth are the same. There was no expounding of the doctrine because it was so commonly understood.

> *The bodies of all men are, indeed, mortal, and are created out of corruptible matter; but the soul is ever immortal, and is a portion of the divinity that inhabits our bodies... Do not you know, that those who depart out of this life according to the laws of nature...enjoy eternal fame; that their houses and posterity are sure; that their souls are pure and obedient, and obtain a most holy place in heaven, from whence, in the revolution of ages, they are again sent...into bodies; while the souls of those whose hands have acted madly against themselves are received by the darkest place in Hades?*
> THE WORKS OF FLAVIUS JOSEPHUS, TRANSLATED BY WILLIAM WISTON

Going back to the time of Christ, we do not have to look far to discover a large cheering section for the doctrine of rebirth among the orthodox Jewish leaders of that period. There are three learned Jewish philosophers appearing just before or at the time of Christ who taught the doctrine of reincarnation. They were

Philo Judaeus, a. k. a. Philo of Alexandria, c. 20 B.C.E.- c. 50 C.E., who was the greatest Jewish philosopher and theologian of the Greco-Roman period whose writings have survived; the Jewish sage Hillel, the great Chaldean teacher who was the leading Pharisee in Jerusalem during the late 1st century B.C.E. and early years of the present era; and the great Jewish sage Jehoshuah ben Pandira. Today, these three men are household names in Judaism and garner enormous respect from all orthodox Jews, regardless of sect. They are prominent fixtures in Jewish religious history, and they all taught the doctrine of reincarnation.

THE KABBALAH

The Holy Kabbalah is the "hidden" or "secret" teaching of Judaism. It is the mystic path appearing in Judaism, just as the Sufis are to Islam and the Gnostics are to Christianity. In the same tradition, Jesus did not reveal all of his teachings in his public sermons. There was a hidden or direct teaching that was revealed privately, and there was a teaching for the multitudes who would not be capable of understanding deeper truths.

> *When he was alone, the Twelve and the others around him asked him about the parables. He told them, "The secret of the kingdom of God has been given to you. But to those on the outside everything is said in parables."*   MARK 4:10-11, NIV

In another instance Judas (not Judas Iscariot) asks Jesus why he intends to show himself to them but not to others, implying a hidden revelation.

> *Then Judas (not Judas Iscariot) said, "But, Lord, why do you intend to show yourself to us and not to the world?"*
> JOHN 14:22, NIV

Jesus follows with a long commentary and tells Judas that even though he (Jesus) is giving Judas (and others) special insight, there are yet even more things which Jesus will not reveal to them because they are not ready for them. That would make two layers of insight beyond the multitudes.

I have yet many things to say unto you, but ye cannot bear them now.   JOHN 16:12, KJV

There are hidden teachings which Jesus discussed openly with the disciples but not with the masses simply because the masses were not spiritually prepared. To do so would have been to cast pearls before swine. How could a barnyard animal appreciate the value of a pearl? Paul indicates that he too adjusts the directness of his teachings according to the understanding of the audience. Paul clearly states that there are teachings which he holds back because the listeners lack the spiritual depth to comprehend them.

Brothers, I could not address you as spiritual but as worldly— mere infants in Christ. I gave you milk, not solid food, for you were not yet ready for it. Indeed, you are still not ready.
                                    1 CORINTHIANS 3:1-2, NIV

Today, what remains of Paul's teachings, his public letters, are milk for spiritual infants. The "meat" was not recorded as open letters to churches but was taught by Paul directly to those whom he considered qualified. His revelation of Melchizedek is another indication of this.

The Holy Kabbalah is the hidden or secret tradition of Judaism not because it was forbidden but because it requires a high degree of spiritual maturity and insight to grasp. The Kabbalah is solid spiritual food that cannot be given to milk-drinking babes. Also, early Kabbalists did not want the teachings corrupted and perverted by well-meaning but immature souls. In centuries past, one had to prove worthiness to be taught the Kabbalah. The divine teaching and the spiritual practices such as ecstatic communion with God and meditation were transmitted orally under the careful and watchful guidance of an accomplished master, much like the guru/disciple relationship that exists between Hindu, Buddhist and Islamic Sufi masters and their disciples. For the most part, the Kabbalah was first committed to print and published in the Middle Ages, releasing it for the first time into the grasp of the secular body of mankind. Today, the Kabbalah is studied and practiced by many Jews, and it holds the doctrinal center stage for Hasidic Jews.

Hebrew theology was divided into three aspects, which are the *law*, the *soul of the law* and the *soul of the soul of the law*. The law was taught to every Jew; the soul of the law, or Mishna, was revealed to Rabbis; while the soul of the soul of the law, the Kabbalah, was revealed only to the highest initiates. We have just read that Jesus and Paul both referred to knowledge that is given to the many as distinct from knowledge that is given to the few.

According to Kabbalistic history, the teachings of the Kabbalah were given to a school of angels prior to the fall of man. The angels later revealed these teachings to Adam so that the fallen state of mankind might be redeemed. Specifically, the angel Raziel was sent from heaven by God to tutor Adam in the divine principles of the Kabbalah. Various angels were then sent to the Jewish patriarchs to clarify and intensify the understanding of this profound divine science. The angel Tophiel taught Shem, Raphael taught Isaac, Metatron taught Moses, and Michael taught David. Solomon was also a very high initiate in Kabbalistic wisdom.

The Kabbalistic torch was passed from Adam to Noah and then to Abraham, who immigrated to Egypt where he allowed a portion of the divine doctrine to be revealed to the Egyptians. Moses, who was adept in all the wisdom of Egypt, first learned the Kabbalah there but became most proficient in it while wandering for forty years in the wilderness. Moses also initiated the Seventy Elders into the way of the Kabbalah, which they, in turn, transmitted orally to their students.

In centuries past the teachings of the Kabbalah were closely guarded, but the sacred texts also predicted a time when the teachings could be accessed by anyone. Today, the Kabbalah is experiencing a tremendous resurgence of popularity and is being taught by Rabbis in living room study groups or classes offered through local synagogues. Non-Jews are also flocking to Kabbalah classes being held in local libraries and adult education programs. While most mainstream Jews in our modern world do not court reincarnation, Kabbalists are unshakably wedded to it. The three greatest books of Kabbalism are *Sepher Yetzirah*, The Book of Formation; *Sepher ha Zohar*, The Book of Splendor; and *Apocalypse*, The Book of Revelation. The following is a quote from the *Sephar ha Zohar.*

The souls must re-enter the Absolute, from whence they have emerged. But to accomplish this end they must develop the perfections; the germ of which is planted in them. And if they have not developed these traits in this one life, then they must commence another, a third, and so forth. They must go on like this until they acquire the condition that allows them to associate again with God. THE ZOHAR

The "germ" that is planted *in them* which leads to the "perfections" is the I AM; it is our oneness in Christ.

ORIGEN VS. JUSTINIAN AND THEODORA

In the first five hundred years of Christianity, reincarnation was most certainly on the main stage. It was a prominent and well-respected merchant in the bazaar of Christian theology.

A significant number of early church pillars such as St. Augustine, Clement of Alexandria, St. Gregory of Nyssa, Justin Martyr and St. Jerome believed in the doctrine of reincarnation. In his *Confessions*, St. Augustine ponders the common sense viability of reincarnation:

Did my infancy succeed another age of mine that dies before it? Was it that which I spent within my mother's womb? ... And what before that life again, O God of my joy, was I anywhere or in any body? CONFESSIONS OF ST. AUGUSTINE, EDWARD PUSEY, TRANSLATOR, BOOK I.

There is one early church father who is the central figure in this complex story of intrigue and deception. According to the *Encyclopedia Britannica*, Origen (C.E. 185-254) was the most prominent, most distinguished and most influential of the early church fathers. We would do well to consider the enormity of this statement. The *Encyclopedia Britannica* also declares that he was the most prolific writer and theologian of early Christianity, with works numbering around 6,000. St. Jerome asks, "Which of us can read all that he has written?" It is important to understand that Origen's story is not about the trials and tribulations of an obscure backwoods rogue theologian. How such an important and prominent luminary receded into the blackness of obscurity is a fascinating story and underscores the ego's perennial effort to have its own way.

The *Encyclopedia Britannica* describes Origen as both a Neo-Platonist and a Gnostic. Socrates and Plato were arguably the most important bearers of the doctrine of reincarnation to the Western world. The first clear presentation of reincarnation by these two is in Plato's *Meno* and later in the *Phaedo,* where the concept is fully articulated. In the *Phaedo,* Socrates (under the pen of Plato) goes to great lengths to explain the philosophy, proposing that the soul is immortal and does not cease to exist when the body expires. In Plato's *Republic,* the character Er describes the after death journey of the soul in graphic detail before "coming back." These ideas are expanded in the *Timaeus* and the *Phaedrus,* in which Socrates presents reincarnation in the strongest terms.

Aristotle emphasized a more empirical materialism which focused on the here-and-now, the observable. It should be pointed out that through the centuries many philosophers have strongly disagreed with Aristotle's "logic of categories" axiom which proposes a tidy compartmentalization of all aspects of existence, both cosmic and human. This theory supposes no overlapping connection of the various categories of knowledge such as science, history and religion. Thomas Aquinas, who played a large role in shaping Christianity as we know it today, based his entire view of life on Aristotelian logic, thus abandoning the mystical experiential traditions altogether. In this light we can understand more clearly the *Encyclopedia Britannica's* categorization of Origen as a Neo-Platonist with a decidedly Gnostic flavor. The Gnostics, as described earlier, believed that truth could be gained only through "Gnosis" or direct experience of God. They emphasized ecstatic communion and the inward path toward God. About reincarnation, Origen has this to say:

> *If it can be shown that an incorporeal and reasonable being has life in itself independently of the body and that it is worse off in the body than out of it, then beyond a doubt bodies are*

*only of secondary importance and arise from time to time to
meet the varying conditions of reasonable creatures. Those
who require bodies are clothed with them, and contrawise,
when fallen souls have lifted themselves up to better things
their bodies are once more annihilated. They are thus ever
vanishing and ever reappearing.*
ORIGEN, FROM A SELECT LIBRARY OF THE NICENE AND POST-
NICENE FATHERS OF THE CHRISTIAN CHURCH, P. SCHAFF AND
H. WACE EDITORS

*By some inclination toward evil, certain spirit souls come into
bodies, first of men; then, due to their association with the irra-
tional passions after the allotted span of human life, they are
changed into beasts, from which they sink to the level of plants.
From this condition they rise again through the same stages and
are restored to their heavenly place.*
ORIGEN, ON FIRST PRINCIPLES, B. W. BUTTERWORTH, TRANSLATOR.

As with many great saints of the past, there was nothing luke-
warm about Origen. While his supporters were passionate in her-
alding his views, his detractors passionately pursued his
destruction. Origen was banished forever from official church
recognition at the Second Council of Constantinople (the Fifth
Ecumenical Council) amidst a back drop of swirling political intrigue and dissension that was so severe it leaves many students
of the event to question whether or not Christians are bound by
the edicts and anathemas that were adopted there.

Emperor Justinian wrote a letter to the Patriarch of Constantinople
naming Origen as one of the pernicious heretics. To be a heretic is
bad enough, but *pernicious* means "1. insidious harm or ruin; 2.
deadly or fatal." In other words, there are no human beings worse
than this. Justinian then convened a synod at Constantinople in
543 C.E. which issued an edict refuting Origen. Pope Vigilius opposed the edict and promptly suspended all communication with
the Patriarch of Constantinople. When the Pope arrived in
Constantinople, he reversed himself, issuing a document support-
ing the Justinian edict. Many speculate that this document was issued at the gunpoint of intense political pressure. These
speculations are confirmed by the fact that Pope Vigilius withdrew

the document seven years later in 550 C.E. After much rancorous discussion and many maneuvers, Justinian called for a meeting of the entire Church in 553 C.E., known as the Fifth Ecumenical Council or the Second Council of Constantinople. The Church was geographically divided into East and West, with these lines of division also extending into religious and philosophical matters. In general, the West was supportive of Origen while the East was not. Justinian himself presided over the meeting because Pope Vigilius had boycotted the gathering as an act of protest over irregularities such as stacking the arrangements for attendance against the West. It was highly irregular for Justinian and not the Pope to preside over this conclave. Of the 165 bishops who signed the acts of the Council, not more than six were from the West because they were not in attendance. Let us recap for emphasis. The Pope refused to attend, Justinian ran the meeting and half of the bishops, the ones most likely to support Origen, did not attend the Council meeting.

In the long run, Pope Vigilius accepted the Council, but the West did not recognize the Council as legitimate for some time. Several Western dioceses even broke off communication with Rome. Milan was so righteously indignant over this blatant skewering of propriety that they did not rejoin Rome until the end of the sixth century. To add to the vagary of Origen's demise, it should be noted that in the end of the Fifth Ecumenical Council's fourteen anathemas, Origen's name is mentioned in only one of them, nestled in a list of heretics. There is some evidence that even this was an error. The tragedy is that Christians have been led to believe that the doctrine of reincarnation has never been part of Christian faith. Others have supposed that the question of reincarnation was forever closed at the Fifth Ecumenical Council.

To further clarify the picture of Origen's crucifixion, it is important to understand his principle antagonist, emperor Justinian. The *Encyclopedia Britannica* has interesting things to say about him.

> *The truth seems to be that Justinian was not a great ruler in the higher sense of the word, that is to say, a man of large views, deep insight...*

Justinian was quick rather than strong or profound; his policy
does not strike one as the result of deliberate and well-considered
views, but dictated by the hopes and fancies of the moment.

In contrast, no previous ruler had taken such an interest in church policy as did Justinian. In what way is a man who is a shallow-minded opportunist (to summarize the *Encyclopedia Britannica's* characterization) interested in deeper spiritual matters? This question has left many to speculate that Justinian saw the Church as a means of control and exploitation, with the whip being his "one life then heaven or hell" policy.

While Justinian is portrayed as soft and indecisive, his wife, the empress Theodora, was an indomitable freight train of decisiveness and strength. It should be clearly understood that she was not merely his consort but was empress regnant, which means she had the legal right to interfere and run the empire. Officials took an oath to her as well as to Justinian. In the great Nika insurrection of 532, her courage alone saved her husband from being overthrown.

According to Procopius the historian,

> *"Theodora was the daughter of a bear feeder of the amphitheater at Constantinople, and she began working as an actress (regarded as an extremely low vocation) while still a child. Later she became a well-known courtesan and eventually met Justinian in Constantinople. Justinian's aunt, who was the empress at the time, forbade the marriage but upon her death Justinian repealed a law which prohibited senators from marrying women of the stage. In 527, at the death of Justinian's uncle the emperor Justin, Justinian and Theodora became rulers of the Roman Empire. He was forty-four and she was twenty-four."*

According to Procopius as written in the *Encyclopedia Britannica,*

> *"She surrounded herself with ceremonious pomp, and required all who approached to abase themselves in a manner new even to that half-Oriental court. She constituted herself the protectress of faithless wives against outraged husbands, yet professed great zeal for the moral reformation of the city, enforcing se-*

verely the laws against vice, and confining five hundred courte-
sans, whom she had swept out of the streets of the capital, in a
'house of repentance' on the Asiatic side of the Bosphous strait."

Procopius portrays her as acting with the greatest cruelties. The *Encyclopedia Britannica* goes on to state that we are able to gather from other writers that Theodora was indeed extremely harsh and tyrannical.

The following is an excerpt from the *Anecdota* by Procopius, describing Justinian.

I think this is as good a time as any to describe the personal appearance of the man. Now in physique he was neither tall nor short, but of average height; not thin, but moderately plump; his face was round, and not bad looking, for he had good color, even when he fasted for two days. To make a long description short, he much resembled Domitian, Vespasian's son....

Now such was Justinian in appearance; but his character was something I could not fully describe. For he was at once villainous and amenable; as people say colloquially, a moron. He was never truthful with anyone, but always guileful in what he said and did, yet easily hoodwinked by any who wanted to deceive him. His nature was an unnatural mixture of folly and wickedness. What in olden times a peripatetic philosopher said was also true of him, that opposite qualities combine in a man as in the mixing of colors. I will try to portray him, however, insofar as I can fathom his complexity.

This Emperor, then, was deceitful, devious, false, hypocritical, two-faced, cruel, skilled in dissembling his thought, never moved to tears by either joy or pain, though he could summon them artfully at will when the occasion demanded, a liar always, not only offhand, but in writing, and when he swore sacred oaths to his subjects in their very hearing. Then he would immediately break his agreements and pledges, like the vilest of slaves, whom indeed only the fear of torture drives to confess their perjury. A faithless friend, he was a treacherous enemy,

insane for murder and plunder, quarrelsome and revolution-
ary, easily led to anything, but never willing to listen to good
counsel, quick to plan mischief and carry it out, but finding
even the hearing of anything good distasteful to his ears.

How could anyone put Justinian's ways into words? These
and many even worse vices were disclosed in him as in no
other mortal: nature seemed to have taken the wickedness of
all other men combined and planted it in this man's soul. And
besides this, he was too prone to listen to accusations; and too
quick to punish. For he decided such cases without full exami-
nation, naming the punishment when he had heard only the
accuser's side of the matter. Without hesitation he wrote de-
crees for the plundering of countries, sacking of cities, and sla-
very of whole nations, for no cause whatever. So that if one
wished to take all the calamities which had befallen the Ro-
mans before this time and weigh them against his crimes, I
think it would be found that more men had been murdered by
this single man than in all previous history.

He had no scruples about appropriating other people's property,
and did not even think any excuse necessary, legal or illegal, for
confiscating what did not belong to him. And when it was his,
he was more than ready to squander it in insane display, or give
it as an unnecessary bribe to the barbarians. In short, he nei-
ther held on to any money himself nor let anyone else keep any:
as if his reason were not avarice, but jealousy of those who had
riches. Driving all wealth from the country of the Romans in
this manner, he became the cause of universal poverty.

Now this was the character of Justinian, so far as I can por-
tray it.
Translated by Richard Atwater, in Procopius, Secret History, (Chicago: P. Covicii; New York: Covicii Friedal,
1927), reprinted by University of Michigan Press, 1961

The historian Procopius, who wrote the above narrative, was appointed secretary to General Belisarius in 527 C.E. The General
was Justinian's right-hand man and personal confidant.
Procopius also wrote the well known *Histories* in eight books, the

Buildings of Justinian in six books and the *Anecdota*. For obvious reasons, the *Anecdota* was not published until after the death of Procopius. As a historian and chronicler of Justinian and his court, he was constrained to write only positive accounts while everyone concerned was still alive. Secretly, he wrote the *Anecdota* to expose the utter immorality and disregard for decency expressed in the lives of Justinian and Theodora. The *Encyclopedia Britannica* says:

> *Owing to the ferocity and brutality of the attacks upon Justinian, the authenticity of the "Anecdota" has been called in question, but the claims of Procopius to the authorship are now generally recognized.*

In other words, the *Anecdota* reflected so badly on Justinian and Theodora that it was difficult to believe it could be true. It is not the intent of this book to serve as an indictment of these two souls – may they find peace and love wherever they are. The information about Justinian and Theodora and the demise of Origen is printed here as an aid to understanding that the fortunes of the Holy Scriptures and Christian doctrine in general have not always been in the hands of God's servants. The removal of the doctrine of reincarnation may not have been God's doing. God may have originated or inspired the scriptures that we have now accepted to be Christian, but since then, they have, on occasion, been placed in the hands of those with little understanding. Because of this, we should abandon the expectation that these scriptures would arrive in the twenty-first century unscathed.

The doctrine of reincarnation was banished because it gives power and authority to the people. Reincarnation contradicted the aspirations of a few bishops and deacons who felt they alone should dispense the truth to the multitudes. This authoritarian strangle-hold is strengthened by the doctrine of "one chance-one life" because a person who wrongly chose to think for him/herself, dismissing the authority of the hierarchy, would not get another chance to put things aright if s/he guessed wrongly. The position of the hierarchy is that eternal damnation without parole would be the irrevocable fate of those who dared to question the hierarchy's authority.

13

The Resurrection

When the Truth shines in your consciousness, all this that is
seen here becomes meaningless. The Universe will be known to
be like a picture on a wall.

AMMACHI, OMKARA DIVYA PORULE, PART 2

Because the ego originates from the I-am-the-body thought, it will
want to associate every aspect of our nature, in the present and in
the hereafter, with the body. Herein lies the source of the perversion of the resurrection. We are not able to see that we are not the
body, and so we are not able to comprehend ourselves as anything but the body. What goes to heaven? A body. What goes to
hell and burns in the fires? A body. What is Jesus? A body. What
do we want to keep more than anything? Our bodies. What is the
central orthodox issue of the resurrection of Christ? His body is
resurrected. What is the central issue of the judgement day? Our
bodies will be resurrected.

The truth is we are spirit and not body. We were created by God,
from God's very breath and in God's image, and God is spirit.
Therefore, we are also spirit. The body is the container and not
the contents. We suffer because we confuse the two.

God is a Spirit: and they that worship him must worship him
in spirit and in truth. JOHN 4:24, KJV

Jesus answered, "Verily, verily, I say unto thee, Except a man
be born of water and of the Spirit, he cannot enter into the
kingdom of God. That which is born of the flesh is flesh; and
that which is born of the Spirit is spirit." JOHN 3:5-6, KJV

Flesh cannot enter the kingdom of God, but Spirit can. When we go to heaven, we will be like the angels who are not fleshly beings and who have no gender. They are without sex because they are not fleshly bodies. Our true nature is somewhat like the angels, but we have forgotten it like the prodigal son.

The ego is troubled when confronted with the idea that our existence may not require a body. This is understandable because the ego revolves around our identification with the body, and this identification gives rise to the illusory appearance that we are all separate from one another. The idea of not having a body causes the ego to feel it has been set adrift, floating in the empty space of impermanence. There is an unsettling feeling of being ungrounded, naked and not in control. The ego would rather not think the body is transitory and impermanent.

In one event the Sadducees tested the idea of the resurrection by using a Mosaic law which stated that if a man were to die having no children, then his widow should marry the man's brother (the widow's brother-in-law). The Sadducees wanted to know what would happen if the woman married seven times to seven brothers with the preceding one dying each time. Whose wife would she be in the resurrection because they had all seven been her husband.

> *Jesus replied, "You are in error because you do not know the Scriptures or the power of God. At the resurrection people will neither marry nor be given in marriage; they will be like the angels in heaven."* MATTHEW 22:29-30, NIV

Jesus is explaining that we are not fleshly human beings and therefore do not marry one another in the resurrection. Rather, we will exist as spiritual beings like the angels. We will be liberated from the cycle of birth and death. No further physical body will be needed.

In the next scripture, Jesus goes on to explain that the resurrection has nothing to do with reconstituting dead flesh and parking it in heaven. Since the multitudes are blind and see spirituality only in terms of the flesh, he begins his sentence by saying he would like to touch on the subject of resurrecting the dead. Then he goes on to dispute resurrecting dead bodies. He says that God is not for the dead but for the living. In other words the resurrection happens to the living as a profound experience or change. The resurrection is the resurrection of the spirit and not the flesh. It has nothing to do with raising dead bodies. It is clear that his statement contradicted the conventional understanding of the resurrection. The multitudes were astonished.

> *"But about the resurrection of the dead—have you not read what God said to you, 'I am the God of Abraham, the God of Isaac, and the God of Jacob?' He is not the God of the dead but of the living." When the crowds heard this, they were astonished at his teaching.* MATTHEW 22:31-33, NIV

To paraphrase, Jesus says, "I want to comment on this idea of resurrecting the dead body. God is the living God of the prophets. God has nothing to do with dead bodies. God's only concern has to do with what is alive." This means our lives are more than our bodies, and the resurrection has to do with our spirits or souls and not the body. Jesus comments on this:

> *His disciples said to him, "When will the repose of the dead come about, and when will the new world come?"*
>
> *He said to them, "What you look forward to has already come, but you do not recognize it."*
> GOSPEL OF THOMAS, NAG HAMMADI LIBRARY, VERSE 51

Paul agrees that there is no place in heaven for fleshly bodies.

> *I declare to you, brothers, that flesh and blood cannot inherit the kingdom of God, nor does the perishable inherit the imperishable.*
> 1 CORINTHIANS, 15:50, NIV

Jesus says:

> *"If spirit came into being because of the body, it is a wonder of wonders. Indeed, I am amazed at how this great wealth [the spirit] has made its home in this poverty [the body]."*
> GOSPEL OF THOMAS, NAG HAMMADI LIBRARY, VERSE 29

The resurrection is referred to in Hinduism and Buddhism as enlightenment or liberation. It is a dramatic change in one's life and one's perspective. It is the unshakable realization that we are not the body, and that we are one with Christ.

Jesus was an incarnation of God. His command of the elements was perfect while he walked in the world. He could raise Lazarus from the dead, walk on water and change water into wine. He was captured and crucified only because he allowed it to happen. We have no reason to suspect his command of the elements would be diminished when he had left this world. When his ministry was completed by the crucifixion and resurrection, he had no further need of a physical body. However, being one with God and like Melchizedek, he could materialize and dematerialize a fleshly body at will or appear in a more ethereal form like a ghost depending on how he needed to affect those to whom he appeared. In the next scripture Jesus materializes a physical body.

> While they were still talking about this, Jesus himself stood among them and said to them, "Peace be with you." They were startled and frightened, thinking they saw a ghost. He said to them, "Why are you troubled, and why do doubts rise in your minds? Look at my hands and my feet. It is I myself! Touch me and see; a ghost does not have flesh and bones, as you see I have."   LUKE 24:36-39, NIV

In the following passage, two of the party of devotees who had just inspected Jesus' sepulchre set out that day walking to a village called Emmaus, and on the way Jesus joins them and engages them in conversation. They don't recognize him as the Lord but think he is a stranger. So Jesus appears to them, but his body and facial features are unrecognizable. When they arrive at the village, Jesus is still with them, and the devotees ask him to join them for dinner. At the dinner table, Jesus causes them to realize who he is and then vanishes into thin air.

> And it came to pass, as he sat at meat with them, he took bread, and blessed it, and brake, and gave to them. And their eyes were opened, and they knew him; and he vanished out of their sight.   LUKE 24:30-3; MARK 16:12, KJV

In another instance in John 20:14, Mary Magdalene remained outside the sepulchre after the others had come to see that it was empty. She was weeping. Again, Jesus appeared in a form that was not recognizable to Mary, and she assumed he was a gardener. He talked with her and tried to console her. Only after he addressed her as Mary did she understand who the gardener was. If Jesus had taken his old body with him in the resurrection, why did Mary Magdalene and the other two devotees not recognize him?

> *Then the disciples went back to their homes, but Mary stood outside the tomb crying. As she wept, she bent over to look into the tomb and saw two angels in white, seated where Jesus' body had been, one at the head and the other at the foot. They asked her, "Woman, why are you crying?"*
>
> *"They have taken my Lord away," she said, "and I don't know where they have put him." At this, she turned around and saw Jesus standing there, but she did not realize that it was Jesus.*
>
> *"Woman," he said, "why are you crying? Who is it you are looking for?"*
>
> *Thinking he was the gardener, she said, "Sir, if you have carried him away, tell me where you have put him, and I will get him."*
>
> *Jesus said to her, "Mary."*
>
> *She turned toward him and cried out in Aramaic, "Rabboni!" (which means Teacher).*   JOHN 20:10-16, NIV

For centuries, bi-location among living saints has been a well documented occurrence. There are countless stories in which the physical presence of a saint will appear to a devotee who may be on the opposite side of the earth. A western account of bi-location can be found in the life of Padre Pio, a Roman Catholic priest who died only recently. Padre Pio, a humble Capuchin priest from San Giovanni Rotondo, Italy, was blessed by God in many ways. The most dramatic was the stigmata. Padre Pio bore the wounds of Christ for fifty years! He also had the divine gifts of creating fragrances, prophecy, conversion, reading of thoughts and miraculous cures. People are still being cured through his intercession in ways that cannot be explained by medicine or science. Accounts of these divine gifts are also quite common with saints and monks of India and Tibet. Also, there are several accounts of bi-location in the book *Autobiography of a Yogi* by Paramahamsa Yogananda. Sri Yukteswar, Yogananda's teacher, appeared to Yogananda and talked with him after Sri Yukteswar had passed on, much like Jesus appeared to his disciples.

The resurrection that we are to experience is to be reborn in the oneness of the infinite Christ. That is the truth which destroys death because we realize that our nature is and has always been immortal. We have been living an unreal dream of being a body, which is born and which dies again and again. To think that we are bodies is the original sin (original ignorance). To think that the body should be preserved in a resurrection is simply more ignorance. The resurrection means that we are to be liberated from the ceaseless round of births and deaths, with the engine of those births and deaths being our desires. Paul asks where is the sting of death:

> *Behold, I shew you a mystery; We shall not all sleep, but we shall all be changed, In a moment, in the twinkling of an eye, at the last trump: for the trumpet shall sound, and the dead shall be raised incorruptible, and we shall be changed. For this corruptible must put on incorruption, and this mortal must put on immortality. So when this corruptible shall have put on incorruption, and this mortal shall have put on immortality, then shall be brought to pass the saying that is written, Death is swallowed up in victory. O death, where is thy sting? O grave, where is thy victory? The sting of death is sin; and the strength of sin is the law.*   1 CORINTHIANS 15:51-56, KJV

We are all asleep, dreaming that we are mortal bodies. Being asleep in this way, we have eyes but do not see, and we have ears but do not hear. We have no spiritual awareness. Eventually, we will all awaken but not all at the same time. That quickening or awakening is the enlightenment experience that happens in the twinkling of an eye when we have surrendered the last vestige of our personal minds, egos and identities. This is the last trump (trumpet in Greek). That is the final laying down of everything we consider to be ourselves, for it is only by losing our lives that we gain our lives (Luke 9:24). It is only in surrendering our selves that we realize our Self. This is the final giving up of everything to God. At this point we discover that our core being is incorruptible and immortal, and we are forever changed. We see clearly that we are the I AM and not a body or a bundle of thoughts and identities. We discover that we are the I AM and not I-am-this and I-am-that. The last line in Paul's statement is interesting, "...and the strength of sin is the law." The Pharisees were convinced that they could attain heaven by following all of the scriptural injunctions or Jewish laws which include the ten commandments. Living a moral life is a necessary ingredient for arriving at enlightenment or resurrection, but living a moral life and observing the law in itself is not the goal. Without the love and compassion that arises out of experiencing our oneness in Christ, morality quickly degenerates into more egotism, and the fires of criticism, condemnation, judgement and hatred will quickly rage out of control as they did with the Pharisees then and continue to do now.

> *Those who say they will die first and then rise are in error. If they do not first receive the resurrection while they live, when they die they will receive nothing.*
> THE GOSPEL OF PHILIP, 73:1-5, THE NAG HAMMADI LIBRARY

14

Eternal Damnation and Hell

Hatred makes the mind a hell. Likewise, anger, jealousy and uncontrollable craving for name and fame make life equal to hell. You lose your peace of mind. You lose the love in you, the beauty in you, and your mind becomes a madhouse.

AMMACHI, AWAKEN CHILDREN, VOL. 5

There is a hell, but it is not forever. The current orthodox view of eternal damnation to hell says that this unfortunate circumstance is simply the result of having been given free will. It's not God's fault that we will be painfully tortured in a world of gnashing teeth for all eternity. Somehow free will is supposed to make sense of this eternal torture chamber. God gave us free will, and so God stands back with hands in the air, palms facing us, looking blankly a little off to the side, telling us that our decent into hell is beyond his control. "I'm sorry, my dear ones, but there is nothing I can do to help you. I gave you free will." The pitfall in the "free will" line of reasoning is that if God gave us free will he can also take it back.

In the following scripture it is revealed that Jesus descended into a "prison" to preach to disembodied persons (spirits) who disobeyed at the time of Noah. A prison is probably not heaven, and therefore, it is safe to assume this "prison" is hell. Why would the Lord bother to preach to them if they were doomed to hell for all eternity? What difference would it make if there were no way out? At the very least, the following scripture indicates the existence of the soul in some sort of prison after the body has fallen away. It also indicates that they are able to receive a sermon without a body.

For Christ died for sins once for all, the righteous for the un-
righteous, to bring you to God. He was put to death in the
body but made alive by the Spirit, through whom also he went
and preached to the spirits in prison who disobeyed long ago
when God waited patiently in the days of Noah while the ark
was being built.   1 PETER 3:18-20, NIV

In the entire New Testament the word "hell" appears twenty-three times. Fifteen of these were spoken by Jesus and were translated from the Greek word *Gehenna* (Matthew 5:22, 5:29, 5:30, 10:28, 18:9, 23:15, 23:33, Mark 9:43, 9:45, 9:47, and Luke 12:5). *Gehenna* is also used in James 3:6. Jesus used the word hell translated from the Greek word *Hades* four times (Matthew 11:23, 16:18, Luke 10:15, and Luke 16:23). *Hades* is also used in Revelations 6:8, 20:13, and 20:14. In 2 Peter 2:4 the Greek word for hell is *Tartaros,* which is the deepest level of Hades.

As we can see the most common occurrence of the word hell in the New Testament is translated from *Gehenna.* Gehenna has been translated from the Greek word "Ge-Hinnom" which is, in turn, translated from a combination of the Hebrew word "gay" and "Hinnom." Gehenna was a dump, a refuse pit on the out-skirts of Jerusalem which contained rotting carcasses, trash and other foul items. A fire was often burning in it to consume the garbage. The stench of the smoke made it a very unpleasant place to be. Why does Jesus use the metaphor Gehenna when referring to hell instead of Hades, the literal word for hell? That his meta-phorical use of Gehenna is intentional is indicated in four other scriptures where the Lord opted to use the word Hades, which in Greek, can more properly be translated as an actual location. The most reasonable explanation is that hell is a state of mind, and like the kingdom of God (heaven), it is within us (Luke 17:21). He is referring to the mental and emotional torment that we experi-ence now in this world when we become deluded by the ego and thus separated from God.

Christianity, Hinduism, Judaism, Islam and Buddhism all agree that when the body passes away, we go to heaven or hell accord-ing to our merits. The difference in these religions is only the du-ration. If Jesus tells us in Luke 17:21 that the kingdom of God is within us, then where does that put hell? Heaven and hell are both within us. If we remember that "within" is as infinite as "without," this is easier to grasp.

When the soul is mired in the ego, it is in hell, whether in this world or the next. That is why the first of Buddha's Four Noble Truths is "Life in this world is suffering," meaning that most everyone in this world is suffering from the delusion of the ego and its attachments. The world around us will reflect our hellish state of mind here and also in the hereafter. People whose minds are absorbed in selfishness and self-centered desires will attract hellish surroundings. When they are reborn, they will be born into circumstances that mete out suffering, and this suffering is simply the return or reflection of their own selfish actions. When they die, they will again gravitate towards a hell world that fits their egoistic point of view.

In the last week of July, 1999, Pope John Paul II, in a radical departure from the common Christian concept of hell, declared the following:

> Hell is not a punishment imposed externally by God, but the condition resulting from attitudes and actions which people adopt in this life. More than a physical place, hell is the state of those who freely and definitively separate themselves from God, the source of all life and joy.

When the word "eternal" or "everlasting" appears in the sayings of Jesus, it is the from the Greek word *aionios*, which means "into the age of ages" or "into the age." The Greek word *aionios* is derived from the root word *aion,* which means age. Our own English word eon (sometimes spelled aeon) comes from the Greek word *aion. Aionios* is an ambiguous word that can mean a very long time or forever. Jesus originally spoke the sayings in Aramaic, his native language. After he passed from this world, the stories of Jesus and what he said were handed down by word of mouth for about seventy years. Finally, they were translated from Aramaic and committed to writing in the Kione language, which was a Greek "market place" or common language. That language is now dead. From there it was again translated into the Greek we know today, and from there it was translated to English. As we can see, there was ample opportunity during the word-of-mouth era and through the various translations for embellishment and coloring of the stories before they were committed to written script. For example, the story of the virgin birth of Mary only occurs in Luke and not in the other three gospels. Regarding this, it is interesting to note that Luke the physician was a Greek, and similar stories of virgin births are also found in Greek mythology. How are we to know that the writers of the gospels themselves did not misconstrue any meaning or attach any personal bias in their rendering of scripture that was passed down by word of mouth for seventy years? We saw exactly this type of twisting and warping when we compared the "If your eye be single" scripture in the New International Version and the King James Version earlier. An ambiguous word such as *aionios* gives cause for speculation.

> *And surely I am with you always, to the very end of the age.*
> MATTHEW 28:20, NIV

In the above scripture we read the last word of the sentence as "age," and it means a finite amount of time with an end. The Greek word for "age" in this scripture is again *aionios*, which is the same word that is translated as "eternal" or "everlasting" in other New Testament scriptures. Translators have been assigning meaning to *aionios* to suit their own beliefs. The above scripture shows that *aionios* can definitely be interpreted as a finite amount of time. Thus, we must pause to consider that going to hell may not be forever. If we are to reincarnate, then our stay in hell will end.

Whenever Jesus uses the word damnation, it is from the Greek word *krisis* which means a decision with reference to subject or object, for or against. The transliteration for *krisis* is "judgement" and not damnation. The translators of the New Testament assumed "judgement" meant "damnation," but that is their own projection or interpretation. In the light of what we have considered, let's examine the following scripture.

> *Ye serpents, ye generation of vipers, how can ye escape the*
> *damnation of hell?* MATTHEW 23:33, KJV

The transliteration from Greek reads: *Snakes, offspring of vipers, how [can] you escape from the judgement of Gehenna.* This can just as easily be translated as: Snakes, offspring of vipers, how will you avoid reaping the suffering that you have sown, thus being tormented in your mind and heart as though having to live in the stench and filth of the town dump?

Only someone who does not know God would maintain the idea of an eternal hell. God is mercy, love and compassion and loves all of his children intensely. God *is* love (1 John 4:8 & 4:16). For all eternity, this is God's nature.

SHEATHES OF THE SOUL

According to Hindu scripture, we have five "bodies" which can be compared to layers of an onion. The Jewish Kabbalah also holds this concept of layered bodies to be true. The soul functions through these bodies or vehicles simultaneously. In the ancient Sanskrit language they are called *kosha,* which means "sheath." The outermost and coarsest layer, the *annamaya kosha*, is the dense physical body. The next layer, the *pranamaya kosha*, is a subtle form of matter and consists of the vital life force called *prana* in India and *chi* (pronounced chee) in China. Next is the *manomaya kosha,* which is the mind with its thoughts, emotions and desires. More subtle yet is the *vijnanamaya kosha,* which is the body of cognition and intuition. It is the vehicle of direct knowing, wisdom, intuition, gnosis, and creativity. The fifth and innermost body is the *anandamaya kosha* or body of bliss. It is not a sheath in the sense of the other *koshas* but is the soul itself, and it is from the *anandamaya kosha* that all the other *koshas* or "sheaths" are projected.

At the point of death, the subtle sheaths withdraw from the physical body, and the soul functions with complete continuity and is cognizant primarily through the mental, emotional, and intuitive bodies. The soul and its subtle bodies then inhabit another realm or plane of existence, which is like the western version of heaven and hell but with a little more definition. These levels are called *lokas* in Sanskrit. At the death of the physical body the soul leaves the *Bhuloka* or "Earth world." The *Bhuloka* is perceived through the five senses of the physical body, and it is the most coarse and most dense of the worlds. Most souls then inhabit the *Antarloka,* which means "Inner or in-between world." The *Antarloka* can be further subdivided into three worlds. The first and highest of these subdivisions is the *Devaloka* or "Place of radiant beings." It is the most subtle mental realm and is the abode of angels. Next is the *Pretaloka,* which means "World of the departed." It is more gross than the *Devaloka* and is the world inhabited by earth-bound souls sometimes referred to as ghosts. It is a duplicate of the physical world but composed of subtle substance. At the bottom is the hell world of *Narakaloka* or "Abode of darkness," which is the home of demons. This is the distressful world that Jesus describes as being like the foulness of Gehenna where souls suffer as the result of their own misdeeds in previous lives. Here souls experience torment, confusion and darkness. No one stays here forever.

Going further inward beyond the *Antarloka,* we have the *Karanaloka* or "World of God." Highly evolved souls go here. This world is also inhabited by cosmic archetypal beings sometimes referred to as gods, goddesses or archangels. This world is very subtle and composed of light.

Karanaloka   World of God; home of very evolved souls, archangels and celestial beings

Antarloka — *Devaloka* – Place of radiant beings; abode of angels
— *Pretaloka* – World of the departed; inhabited by earth-bound souls (ghosts)
— *Narakaloka* – Abode of darkness; home of demons

Bhuloka   World of physical matter

When the physical body drops away, the soul continues to experience existence through the subtle sheaths and is naturally attracted toward worlds and beings that mirror the soul's own disposition. Souls of a feather flock together. Angry people will go to worlds full of other angry souls, whereas a loving soul will ascend toward worlds occupied by other loving and compassionate souls.

As the soul evolves over many eons, it will eventually exhaust its desire for external pleasures and sensations. The illusion that happiness lies somewhere outside of itself will begin to fade. At that time it will become ripe for liberation or the resurrection. It will experience the final death, which is the death of the ego. At this point the soul merges with God forever and does not engage in any more incarnations unless it chooses to for the purpose of expressing compassion and love towards those souls still bound by the ancient wheel of birth and death.

In summary, we are seeing another way to interpret the teachings of Jesus. First, the soul is bound to the wheel of birth and death, assuming many bodies and incarnations, and second, hell is not for all eternity. Hell, like heaven, exists within us, and we all share this inner reality in the collective unconscious that lies below the surface of our perceived mortal existence.

15

The Messiah Comes Again

*Forget not the Truth. Be not fascinated on seeing the wonders
of the world. Remember that if you miss the Existence-Aware-
ness-Bliss (Satchidananda) Death will be just behind you.*
AMMACHI, OMKARA DIVYA PORULE, PART 2

The Second Coming of Christ is the recognition of Christ as the
living presence at the center of one's own being and has nothing
to do with the physical body of Jesus making another appearance.
Even if Christ were to return in the same body, this would not be
more important than the direct realization of Christ within us.
The Christ within us is immanent, ever present and cannot be
taken away from us. Many people saw the first body of Jesus and
were not moved. So it will be if he comes again in a second body.
Conversely, the direct realization of the universal Christ that
dwells deep in the heart of all beings forever changes one. It is, in
fact, the very salvation that Christians seek.

The following passage, which appears in three of the four gospels, is what most Christians regard to be a description of the
Second Coming of Christ.

> As he was leaving the temple, one of his disciples said to him,
> "Look, Teacher! What massive stones! What magnificent build-
> ings!" "Do you see all these great buildings?" replied Jesus. "Not
> one stone here will be left on another; every one will be thrown
> down." As Jesus was sitting on the Mount of Olives opposite the
> temple, Peter, James, John and Andrew asked him privately,

"Tell us, when will these things happen? And what will be the sign that they are all about to be fulfilled?"

Jesus said to them: "Watch out that no one deceives you. Many will come in my name, claiming, 'I am he,' and will deceive many. When you hear of wars and rumors of wars, do not be alarmed. Such things must happen, but the end is still to come. Nation will rise against nation, and kingdom against kingdom. There will be earthquakes in various places, and famines. These are the beginning of birth pains. You must be on your guard. You will be handed over to the local councils and flogged in the synagogues. On account of me you will stand before governors and kings as witnesses to them. And the gospel must first be preached to all nations. Whenever you are arrested and brought to trial, do not worry beforehand about what to say. Just say whatever is given you at the time, for it is not you speaking, but the Holy Spirit. Brother will betray brother to death, and a father his child. Children will rebel against their parents and have them put to death. All men will hate you because of me, but he who stands firm to the end will be saved.

"When you see 'the abomination that causes desolation' standing where it does not belong—let the reader understand—then let those who are in Judea flee to the mountains. Let no one on the roof of his house go down or enter the house to take anything out. Let no one in the field go back to get his cloak. How dreadful it will be in those days for pregnant women and nursing mothers! Pray that this will not take place in winter, because those will be days of distress unequaled from the beginning, when God created the world, until now—and never to be equaled again. If the Lord had not cut short those days, no one would survive. But for the sake of the elect, whom he has chosen, he has shortened them.

"At that time if anyone says to you, 'Look, here is the Christ!' or, 'Look, there he is!' do not believe it. For false Christs and false prophets will appear and perform signs and miracles to deceive the elect—if that were possible. So be on your guard; I have told you everything ahead of time.

"But in those days, following that distress, the sun will be darkened, and the moon will not give its light; the stars will fall from the sky, and the heavenly bodies will be shaken. At that time men will see the Son of Man coming in clouds with great power and glory. And he will send his angels and gather his elect from the four winds, from the ends of the earth to the ends of the heavens.

"Now learn this lesson from the fig tree: As soon as its twigs get tender and its leaves come out, you know that summer is near. Even so, when you see these things happening, you know that it is near, right at the door. I tell you the truth, this generation will certainly not pass away until all these things have happened. Heaven and earth will pass away, but my words will never pass away. No one knows about that day or hour, not even the angels in heaven, nor the Son, but only the Father. Be on guard! Be alert! You do not know when that time will come. It's like a man going away: He leaves his house and puts his servants in charge, each with his assigned task, and tells the one at the door to keep watch. Therefore keep watch because you do not know when the owner of the house will come back—whether in the evening, or at midnight, or when the rooster crows, or at dawn. If he comes suddenly, do not let him find you sleeping. What I say to you, I say to everyone: 'Watch!'" MARK 13:1-37. NIV [emphasis added]

Are we to take this scripture literally or as metaphor or both? As a description of the long awaited "Second Coming," this scripture has one rather cumbersome and intractable problem. In the third sentence of the last paragraph, and in all of the three gospels in which this scripture appears, the Lord says that this generation, meaning those to whom he was talking at that moment, would not pass away until all these things had happened. Obviously that generation passed away and many more generations, and these things did not happen in the literal sense. The stars did not fall from the sky, and Jesus did not appear in the clouds. There are only two things we can say about this. Either Jesus was wrong, or we have made a mistake in interpreting this scripture to be a literal end of the world which has yet to come.

In another scripture Jesus refers to destroying the temple and raising it back in three days.

> *Then the Jews demanded of him, "What miraculous sign can you show us to prove your authority to do all this?"*
>
> *Jesus answered them, "Destroy this temple, and I will raise it again in three days."*
>
> *The Jews replied, "It has taken forty-six years to build this temple, and you are going to raise it in three days?" But the temple he had spoken of was his body.* JOHN 2:18-21

The Jews were incredulous because it had taken them forty-six years to build the temple in which they were all standing and having the conversation. John goes on to tell us that Jesus had been speaking metaphorically.

We can also apply a metaphorical interpretation to the "last days" scripture above. In the beginning, throwing down all of the stones of the buildings represents the destruction of the old religious order. Internally, it represents the destruction of the ego and its false identities. The apocalyptic circumstances represent the turmoil and the great internal battles that must be fought to cast the ego out of our lives. The darkening of the sun and moon, stars falling from the sky and the shaking of heavenly bodies brings us back to an understanding of the inner turmoil or the dark night of the soul prior to enlightenment. The Son of Man comes in clouds with great power and glory, indicating he comes not from this world but from heaven, which we understand from Luke 17:21 to be within us. The remainder of the Lord's commentary has to do with alertness and mental preparedness that is necessary to make the leap when the opportunity of inner ripening offers to take us into the infinite. Only if we take this scripture as a metaphor describing the process of enlightenment do we avoid having to say Jesus made a mistake concerning the reality of the apocalypse happening to the generation that was present at the time of Christ.

In another instance Jesus tells his audience that the kingdom of God is immanent for some who are standing with him listening to him speak. He tells them that they will see the kingdom of God before they die.

> *I tell you the truth, some who are standing here will not taste death before they see the kingdom of God.*   LUKE 9:27, NIV

Clouds of glory did not sweep the earth, and the graves did not open, yielding up their bounty of bones and rotting flesh to heaven or hell. Yet there can be no doubt, because Jesus said it, that there were some at that gathering who saw the kingdom of God before they died. In the *Gospel of Thomas* we read:

> *The disciples said to Jesus, "Tell us how our end will be."*
>
> *Jesus said, "Have you discovered, then, the beginning, that you look for the end? For where the beginning is, there will the end be. Blessed is he who will take his place in the beginning; he will know the end and will not experience death."*
> GOSPEL OF THOMAS, NAG HAMMADI LIBRARY, VERSE 18

This scripture agrees with the statement by Jesus that all these things (the end-of-days) will happen before this generation passes. The "end" is not a physical end, according to Jesus, but a spiritual "end." When one transcends duality by the dissolution of the ego, the beginning and the end merge in the eternal now. Again in the *Gospel of Thomas* we read:

> *His disciples said to him, "When will the kingdom come?"*
>
> *[Jesus said,] "It will not come by waiting for it. It will not be a matter of saying 'here it is' or 'there it is.' Rather, the kingdom of the father is spread out upon the earth, and men do not see it."*   GOSPEL OF THOMAS, NAG HAMMADI LIBRARY, VERSE 113

It is also possible that the apocalyptic events in Mark 13:1-37 were a description of the destruction of Jerusalem and the Jerusalem Temple. Two times in the same century, the Romans put down armed rebellions in Palestine–in 66-77 C.E. and in 132-136 C.E.–with tremendous suffering to the poor. Various Jewish sects also warred against each other and inflicted as much damage and death on themselves as did the Romans. In 70 C.E. the Jerusalem temple was completely destroyed by the Romans, and a war tax was imposed on all the people, including Jewish Christians. In 136 C.E., the entire city of Jerusalem was reduced to rubble, and further access to the city was forbidden to anyone who looked like a native. Was this the judgement day Christ foretold?

Some may contend that Acts 1:9 shows Jesus being received into a cloud in the sky, and therefore, the kingdom is not within us. Let's examine that scripture.

> After he said this, he was taken up before their very eyes, and a <u>cloud</u> hid him from their sight. They were looking intently <u>up</u> into the <u>sky</u> as he was going, when suddenly two men dressed in white stood beside them. "Men of Galilee," they said, "why do you stand here looking into the <u>sky</u>? This same Jesus, who has been taken from you into <u>heaven</u>, will come back in the same way you have seen him go into heaven."
>
> ACTS 1:9-11, NIV [emphasis added]

The Greek word for cloud in this scripture, *nephele*, actually means cloudiness. It could be translated as a literal cloud, but it can be equally translated as obscurity, as in, "My thoughts became cloudy."

Where it says "sky," the Greek word from which "sky" is translated is *ouranon*. This word may be translated as sky, heaven as the abode of God or happiness, power and eternity, according to Strong's Greek Dictionary. In fact there are two other occurances of the word heaven in the last sentence, which in Greek is again the same word *ouranon*. All occurances of "sky" and "heaven" in this scripture are from the same Greek word *ouranon*. When we read the direct Greek transliteration for Acts 1:9-11 this is what it says:

> And these things having said, [while] [were] looking they he was taken up and a cloud took up him from the eyes of them. And as looking intently they were into heaven going he and behold men two had been present with them in clothing white, who also said, men of Galilee why have you stood looking into heaven? This Jesus, the one having been taken up from you into heaven thus will come in which manner you saw him going into heaven.   GREEK ENGLISH INTERLINEAR NEW TESTAMENT

The word "up," appearing in "up into the sky," does not exist at all in the original Greek. And the word "sky" should properly be translated as "heaven." In the above transliteration, the choice of "cloud" for the Greek *nephele* was the interpretation in this particular transliteration. We can also choose the figurative translation as meaning obscurity.

The Second Coming of Christ is an affair of the heart. For someone who is wholly absorbed in a materialistic, body-oriented point of view, this will seem shallow because, for such a person, the heart is a shallow place. Such a one perceives the heart to be six inches below the breastbone. We should remember that the "heart" means the collective underpinning. The heart is the universal dynamo of God pumping the electricity of love, light and life through the light bulbs we know as our individual selves.

16

Forgive and Be Happy

Jesus Christ set an unforgettable example of how to respond.
He let His body be tortured and crucified, and even when He
was dying on the cross, Christ prayed for those who were
against Him: He prayed for their own good—that they might
be forgiven.   AMMACHI, AWAKEN CHILDREN, VOL. 5

Jesus' uncompromising forgiveness can only be understood in the
light of our unity in the I AM. We must forgive others because they
are us. If we allow anger and hatred to infect our minds we will obscure and block the grace of God that flows from within us. The
cancerous feelings of anger and hatred will grow and expand, in-
fecting our lives more and more with each passing day. Our blindness and delusion will become deeper and more entrenched,
causing our errors to multiply, bringing even more darkness. This
becomes a vicious cycle from which it is very difficult to escape.

Let us think about the following childhood phrase: *Sticks and*
stones may break my bones, but words will never hurt me. Why do we
feel hurt if someone says something hurtful to us? After all, they
are only words. It is not as if the hurler of insults has physically
hit us. Only words! The truth is, if we become angry because of
what someone says, we do as much or more harm to ourselves
than to the person with whom we are angry. We slide deeper into
ignorance of our own Self or God. It is because of our own ego
(ignorance of our unity) that we are offended and become angry.

When we see how deluded we have become by our own ego and
how much we suffer because of it, we will have compassion and

understanding for others even when they curse us and revile us. We will not become angry with them because we understand that they are steeped in ignorance and suffering just like us. How could one be born into this world and come out otherwise? Our parents are deluded, our teachers are deluded, and media convince us that happiness is in gratifying the senses, having power and being popular. We are taught to *buy* in order to *be,* and so the merry-go-round of our hollow and baseless existence spins around and around like a mad dog chasing its tail. Jesus demonstrated the depth of forgiveness that comes from one who is absorbed in the divine reality of our oneness when he was crucified. Imagine the horror of being nailed to a wooden cross, then being left to die of thirst. What a horrible cruel death he had. Even as he was hanging from the cross in excruciating pain he said:

> *Then said Jesus, "Father, forgive them; for they know not what they do." And they parted his raiment, and cast lots.*
> LUKE 23:34, KJV

Jesus had only love, compassion and forgiveness for those who crucified him. He understood that they were deluded and simply didn't know any better. He had not even an iota of hatred or anger for them.

If our minds become angry when someone says something unkind to us, then why is it not possible to simply *not* get angry? After all, they are just harmless words. Nobody has caused us any physical harm or discomfort. Ammachi explains the Christ-like attitude that we should work to develop.

> *Son, suppose somebody is talking to us angrily. Listen to everything with patience. Don't feel angry at him. Anger comes when we think that we are the body. No anger or hatred will be felt if you think that "I am not the body but the Supreme Self." Who is there to be angry at then? There is only one Self that is all-pervading. It is in everyone. We must perfectly understand that we are not the body but the Atman.*
> AMMACHI, AWAKEN CHILDREN, VOL. 1 [NOTE: THE SUPREME SELF IS TO THE ATMAN AS GOD IS TO THE ETERNAL SOUL]

Questioner: Amma, I cannot control hatred and anger.

Amma: Son, no hatred or anger will come if you consider others as your own. A mother will not consider the odor from the excreta of her own children as foul-smelling, bad or harmful. An infected, putrid smelling wound full of pus on our own body is not a problem for us because it is our own body. We can bear the smell. But if it is on somebody else's body, we cannot stand it. We don't feel any anger or hatred towards our son or daughter even if they scold or hit us. Why? Because of the feeling that they are our own. Thus, if we hold the attitude that all beings are "my own," hatred and anger will go. We can overcome these negative traits if we become aware of their terrible consequences. Anger will make us do all kinds of evil deeds. It will dissipate all our good energies. It will take away our discriminative power and make us bitter, mad and even insane. Consider anger as your first and foremost enemy. If you become aware that you are going to get angry, leave that place immediately and try to contemplate in solitude.

AMMACHI, AWAKEN CHILDREN, VOL. 3

Amma continues:

The past is a dictionary or a thesaurus. Whenever we hear, experience or do something, we automatically refer to these old pages. Through them we find meanings, interpretations or uses that were utilized before. Then we speak or act according to such references. This is reaction.

For example, someone abuses us. Suddenly the past comes to the foreground. Even without waiting for our permission, even without our knowledge, it gives references. It says, "You have been abused countless times by different people. Each time you were abused by someone, you retaliated. So do it again, abuse him back. Use stronger words and expressions." Thus, the chain of the past reveals itself: When someone offends you, you offend him in return. If someone gets angry at you, you return the anger. This is how it happens. The habitual reaction stored in the past comes up again and again. And each time you react, it becomes stronger and stronger. You and your vic-

tim each have a past. Both of you react to each other. The
other person has also been abused a number of times. Each
one reacts according to the strength and density of his past re-
actions. Both of you have volumes and volumes of giant-sized
books to which you unknowingly refer. A Mahatma (saint)
remains a blank sheet of paper, while an ordinary person
keeps on writing on the pages, continuing to add to those gi-
gantic books each time he reacts.

AMMACHI, AWAKEN CHILDREN, VOL. 5

If we can begin to glimpse the tangled tapestry of torture that simmers deep within our own psyches, then we will be able to be more gracious in forgiving others. It requires great courage to face the truth of our own egos. It takes great courage to accept responsibility for our own mental sufferings such as anger, hatred, jealousy and fear. Yet unless we do exactly that, we are doomed to suffer again and again, living in a hellish world of our own creation. It is not other persons, places or things that are to blame. God is not to blame. It is the condition of our own minds that is to blame.

If someone is unkind to us we will defend the ego and eliminate the person by avoiding him/her, removing that person from our circle of acquaintances or persecuting him/her until s/he leaves. But the same situation will repeatedly appear as other persons. Life will continue to present us with the same circumstance until we learn the lesson. If suffering is part of an identity that our egos have adopted, we will not be willing to let go of the circumstances of the suffering. For instance, if the ego believes it is a victim, then the "victim" becomes an identity, and we will believe, "I am a victim—that is who I am." The ego will seek out circumstances in which to be victimized, whether real or imagined, so that the ego can sustain its identity and, therefore, its existence. There is no end to our tangled web of numberless identities which the Buddhists call the endless knot. Once we realize the enormity and the gravity of our plight, we will surrender to God as helpless children in the dawning awareness that we are not capable of removing it alone.

Once we realize our own plight, we will see that others are suffering too, and this is why they act unkindly. They are also miserable. We may say, "But I am not miserable!" What most of us really mean when we say we are happy is that we are expecting to be happy in the future, and so we are content to endure our sufferings with the dream that we will soon get to the proverbial grass that is greener on the other side. We live in a fantasy world of expectation for cars, homes, perfect mate, perfect kids, perfect job, vacations, comfort, attention, security, ad infinitum. When we say "suffering," what we are talking about is mental suffering such as anger, hatred, fear, jealousy, insecurity, pride, anxiety, boredom, apathy and no peace. The foundation of Buddhism is the Four Noble Truths presented by the Buddha. The first Noble Truth is Life is suffering. The second Noble Truth is Suffering is caused by desires. The third Noble Truth is Suffering ends when desires end. The forth Noble Truth is Practicing the Eight-fold Path brings an end to desires.

There is a story about a young man in his early twenties who went to a fortune reader. The fortune reader studied his hands carefully for a few moments and then said, "I'm afraid I have some bad news." "What is it?" the man responded cautiously. She replied, "You will have much suffering and torment until you are fifty years old." "And then?" the man asked. The fortune reader shot back, "And then you will get used to it." We are all so accustomed to mental suffering, fear, stress and anxiety that we think it is normal. In Plato's *Cave Allegory* a group of people are born and live in a dark cave, never having any knowledge of the outside world. They live in awful conditions. One day, one among them finds a way out and discovers a much better world full of sunshine, trees, warm dry beds and good food. Returning to the cave, he tries to convince the others to leave the cave, but none of them would believe him. They were afraid to consider such a thing. After all, their condition was how it had always been for them and their fathers and mothers before them. They are suspicious and refuse to leave the cave. In the same way, there is a better way to live our lives in a fearless, stress free and blissful state of mind. That is merging with Christ.

There are two keys to forgiving. One is to realize we are all deluded and suffering from the same delusions, and the second is to try to realize that we are all connected as one whole. Regarding the latter point, we must try to come to an understanding that the

I AM that is in you is the same I AM that is in me and everyone else. It is the ego that makes us feel that others are separate from us. Peter asked Jesus about forgiving.

> *Then came Peter to him, and said, "Lord, how oft shall my brother sin against me, and I forgive him? Till seven times?"*

> *Jesus saith unto him, "I say not unto thee, until seven times: but, until seventy times seven."*   MATTHEW 18:21-22 - KJV

By seventy times seven, Jesus was actually saying we should forgive an endless amount of times (who is going to count to 490 efforts to forgive). Jesus is trying to tell us how to be happy. If we carry anger, hatred and enmity in our hearts toward anyone, no matter what they have done, it will poison us, and destruction and suffering will be our bitter fruit. We will reap what we sow.

Jesus says if we don't forgive others, then God will not forgive us.

> *For if ye forgive men their trespasses, your heavenly Father will also forgive you: But if ye forgive not men their trespasses, neither will your Father forgive your trespasses.*
>   MATTHEW 6:14-15 - KJV

In other words, if we allow anger and hatred to ferment and grow in our minds, it will close the door to our hearts and that is where God lives. We ourselves will unwittingly turn the valve which shuts off God's grace. God, as the life presence of the I AM, is really the source of true happiness. The more negative mental feelings we have, the more that God is pushed out of our lives. The more this happens, the more alone we feel, the more afraid we become, the more hatred we harbor, and so it is a dizzying downward spiral into our own self-created hell. We may think we are justified in hating someone, but in so doing we only destroy our own happiness.

If we judge others, our hearts will become as stone. Judging others denies the truth of our unity in God. Compassion and love cannot survive in a judgmental mind in the same way that grass will not grow in a desert. Again Jesus says about judging others:

> *"Be ye therefore merciful, as your Father also is merciful.*
> *Judge not, and ye shall not be judged: condemn not, and ye*
> *shall not be condemned: forgive, and ye shall be forgiven...*
> LUKE 6:36-37, KJV

The ego likes to judge others and to find fault with them because the ego is basically insecure, and so it must debase others in order to exalt itself. The ego is adept at finding faulty, nasty, broken people everywhere. The ego comes equipped with the latest state-of-the-art sinner radar.

Most of us are blind when it comes to seeing our own faults. If we could see and accept our own faults, we would not be so quick to judge and condemn others. The Lord says:

> *And why beholdest thou the mote that is in thy brother's eye,*
> *but perceivest not the beam that is in thine own eye? Either how*
> *canst thou say to thy brother, Brother, let me pull out the mote*
> *that is in thine eye, when thou thyself beholdest not the beam*
> *that is in thine own eye? Thou hypocrite, cast out first the beam*
> *out of thine own eye, and then shalt thou see clearly to pull out*
> *the mote that is in thy brother's eye.*   LUKE 6:41-42, KJV

Jesus is saying we are so focused on the little faults in someone else but fail utterly to see our own giant faults. Jesus gives more good advice as to how to deal with those who torment us or invoke our anger:

> *Ye have heard that it hath been said, "An eye for an eye, and a*
> *tooth for a tooth:" But I say unto you, "That ye resist not evil:*
> *but whosoever shall smite thee on thy right cheek, turn to him*
> *the other also. And if any man will sue thee at the law, and*
> *take away thy coat, let him have thy cloke also. And whoso-*
> *ever shall compel thee to go a mile, go with him twain. Give to*
> *him that asketh thee, and from him that would borrow of thee*
> *turn not thou away."*

> *Ye have heard that it hath been said, "Thou shalt love thy*
> *neighbour, and hate thine enemy." But I say unto you, "Love*
> *your enemies, bless them that curse you, do good to them that*

hate you, and pray for them which despitefully use you, and
persecute you; That ye may be the children of your Father
which is in heaven: for he maketh his sun to rise on the evil
and on the good, and sendeth rain on the just and on the un-
just. For if ye love them which love you, what reward have ye?
do not even the publicans the same? And if ye salute your
brethren only, what do ye more than others? do not even the
publicans so? Be ye therefore perfect, even as your Father
which is in heaven is perfect."   MATTHEW 5:38-48, KJV

Love our enemies, bless them that curse us, do good to those that hate us and pray for those who persecute us. Why? The main reason is this course of action will reflect the truth of our own beings, our oneness and unity in God, and we can be instrumental in putting an end to hatred as an act of compassion. But there is also a good self-serving reason to love our enemies. Without detractors and persecutors to revile us, it would be more difficult to make any spiritual progress. We are in need of circumstances that test our humility and our surrender to God. There is a story about a holy man. In the village where he lived, a certain man who was an atheist was always persecuting him and antagonizing him. For years this went on, and even though the holy man's congregation was often angered by the atheist's actions and sharp words, the holy man never complained. One day the atheist died suddenly, and the holy man and only a few of the congregation and villagers attended the funeral. The disciples were astonished to see the holy man weeping and grieving. Later they asked him about this. He replied that the congregation and villagers only said or did what they thought would please the holy man. The atheist was the only one available to test the holy man's detachment, compassion, forgiveness and patience. So he truly was grieving to see him depart.

To be less important does not mean to be self-demeaning or to look critically or in an unforgiving way at ourselves. That would still be focusing on I...I...I. If we stop thinking about ourselves we will have space to love others, forgive others and have compassion for others. If someone says something unkind we will simply think, "So what?" We might even think, "Maybe he's right. I'll think about it." Wouldn't that be wonderfully liberating? The idea that someone has criticized us will not be important because we will no longer have an exaggerated sense of self-importance. This is the power and the wonder of humility. True humility arises out of the understanding of our oneness in God.

As the saying goes, "To err is human, but to forgive is Divine." Forgiveness is another way to express our unity in the one living God.

17

Love Rules

Innocence comes when there is love. Divine Love makes you like a child. Love makes you accept anything and everything. The lover does whatever the beloved says. We can see this even in ordinary love. When one really loves, one's intellect becomes empty; one stops thinking. No thoughts, no mind, nothing. Only love remains. This forgetting-all-else kind of love culminates in innocence." AMMACHI, AWAKEN CHILDREN, VOL. 4

The author will feel this book to be a success if the reader will come away from it with the conviction that, according to Jesus, the practice of love is the most important aspect of our spiritual path: love for God and love for others. This is the road to true and lasting happiness. In love there is peace, and in peace there is love. Love is the light of the world. Where there is no love, darkness prevails, and there can be no peace.

Every act of love is a work of peace no matter how small.
MOTHER TERESA

Jesus makes it very clear that the most important activity for any person is loving God and loving others:

Love the Lord your God with all your heart and with all your soul and with all your mind. This is the first and greatest commandment. And the second is like it: Love your neighbor as yourself. All the Law and the Prophets hang on these two commandments. MATTHEW 22:36-40, NIV

In order to be a follower of Jesus, we are required to take the practice of love more seriously than anything else. This is also true in other religions such as the path of the Bhaktas (devotion to God) in Hinduism and the devotional ecstasy practiced by the Sufis in Islam. In Buddhism it is the practice of compassion for others and devotion to the teacher.

Buddha comments on love for others:

> *Just as a mother would protect her only child at the risk of her*
> *own life, even so, cultivate a boundless heart towards all beings.*
> *Let your thoughts of boundless love pervade the whole world.*
> SUTTA NIPATA, 149-150

In addition to Jesus, other saints in this tradition include Narada who wrote the Bhakti Sutras, Hafiz, Ramprasad, Rumi, Ramakrishna and Ammachi. All of these great saints taught the path of love for God and others as a path to liberation.

Once love is felt, it will become obvious that we have gotten off-track to a great degree. Having been seduced by the ego at an early age, we have long forgotten how to love or even what love feels like. This is why the many scriptures and sayings of Jesus which direct us to the practice of love are ignored. It is as if they were written in every Bible with invisible ink. Only people who have discovered love will notice these scriptures. When we say, "Let's talk about loving God and others," it is as though the audience becomes so many stone statues. Then a voice whispers from behind the curtain and says, "They can't hear you." We become the proverbial deer staring with glazed eyes into the approaching headlights of divine love. There are numerous websites that offer ready made sermons, and yet the subject of the universal nature of love and how to go about becoming a loving person is almost non-existent. This is astonishing when viewed from the perspective that the practice of love is the most important spark of wisdom that Jesus had to give us. This is what he talked about the most. In Mark 12:31 the Lord tells us there are no commandments greater than loving God and loving our neighbors. A few paragraphs back, we read in Matthew 22:36-40 that there is *no commandment greater* than loving God with everything we can muster, and the second commandment, to love our neighbor, is like it. All the law and all the prophets, meaning everything and anything of a religious or spiritual nature, hang on these two commandments. How could this be said any more clearly? And yet there are few who give even a thought to worshipping in the church of the heart. Preachers do not mention it from the pulpit. In contrast, Jesus says there is not much point in talking about anything else. There are few books written about love. The reason for this is simple. We have no love in our hearts, and we do not know that we have no love. We don't relate to love or understand love or have any awareness of love. We are unable to feel love. Because of this, we have become the walking dead that Jesus referred to when he told the man to "...let the dead bury their dead" (Matthew 8:22). This was the condition of the Pharisees and the condition of many who claim to be followers of Jesus today.

Jesus' very life and his willingness to die on the cross for our benefit is an expression of his boundless love. Even as he was hanging with nails in his hands and feet, tormented and suffering, he asked God to forgive his accusers and executioners because they did not know what they were doing. Who among us has that much love? Are we able to love our enemies and pray for those who curse us?

Jesus tells us that unless we become innocent as a little child, we are not getting into heaven (Matthew 18:3). As Amma says in her previous quote, innocence comes when there is love. Love and innocence go hand in hand. Love is the measure of all things. If love is absent, then scripture, other persons and even our own beings are meaningless. When love is present, the most insignificant of actions, people, things and events have meaning and are endowed with sublime beauty. Love makes life full and complete. Without love, there is only the dry, barren wasteland of living death. We have eyes but do not see, ears but do not hear. Without love, life becomes death, and the intellect becomes the executioner.

In this world where time and space appear to be temporarily permanent, there is an unseen glue that binds all things. This invisible glue is love. It is the web of eternity in which we and every object and creature in this universe are perpetually bound. Love is the stage upon which the dance of time and space play out their eternal dramas. It is as if all of the beings and objects of the universe exploded out of the singularity of God's formless nature but were tethered to each other and to God by rubber bands of love. Love is the unseen attracting force. Love is the all-encompassing resonance of God's being which binds everything together. Love is the expression of unity in diversity, and therefore, love is the direct presence of God in this world of duality. If we fail to know or experience this then we become deluded and self-centered, buying into the deception that we are all separate – every man for himself. Wherever there is genuine and sincere love, there we will find God. Wherever compassion and mercy are expressed, there also is God.

The existence of love cannot be confirmed by the five senses, but rather it must be felt to be known. Like electricity, love cannot be seen, but we can feel it. We can also observe its effects and thereby induce its presence or its reality. Love is spiritual and is of the heart, whereas the mind and intellect are of the world of duality. When our minds are removed from the senses and absorbed by the heart, we see only unity and oneness. When the mind is foreign to love and absorbed only in the intellect and its five windows of the senses, we see the universe and all beings as diversity, division and separation. Out of this separation arises the ego.

The scriptural evidence to support our position that love is the capstone on the pyramid of life and the single-minded goal of spiritual practice, is overwhelmingly complete. The following is a presentation of these key New Testament scriptures.

According to Jesus:

> You have heard that it was said, "Eye for eye, and tooth for tooth." But I tell you, do not resist an evil person. If someone strikes you on the right cheek, turn to him the other also. And if someone wants to sue you and take your tunic, let him have your cloak as well. If someone forces you to go one mile, go with him two miles. Give to the one who asks you, and do not turn away from the one who wants to borrow from you.
>
> MATTHEW 5:38-42, NIV

You have heard that it was said, "Love your neighbor and hate your enemy." But I tell you: Love your enemies and pray for those who persecute you, that you may be sons of your Father in heaven. He causes his sun to rise on the evil and the good, and sends rain on the righteous and the unrighteous. If you love those who love you, what reward will you get? Are not even the tax collectors doing that? And if you greet only your brothers, what are you doing more than others? Do not even pagans do that? Be perfect, therefore, as your heavenly Father is perfect. MATTHEW 5:43-48, NIV

...honor your father and mother, and love your neighbor as yourself. MATTHEW 19:19, NIV

"Teacher, which is the greatest commandment in the Law?"

Jesus replied: "'Love the Lord your God with all your heart and with all your soul and with all your mind.' This is the first and greatest commandment. And the second is like it: 'Love your neighbor as yourself.' All the Law and the Prophets hang on these two commandments." MATTHEW 22:36-40, NIV

One of the teachers of the law came and heard them debating. Noticing that Jesus had given them a good answer, he asked him, "Of all the commandments, which is the most important?"

"The most important one," answered Jesus, "is this: 'Hear, O Israel, the Lord our God, the Lord is one. Love the Lord your God with all your heart and with all your soul and with all your mind and with all your strength.' The second is this: 'Love your neighbor as yourself.' There is no commandment greater than these." MARK 12:28-31, NIV

On one occasion an expert in the law stood up to test Jesus. "Teacher," he asked, "what must I do to inherit eternal life?"

"What is written in the Law?" he replied. "How do you read it?"

He answered: "'Love the Lord your God with all your heart and with all your soul and with all your strength and with all your mind'; and, 'Love your neighbor as yourself.'"

"You have answered correctly," Jesus replied. "Do this and you will live."   LUKE 10:25-28, NIV

But I tell you who hear me: Love your enemies, do good to those who hate you, ...   LUKE 6:27, NIV

If you love those who love you, what credit is that to you? Even "sinners" love those who love them.   LUKE 6:32, NIV

But love your enemies, do good to them, and lend to them without expecting to get anything back. Then your reward will be great, and you will be sons of the Most High, because he is kind to the ungrateful and wicked.   LUKE 6:35, NIV

A new command I give you: Love one another. As I have loved you, so you must love one another. By this all men will know that you are my disciples, if you love one another.
                                JOHN 13:34-35, NIV

My command is this: Love each other as I have loved you. Greater love has no one than this, that he lay down his life for his friends.   JOHN 15:12-13, NIV

This is my command: Love each other.   JOHN 15:17, NIV

And Paul says:

The commandments, "Do not commit adultery," "Do not murder," "Do not steal," "Do not covet," and whatever other commandment there may be, are summed up in this one rule: "Love your neighbor as yourself." Love does no harm to its neighbor. Therefore love is the fulfillment of the law.
                                ROMANS 13:9-10, NIV

The entire law is summed up in a single command: "Love your neighbor as yourself."   GALATIANS 5:14, NIV

But the man who loves God is known by God.
                                1 CORINTHIANS 8:3, NIV

If I speak in the tongues of men and of angels, but have not love, I am only a resounding gong or a clanging cymbal. If I have the gift of prophecy and can fathom all mysteries and all knowledge, and if I have a faith that can move mountains, but have not love, I am nothing. If I give all I possess to the poor and surrender my body to the flames, but have not love, I gain nothing. Love is patient, love is kind. It does not envy, it does not boast, it is not proud.   1 CORINTHIANS. 13:1-4, NIV

Love does not delight in evil but rejoices with the truth.
1 CORINTHIANS. 13:6, NIV

Love never fails. But where there are prophecies, they will cease; where there are tongues, they will be stilled; where there is knowledge, it will pass away.   1 CORINTHIANS 13:8, NIV

And now these three remain: faith, hope and love. But the greatest of these is love.   1 CORINTHIANS 13:13, NIV

Do everything in love.   1 CORINTHIANS 16:14, NIV

The only thing that counts is faith expressing itself through love.
GALATIANS 5:6, NIV

Be imitators of God, therefore, as dearly loved children and live a life of love, just as Christ loved us and gave himself up for us as a fragrant offering and sacrifice to God.
EPHESIANS 5:1-2, NIV

Therefore, as God's chosen people, holy and dearly loved, clothe yourselves with compassion, kindness, humility, gentleness and patience. Bear with each other and forgive whatever grievances you may have against one another. Forgive as the Lord forgave you. And over all these virtues put on love, which binds them all together in perfect unity.
COLOSSIANS 3:12-14, NIV

And James:

If you really keep the royal law found in Scripture, "Love your neighbor as yourself," you are doing right.   JAMES 2:8, NIV

Peter:

> *Now that you have purified yourselves by obeying the truth so that you have sincere love for your brothers, love one another deeply, from the heart.* 1 PETER 1:22, NIV

> *Above all, love each other deeply, because love covers over a multitude of sins.* 1 PETER 4:8, NIV

And John:

> *This is the message you heard from the beginning: We should love one another.* 1 JOHN 3:11

> *We know that we have passed from death to life, because we love our brothers. Anyone who does not love remains in death.* 1 JOHN 3:14, NIV

> *This is how we know what love is: Jesus Christ laid down his life for us. And we ought to lay down our lives for our brothers. If anyone has material possessions and sees his brother in need but has no pity on him, how can the love of God be in him? Dear children, let us not love with words or tongue but with actions and in truth.* 1 JOHN 3:16-18

> *Dear friends, let us love one another, for love comes from God. Everyone who loves has been born of God and knows God.* 1 JOHN 4:7, NIV

> *Whoever does not love does not know God, because God is love.* 1 JOHN 4:8, NIV

> *Dear friends, since God so loved us, we also ought to love one another. No one has ever seen God; but if we love one another, God lives in us and his love is made complete in us.* 1 JOHN 4:11-12, NIV

> *And so we know and rely on the love God has for us. God is love. Whoever lives in love lives in God, and God in him.* 1 JOHN 4:16, NIV

There is no fear in love. But perfect love drives out fear, because fear has to do with punishment. The one who fears is not made perfect in love. 1 JOHN 4:18, NIV

If anyone says, "I love God," yet hates his brother, he is a liar. For anyone who does not love his brother, whom he has seen, cannot love God, whom he has not seen. And he has given us this command: Whoever loves God must also love his brother. 1 JOHN 4:20-21, NIV

And now, dear lady, I am not writing you a new command but one we have had from the beginning. I ask that we love one another. And this is love: that we walk in obedience to his commands. As you have heard from the beginning, his command is that you walk in love. 2 JOHN 1:5-6, NIV

The operative word in these scriptures is love. Love is the central core of the teachings of Jesus the Christ and also the motivation behind his ultimate sacrifice on the cross. We should note that when Jesus advises us to love God, he does not endorse any particular sectarian form of God. Rather he tells us to love "your" god, which is to say love God in whatever form we understand Him to be. In the Greek transliteration it is love, the "God of you." Jesus understood that it was not the form that was important, but rather the loving that was the central issue because God *is* love.

When the ego stands aside, an unbroken stream of pure unconditional love naturally pours out from the depths of our beings, like a fountain or waterfall, to all creatures and persons and all of nature. It does not ask if others are worthy of receiving our love. There is no judgement. This is God's love or the love that *is* God.

We say that God adores the humble, but in reality God's love and grace are always pouring out equally to all. It is our egotism and vanity that shuts off the valve to God's pipeline of grace. God never withdraws. To what place would the omnipresent withdraw?

For most of us, loving God and others is a mechanism to get what we want. We pretend to love God by going to church or by making offerings so that God will bless our business, heal our sickness, find our mate or give us wealth. Few of us have found our way to the river of love for the sake of love alone. We love our spouses as long as our spouses give us what we want in return. We love our friends as long as they make us feel secure or provide us with some other happiness. Our relationships revolve around the ego and its attachments and aversions. Swami Vivekananda called this "shopkeeper's love."

Understandably, there are some who believe that the second of Jesus' two commandments, love your neighbor as your self, was not intended to include *everyone*. For a person who lacks any understanding of our oneness and our inherent unity, loving everyone makes no sense. Such an idea belongs to the realm of love in which all beings and the entire universe are connected. Most of us dwell in the realm of the intellect, which sees only separateness and division. Therefore, the following scripture is sometimes presented as evidence that Jesus did not intend for us to love everyone.

> On one occasion an expert in the law stood up to test Jesus. "Teacher," he asked, "what must I do to inherit eternal life?"
>
> "What is written in the Law?" he [Jesus] replied. "How do you read it?"
>
> He [the expert] answered: "'Love the Lord your God with all your heart and with all your soul and with all your strength and with all your mind'; and, 'Love your neighbor as yourself.'"
>
> "You have answered correctly," Jesus replied. "Do this and you will live."
>
> But he wanted to justify himself, so he asked Jesus, "And who is my neighbor?"
>
> In reply Jesus said: "A man was going down from Jerusalem to Jericho, when he fell into the hands of robbers. They stripped him of his clothes, beat him and went away, leaving him half-dead. A priest happened to be going down the same road, and when he saw the man, he passed by on the other side. So too, a Levite, when he came to the place and saw him, passed by on the other side. But a Samaritan, as he traveled, came where the

*man was; and when he saw him, he took pity on him. He went
to him and bandaged his wounds, pouring on oil and wine.
Then he put the man on his own donkey, took him to an inn
and took care of him. The next day he took out two silver coins
and gave them to the innkeeper. 'Look after him,' he said, 'and
when I return, I will reimburse you for any extra expense you
may have.' Which of these three do you think was a neighbor to
the man who fell into the hands of robbers?"*

*The expert in the law replied, "The one who had mercy on
him." Jesus told him, "Go and do likewise."*
LUKE 10:25-37, NIV (brackets by author)

The deception that we should love only selected people is vanquished for all time by reading in Matthew:

*You have heard that it was said, 'Love your neighbor and hate
your enemy.' But I tell you: Love your enemies and pray for
those who persecute you, that you may be sons of your Father
in heaven. He causes his sun to rise on the evil and the good,
and sends rain on the righteous and the unrighteous. If you
love those who love you, what reward will you get? Are not
even the tax collectors doing that? And if you greet only your
brothers, what are you doing more than others? Do not even
pagans do that?*
MATTHEW 5:43-47, NIV

Buddha also reveals the truth of universal and unconditional love
for all:

*That great cloud rains down on all whether their nature is su-
perior or inferior. The light of the sun and the moon illuminates the whole world, both him who does well and him who
does ill, both him who stands high and him who stands low.*
SADHARMAPUNDARIKA SUTRA 5

If we are to love our enemies, pray for those who persecute us
and love everyone even as the sun equally rises on the good and
the evil, then what are we to make of the parable of the good Samaritan? The central point is the Samaritan loved his neighbor
while the others did not, and so we are advised to do like the
Good Samaritan. Also, Jesus was responding to a question from

an expert in the Jewish religious law. This expert was of the opinion that his religious order was *the* spiritual bowl of cherries. Thus, Jesus is speaking to him between the lines. Not without coincidence, Jesus uses a priest and a Levite as the bad examples. The Levites are the special Jewish tribe from which all priests come. Only a Levite could be a priest or rabbi. In stark contrast is the Samaritan. According to the *Encyclopedia Britannica*, Flavius Josephus (37-96? C.E.) in his historical treatise *Jewish Antiquities* is deliberately defamatory in portraying the Samaritans. The Encyclopedia goes on to tell us that the Jews regarded the Samaritans as mongrels and refused their aid in the building of the Second Temple. By this story, Jesus is again telling us we should love everyone, no matter who they are or what their religion, and not just our own circle of friends.

> *Do not judge, and you will not be judged. Do not condemn, and you will not be condemned. Forgive, and you will be forgiven.*
> LUKE 6:37, NIV

Does this mean we should not judge a person for murder, find him guilty and send him to prison? An offender should be in prison to protect others and to protect him from incurring more sin. What the Lord means is that we should still love this man. We should realize that he too is a spiritual brother that has made an error. He too is a child of God, the I AM, for all eternity. Dealing with his error in a pragmatic way, we nonetheless continue to love him and accept him as one of us. We weep for the suffering that he has made for himself and others, but we never condemn him in spirit. We never judge him in spirit, and this is the difference. The essential nature of the murderer or any transgressor is always good, albeit hidden.

> *"I was a stranger and you did not invite me in, I needed clothes and you did not clothe me, I was sick and in prison and you did not look after me."*

> *They also will answer, "Lord, when did we see you hungry or thirsty or a stranger or needing clothes or sick or in prison, and did not help you?"*

*He will reply, "I tell you the truth, whatever you did not do for
one of the least of these, you did not do for me."*

MATTHEW 25:43-45, NIV

A person who abides in love abides in God. Jesus is saying that if
we neglect any person, even one who is in prison, and in fact the
very least of all people in any regard, we have neglected Him.
This is a radical saying and is not comprehensible unless we understand the underlying unity of all beings.

Buddha echoes this point of view:

*If you do not tend one another, then who is there to tend you?
Whoever would tend me, he should tend the sick.*

VINYA, MAHAVAGGA, 8:26:3

EGO IS ANTI-LOVE

It is not possible for love to manifest within us if the ego is pre-
dominant. When the ego is limited, the flow of love will increase.
Love reaches out to others and to God, while the ego withdraws
into a prison of self-created desires, attachments and afflictions.
The ego is the constant pounding of I-am-this and I-am-that,
while love asserts there is no "I" but only "we" or "you." The ego
is driven by the undercurrent of "what's in it for me," while love
constantly asks "what can I do for you." The ego is me... me... me,
while love is you... you... you. It is very important that we try to
understand the difference between the ego and love and see that
the two points of view conflict each other. In a great master like
Jesus, the ego has become permanently subservient or non-existent. If God is love, then Satan is the ego.

Very few of us experience even a shred of love in our day to day life.
This absence, this darkness, makes it very difficult to comprehend
any discussion about love or the meaning of love. We hear about
love with a blank look in our eyes. This is why we do not notice
Jesus' commandments regarding love and why there are no sermons, books or pamphlets written about it. We have forgotten all
about love, and we are not aware that we have no love in our

hearts. When questioned about it, we may think that we have love. We may say we love the Denver Broncos football team, but what we really mean is we are attached to the pleasure we get from watching them win. We are in it for "me," and pure love has nothing to do with the equation. We may say we love our wives or husbands but we are really in the relationship to have someone cater to our complex menu of needs. As long as both parties agree to this, and as long as both parties feel the other is satisfying their needs, the relationship endures. You scratch my back, and I'll scratch your back. As soon as one of the parties feel they are coming up short, it's off to divorce court, followed by a renewed search to find another co-conspirator in the siege of the ego's insatiable appetite. We may say we love our children, but we are often seeing them as no more than extensions of our ego. We encourage them to do well so that their success will reflect well on us. Or we use them as objects to control and manipulate so the ego can feel dominant. In the latter case the parent may attempt to convince the child that it is a loser so that it will remain the slave of the parent's ego. Most of us have no awareness as to what pure selfless love feels like. Some mothers may have experienced it, but only for their own children and no others, and some have experienced pure love for their pets. Children have pure love, but the ego soon drives it away. So we can begin to understand why there is so little discussion about love and how to practice love in church literature, sermons, doctrine and books.

When the ego is gone, love flows unimpeded from the center of our being as a wellspring, a river of divine grace. This manifests outwardly as pure selfless love for all beings. Compassion is love in action.

> *If the mind is to become pure, love for God should come. Virtues should come. The main obstacle to becoming closer to God is our selfishness. Selfishness automatically falls off when we feel compassion for others. Just as the saline taste disappears when fresh water is constantly added to salt water, the bad will leave us when good is constantly thought of. See how many poor people are suffering around us without shelter, clothes, food or proper medical care. We will lose our selfishness when we become compassionate to them.*
>
> AMMACHI, AWAKEN CHILDREN, VOL. 1

A person who has genuine love has already found the kingdom of God, for the Bible tells us that God *is* Love (1 John 4:8, 1 John 4:16). God and Love are exactly the same thing. Genuine love is fearless. It doesn't care what the other person thinks of us. Genuine love does not expect anything in return for the love we give. Genuine love is like the sun that shines on all people regardless of what they have done. It simply shines for its own sake and expects nothing in return. A person who can step into pure love has arrived at the kingdom of God. If we go away from love by allowing anger and hatred to control our lives, then we go away from Heaven, and we unwittingly become bedfellows with hell. If we destroy love, our lives will become hell as certainly as darkness must fall when the sun disappears from the sky. Love purifies all hearts and makes life sweet and fun. Love turns a dreary dungeon into a sunny day at the county fair. Love is the liberator. Love is the flow of life itself. Love is the destroyer of ignorance, for the ego cannot survive in the presence of pure love. It takes courage to surrender to love because it means the death of the ego. Love only gives and does not take.

The following quote is from the *Dhammapada,* which is a collection of teachings that were spoken by the Buddha 2,500 years ago as he preached to the multitudes that gathered to absorb his wisdom. What follows are the opening lines from Chapter One, called *The Twin Verses.* In it the Buddha, the enlightened one, tells us that hatred can only be cured with love and that what we are is the result of what we think.

> *All that we are is the result of what we have thought: it is founded on our thoughts, it is made up of our thoughts. If a man speaks or acts with an evil thought, pain follows him, as the wheel follows the foot of the ox that draws the wagon.*

> *All that we are is the result of what we have thought: it is founded on our thoughts, it is made up of our thoughts. If a man speaks or acts with a pure thought, happiness follows him, like a shadow that never leaves him.*

> *"He abused me, he beat me, he defeated me, he robbed me,"– in those who harbor such thoughts hatred will never cease.*

"He abused me, he beat me, he defeated me, he robbed me,"—
in those who do not harbor such thoughts hatred will cease.

For never does hatred cease by hatred here below: hatred ceases
by love; this is an eternal law.

The world does not know that we must all come to an end
here; but those who know, their quarrels cease at once.

THE DHAMMAPADA, TRANSLATED BY IRVING BABBITT

If we allow anger and hatred into our hearts for any reason whatsoever then it is we who have lost. In doing so, we deny Christ. If we
learn to accept and love others regardless of their trespasses, regardless of their sins, paying no attention to differences in race,
religion or nationality, then we have won a great and lasting victory.

Love is the true guiding light. One who has found pure selfless
love has found God. Therefore, let us study the ego to understand
how it takes us away from love. Let us struggle to find love so that
we may know peace and happiness in all things and in all worlds.

Conclusion

The path to God is difficult only because it is obscured by our own minds. Possessed of an ego, we see only separation where unity exists. This sense of separation, or I-thought, is an illusion in the same way that the earth appears to be flat but is really round and in the same way that the sun appears to circle the earth, but in fact, it is the earth that orbits the sun. Love, the presence of unity, the antidote, is foreign to us, having long departed along with our childhood innocence. Yet there is hope for us if we are willing to search for the eternal radiance that shines at the center of our own beings. Jesus said the path to salvation is in loving God with all of our hearts, minds and souls, and loving our neighbors as our own selves. Therefore, let us embark upon a path of love, kindness and compassion. Let us embrace this world with all of its evils and infirmities and set a course of selfless surrender and service to the well being of others. There is no other reasonable relationship to this world than to be a servant, an ambassador of love, a friend to all. Let us accept every human being as our brother or sister. Having disinherited our selfish obsessions, may our ego become no more than a corpse bereft of any continuing self-serving desires and aspirations. This is truly the way to help ourselves. Taking refuge in God alone, we gratefully accept everything that comes our way, for better or for worse, as God's will. Having steadfastly entered into the narrow path of love and surrender, God will surely come to guide us.

> Expect nothing from this world
> Not friendship; not romance
> > not wealth
> > not joy
> > not happiness
>
> Never forget that suffering
> > is the nature of this world
> > enslaved as it is
> > > by the ego

Give your love and compassion
    to the world
Be a good friend
    and a soulful companion
Serve the poor
– they are divine
    Do whatever is necessary
    to relieve the suffering of others

Never forget that true happiness
    is found in what you give
    and not what you take

Love comes from within you
    and pours out to the world

This is the Eternal Way

Appendix A

Controversy Regarding the Origin of Paul's Pastoral Letters

Most biblical scholars now agree that several New Testament books attributed to Paul are, in fact, forgeries written by an anonymous person. Compelling evidence reveals that 1 and 2 Timothy and Titus were penned decades after the death of Paul. These three books are often referred to as the "Pastorals" because they deal almost entirely with the office of a Christian pastor. Let us take an overview of the arguments.

1. It was not until 100 years after the death of Paul that the Pastoral letters surfaced. They are conspicuously missing from the earliest manuscripts and the earliest lists of Paul's works. In contrast, the other genuine works of Paul are referenced and quoted in independent works from around 95 C.E. It is believed that Paul died in Rome circa 67 C.E. The sudden appearance of the Pastorals a century later was also accompanied by many other pseudo-Pauline works such as the *Acts of Paul, Correspondence of Paul and Seneca, Prayer of the Apostle Paul and the Acts of Paul and Thecla.* These forgeries and also forgeries written in the name of Peter were common into the second century and until about 400 C.E.

2. The ecclesiastical presentation in the Pastorals, having to do with the structure of the church and clergy, are much more defined and specific than the undoubtedly genuine letters of Paul. The Pastorals echo the tone of Christian literature that was being written in the second century. Paul's genuine letters make almost no reference to church officials except in a vague and open-ended way, such as the word "elders." There is one mention in Philippians 1:1 of "bishops and deacons," but Paul does not indicate that these words are representative of an organizational church hierarchy. There

is very little in Paul's non-Pastoral works that would lead us to believe Paul was endorsing any hierarchical order.

In this regard, the Pastorals are as different as night and day. Bishops, deacons and elders are now revealed as official church offices, and the spiritual gift of prophecy, which was so prominent in the genuine works, is now barely visible. This makes sense because the usurpers, the bishops and deacons, can't have prophets appearing with prophetic revelations outside their own circle of power. Timothy 3 describes the qualifications for bishops and deacons, and 1 Timothy 5:17-18 goes so far as to prescribe payment for church officials.

The idea of apostolic succession, whereby the bishops and deacons derive their power from a successive lineage that is traced back to the apostles, appears for the first time in the Pastorals. For the bishops and deacons this becomes their certificate hanging on the wall.

3. There are many differences in language and diction when comparing the Pastorals with the genuine works of Paul. Religious ideas in the Pastorals are presented with phrases that are common to the Greek world but inconsistent with Paul's genuine works. One example is the phrase "sound teaching" (1 Timothy 1:10, etc.). In the genuine works, Paul consistently uses the term "gospel" to denote teaching. Not only is the phrase "sound teaching" absent from Paul's works, but it appears nowhere else in the New Testament. In another curiosity, Timothy and Titus are treated as underlings in the Pastorals. Timothy is referred to as "my child in the faith" (1 Timothy 1:2). In Paul's genuine letters, Timothy is referred to as an equal with phrases such as "brother" (Colossians 1:1; 2 Corinthians 1:1), "fellow-worker" (Romans 16:21), and "servant" of Christ (Philippians 1:1). The author of the Pastorals relegates Timothy to a subordinate position because the Pastorals attempt to show that Paul was the origin of the concept of a church hierarchy. To be consistent with this hierarchical view, Paul became the boss and Timothy the hired hand. In this way, the insertion of a hi-

erarchy into a fledgling Christianity is presented as being blessed by Paul. Paul's authority is stolen to legalize the lust of a few to have power over the many.

In true fascist form, the author of the Pastorals attacks and abuses those with other views, while the original Paul would discuss and debate with them. In 1 Timothy 6:3-4 anyone who follows a different philosophy is no more than a worm to be crushed under one's heal:

> *If anyone teaches false doctrines and does not agree to the sound instruction of our Lord Jesus Christ and to godly teaching, he is conceited and understands nothing. He has an unhealthy interest in controversies and quarrels about words that result in envy, strife, malicious talk, evil suspicions and constant friction between men of corrupt mind, who have been robbed of the truth and who think that godliness is a means to financial gain.*
> 1 TIMOTHY 6:3-5, NIV

4. On a number of occasions the author of the Pastorals tips his hand and reveals a date of writing that is beyond Paul's time. In 2 Timothy 1:5 the author references Timothy's "grandmother Lois" and mother "Eunice" as being the origin of Timothy's sincere faith. Such a way of referring to 3 generations of Christians is consistent with the early second century but not for Paul's time.

Paul expected the Second Coming to be an event for his own lifetime, while the author of the Pastorals did not. In 2 Timothy 2:2, Paul tells Timothy to present Paul's teaching to *faithful men* who, in turn, *will be able to teach others.*

Because he thought the world would be ending soon, Paul discouraged marriage, while the author of the Pastorals berates any teacher who forbids marriage. The following is typical of Paul's view of marriage:

> *Now about virgins: I have no command from the Lord, but I give a judgment as one who by the Lord's mercy is trustworthy. Because of the present crisis, I think that it is*

good for you to remain as you are. Are you married? Do not seek a divorce. Are you unmarried? Do not look for a wife. But if you do marry, you have not sinned; and if a virgin marries, she has not sinned. But those who marry will face many troubles in this life, and I want to spare you this. 1 CORINTHIANS 7:25-28, NIV

5.   The author of the Pastorals is frequently seen tripping over himself as would be typical of any liar. This suggests a make-it-up-as-you-go mentality. In 2 Timothy 4:10-11 "Paul" complains that all his comrades have deserted him with the exception of Luke. A few verses down the road in 2 Timothy 4:21, we see the author forgetting this, and "Paul" says good-bye to *all the brethren* and specifically names four of them! In 2 Timothy 4:6 "Paul" states that he awaits his execution, but at the letter's end, "Paul" makes an odd request of Timothy:

When you come, bring the cloak that I left with Carpus at Troas, and my scrolls, especially the parchments.
2 TIMOTHY 4:13, NIV

What makes this request raise one's eyebrows is in understanding that it would take months for Timothy to get the items to Paul, and Paul would have been executed by then.

In summary, it is the many glaring inconsistencies between the Pastoral letters and the authentic letters of Paul that leads most scholars to conclude that 1 and 2 Timothy and Titus are forgeries.

Bibliography

The author wishes to thank the following for quotations that appeared in this book:

Quotations from the following used with permission of MA Center
© Copyright MA Center 1989 through 1998

Awaken Children, volumes 1 through 9
by Swami Amritaswarupananda
Mata Amritanandamayi Center
P.O. Box 613, San Ramon, CA 94583
www.ammachi.org

Quotations from the following used with permission of MA Center
© Copyright MA Center 1997 and 1999

Eternal Wisdom, Parts 1 and 2
by Swami Jnanamritananda
Mata Amritanandamayi Center
P.O. Box 613, San Ramon, CA 94583
www.ammachi.org

Quotations from the following used with permission of MA Center.
© Copyright Mata Amaritanandamayi Trust 1989

Bhajanamritam
Omkara Divya Porule
Mata Amritanandamayi Center
P.O. Box 613, San Ramon, CA 94583
www.ammachi.org

Gnostic Gospels
by Elaine Pagels

Trinity Press International
P.O. Box 851, Valley Forge, PA 19482-0851

The Hidden Gospel
by Dr. Neil Douglas-Klotz, Ph.D
The Theosophical Publishing House
P.O. Box 270, Wheaton, IL 60189-0270

Nag Hammadi Library
James M. Robinson – General Editor
Harper San Francisco
HarperCollins Publishers
10 East 53rd Street, New York, NY 10022

The Song of God; Bhagavad Gita
Translated by Christopher Isherwood & Swami Prabhavananda
Vedanta Press
1946 Vedanta Place, Hollywood, CA 90068

Upanishads
Translated by Swami Prabhavananda & Frederick Manchester
Vedanta Press
1946 Vedanta Place, Hollywood, CA 90068

Quotations from the following used with permission of the
publisher, Quest Books, The Theosophical Publishng House,
Wheaton, IL. ©1999 by Neil Douglas-Klotz

Decoding the Spiritual Message of the Aramaic Jesus
Quest Books
PO Box 270, Wheaton, IL 60189

ADDITIONAL SUGGESTED READING

Ammachi – A biography of Mata Amritanandamayi
by Swami Amritaswarupananda
Mata Amritanandamayi Center

P.O. Box 613, San Ramon, CA 94583
www.ammachi.org

Finding God's Love (in preproduction)
The art and science of love and devotion as spiritual practice
by Ethan Walker III
Devi Press
www.devipress.com

Soft Moon Shining: Devotional poetry
by Ethan Walker III
Devi Press
www.devipress.com
(available September, 2003)

Ramakrishna and His Disciples
by Christopher Isherwood
Vedanta Press
1946 Vedanta Place, Hollywood, CA 90068

The Yoga of Spiritual Devotion
A modern translation of the Narada Bhakti Sutras
by Prem Prakash
Inner Traditions International
One Park Street, Rochester, Vermont 05767
www.innertraditions.com

Quantum Reality
by Nick Herbert
Anchor Books
A division of Random House

I'm Not Really Here
by Tim Allen
Hyperion New York

Index

Many are called but few are chosen, Matthew c22 v14 · 97
Master my mouth is wholly incapable of saying whom you are like, Gospel
    of Thomas v13 · 87
Must be born of spirit not flesh to enter kingdom, John c03 v05-06 · 189
Must forgive others to be forgiven by Father · 215
Must give up everything one has to be a disciple, Luke c14 v33 · 68
Must leave home and family, Luke c18 v29-30 · 52
Not everyone who says to me, 'Lord, Lord,' will go to heaven, Matthew c17
    v21-23 · 96
Not good if only love those that love you, Luke c06 v32 · 224
Not one jot and tittle shall pass from the law, Matthew c05 v17-18 · 74
Not what goes in but what comes out of a man's mouth that makes him
    unclean, Matthew c15 VII · 135
Obey everything I have commanded you, Matthew c28 v19-20 · 96
Obey what I command, John c14 v15 · 96
One must surpass Pharisees to get into heaven · 61
One's life does not consist of possessions, Luke c12 v15 · 68
People honor me but their hearts are far from me, Matthew c15 v07-09 · 97
Pharisees clean outside of cup but inside is full of greed, Matthew c23 v25 · 61
Pharisees have hidden the keys of knowledge, Gospel of Thomas v39 · 64
Pharisees justify themselves but God knows better, Luke c16 v15 · 60
Pharisees like whitewashed tombs but unclean inside, Matthew c23 v27 · 61
Pharisees make converts twice as much the son of hell, Matthew c23 v15 · 64
Ravens neither sow nor reap yet God feeds them, Luke c12 v24 · 46
Rebukes OT 'Eye for eye, tooth for tooth', Matthew c05 v38-39 · 136
Remove beam from own eye first, Luke c06 v41-42 · 216
Resurrection is not about the body, Matthew c22 v31-33 · 191
Scripture cannot be broken, John c10-v34-36 · 75
Secret teachings for the disciples, Mark c04 v10-11 · 178
Secrets given to disciples but not masses, Matthew c13 v 10-15 · 31
Seek kingdom of heaven first and all else will be added to you, Luke c12 v22-
    31 · 51
Sell possessions and give to the poor, Luke c12 v33 · 68
Servant is greatest among you, Mark c10-v42-44 · 86
Small the gate, narrow the road, few that find it, Matthew c07 v13-14 · 97
Some may kill you thinking service to God, John c16 v02 · 62
Some standing here will see kingdom before they die, Luke c09 v27 · 207
Son of man has no place to lay his head, Matthew c08 v20 · 69
Son of man not to destroy lives but to save them, Luke c09 v54-56 · 127
Spirit of truth dwells in you, John c14 v17 · 24
Split a piece of wood and I am there, Gospel of Thomas, v77 · 107
Tax collector better than Pharisee, Luke c18 v10-14 · 60
Tax collectors and prostitutes to heaven before Pharisees, Matthew c21 v31 · 61
Tells rich man 6 commandments to get into heaven, Matthew c19 v16-19 · 153
Ten virgins parable, Matthew c25 v01-13 · 26
That all of them may be one, complete unity. John c17 v19-23 · 7
These words are not my own, rather the Father in me, John c14 v10 · 103

As cosmic order or cosmic mind · 74
Definition from Greek · 94
Mistranslation as spoken word · 73
Love · 221
Antithesis of ego · 231
Given equally to all · 32, 95, 147
God is love · 233
More reliable than scripture · 72
Your enemies · 31, 128, 230
Lust
As a form of idolatry, *See* Colossians c03 v05 · 152
In the mind same as the physical act · 54
Obscures vision of oneness · 99
Satan's lieutenant · 54

Magi, pagan sorcerers · 142
Mahabharata, Great Battle · 39
Mammon (riches) · 67
Man
Created in God's image · 16
Nature is spirit · 189
Walking dead (as in a dream) · 18
Mara the tempter tests Buddha · 42
Maya · 53
Mein Kampf · 129
Melchizedek
As another Christ · 115
From another religion · 144
No mother, father or ancestors · 116
Messiah
Prophesied in Old Testament book of Malachi · 83
Second Coming of Christ · 203
Mind
Cleansing · 26
Must control it · 55
Monophysites, Jesus is one with God · 102
Monotheism · 162
Mother Teresa quote
Every act of love is peace · 219

Nag Hammadi Library · 91
Nestorian doctrine, Jesus had two natures · 102
New covenant · 137
Non-duality · 3, 25, 157, 160

Sequels to The Mystic Christ

There are two sequels to *The Mystic Christ*.

It is hoped that the reader of *The Mystic Christ* has arrived at these fundamental points:

1. At the core of our beings, the I AM, we all share a common unity.
2. Ignorance of this results in absence of happiness which we call suffering.
3. It is the ego that prevents us from knowing and experiencing the unity and love of our fundamental nature.
4. The practice of love and devotion is recommended by Jesus and others as an antidote for this ego-ignorance.

If we can agree with these points, then we must ask how we go about practicing love and devotion. How do we fulfill Jesus' two commandments to love God with all our heart, mind and soul and love our neighbors as ourselves? This path has been beautifully articulated in Tibetan Buddhism and Hinduism. One example is the *Bhakti Sutras* by Narada. However, there has been precious little written about this in a western context. With Jesus' two commandments in hand, it is baffling to realize that almost no concrete step-by-step instruction in walking this path is offered in Christian literature.

Finding God's Love is a book just for this. It clearly and concisely leads the reader through a discovery of the simple but powerful practice of devotion and love. It is a how-to book designed to be read by practitioners of any faith and with any concept of God. The practice may also be directed to God's incarnations such as Jesus, Buddha and Krishna or it may be directed toward one's spiritual satguru.

While Finding *God's Love* gives us the theory and practice complete with meditations, visualizations and prayers, *Soft Moon Shining* gives us an actual taste of devotion. It is a collection of devotional poetry offered to God in the feminine form. This medium is more able to communicate *feeling* allowing us to invoke the wellspring of love within our own hearts. Experiencing the feeling of devotion gives us primer we need to begin our practice.

The Mystic Christ brings us to the campfire, *Finding God's Love* tells us how to build and maintain the campfire, and *Soft Moon Shining* is the match.

Additional information may be gathered on-line at www.devipress.com or by writing or calling Devi Press and asking for a free brochure. The phone number and address may be found in the front of this book.

Other Books by Ethan Walker III

SOFT MOON SHINING
Devi Press
P.O. Box 5081
Norman, OK 73071
www.devipress.com

Eight poems from *Soft Moon Shining* have been reprinted in *Finding God's Love*. *Soft Moon Shining* is an invitation to step into the heart of the Divine Mother. Her perpetual dance of cosmic bliss plays out through the eons as the creation and dissolution of worlds within worlds. Yet God, in the feminine form of the Mother - as the Absolute made Immanent - is ready to shower Her love and affection on any who care to turn their gaze toward Her fiery heart. Included are 54 illustrations.

This work of poetry is both profound and beautiful in its ability to arrest the reader's conventional mind, plunging the soul into the cauldron of divine intoxication and immortal bliss. Each poem is a meditation on the Mother of the universe. Feel Her love and Her compassion as the Divine Mother hugs each reader in an embrace of timeless love.

Dance with God in the form of the Mother! Revel in the call of the infinite! Swoon with joy as the heart opens wide to the roaring river of Mother love. *Soft Moon Shining* continues in the tradition of those great poets and lovers of God, Ramprasad, Hafiz, and Rumi.

"Get ready to weep with joy! This book is a pure-light can opener for the heart." *William D.*

"Each poem is a profound meditation. This book is best read every day. It's overflowing with love and wisdom." *Margaret D.*

Sample poems from *Soft Moon Shining*:

Soft Moon Shining

My beloved Divine Mother
Dance with me
  under the soft moon shining
    in the wide open fields
    far beyond the toil and trouble
    of my busy mind

Dance with me
    before the night grows old
    while the winds of love
    still bow the grasses
            and the coyotes cry for you
            to step their way

Dance with me my beloved
  while the Mystery's Edge
    still flirts in the shadow
    of your radiant light

The Book

Mother Kali
Place your seal on this book of mortal existence
    now emptied of words
      from crying to you

I have given this book to you
    to do with as you wish
      as there is no one left
        who wants to write in it

Having tasted your Divine Love
    what else can be of any importance?

I am your laughing schoolboy
　　playing hooky from the ceaseless pounding
　　　　of facts and names

And I am running headlong to swim in your river of
immortal bliss
　　carelessly flinging these clothes
　　　　of concerns and considerations to the ground as I go

Hugging Arms

　　My beautiful Divine Mother
　　This universe is your body
　　　　alive and blushing
　　　　　　with cosmic streams
　　　　　　　　and rivers of love

　　I bow to the rocks
　　　　ancient siblings of boundless love

　　I bow to the sun and the sailing planets
　　　　who whistle songs of love
　　　　　　to one another
　　　　　　　　from deep within the inner spheres

　　And I bow to every atom
　　　　eternally in love with every other atom
　　　　　　all of them whirling dervishes
　　　　　　　　ecstatic in their dance
　　　　　　　　　　of joyous coexistence

　　My heart melts at the sight
　　　　of this endless love feast

　　And I deeply regret
　　　　that my hugging arms
　　　　　　are so few and so short

Draw Another Cup of Joy

Compassionate Mother
who's grace is beyond eternity

My friends and I will draw another cup of joy
from the wellspring
of your radiant heart

And raise it to our lips with a shout
Victory to the Mother!
Victory to the Mother of all beings!

And when this tavern of divine revelry
closes in the morning's wee hours

We will all walk home arm in arm
with faltering steps
to our conventional minds
staggering with the intoxication of love
and waking the neighbors
shouting like bugle blowers

Victory to the Mother!
Victory to the Mother of the universe!

FINDING GOD'S LOVE
The practice of love and devotion as a spiritual path
Devi Press
www.devipress.com

Love is the primal essence. Love is the light of the Divine which fills the vastness of eternity with the sweet fragrance of immortal bliss. The practice of love and devotion is an ancient path leading to direct mystical experience of the Supreme. Notable teachers of this path include Jesus, Hafiz, Narada, Ramprasad, and Ammachi. *Finding God's Love* is suitable for any pilgrim of any faith who wishes to experience a direct and personal communion with the Divine. God's lovers will find immediate access to the living room of God's heart where they will revel in the bliss and joy of the universe; divinely intoxicated in the breath of the eternally radiant now; swept away in an endless celebration of life.

The first part of the book reveals how love works to release the human psyche from the fetters of its own self-imposed limitations. Love is the antidote to all negative emotions. Love heals the festering wounds that lay buried in our past. Love cleans the lens of the soul allowing the light of the Divine to percolate up from the center of our being illuminating our personal world. The second part of the book explains the practical aspects of this path including meditations, visualizations and prayer. The last section is a collection of teachings from Ammachi, the hugging saint, on the practice of love and devotion.

Love is what makes life beautiful because God *is* love. Love nourishes the delicate flowering of the immortal soul vanquishing boredom once and for all in the magnificence of its ever-fresh ever-mysterious river of divine grace. This book is an invitation to ecstasy - to swim in the ocean of God.

DEVI PRESS

PO Box 5081, Norman OK 73070
405-447-0364 • fx 405-360-5277
www.devipress.com

Individuals: We encourage you to ask for Devi Press books at your local bookstore. If you are unable to obtain a Devi Press book from your retailer, you may call or email us or use the form below to order via fax or postal service. Mastercard and Visa accepted. Oklahoma residents please add 8.375% sales tax.

Please make checks payable to DEVI PRESS.

Qty	Title	Amount
_____	The Mystic Christ ($14.95)	_____
_____	Soft Moon Shining ($14.95)	_____
_____	Finding God's Love ($13.95)	_____

Unless otherwise specified books are shipped via US Mail ($3.00 for the first book plus $.50 for each add'l book)

Subtotal _____

Sales Tax _____
OK - 8.375%

Shipping _____

TOTAL _____

Date_____

Name_____

Address_____

City/State_____Zip_____

Phone_____

Credit Card #_____Exp._____

Signature_____